# Accounting Desk Book
for
Manufacturing Companies

# Accounting Desk Book for Manufacturing Companies

PAUL D. LUCAS

PRENTICE-HALL, INC. Englewood Cliffs N.J.

Prentice-Hall International, Inc., *London*
Prentice-Hall of Australia, Pty. Ltd., *Sydney*
Prentice-Hall of Canada, Ltd., *Toronto*
Prentice-Hall of India Private Ltd., *New Delhi*
Prentice-Hall of Japan, Inc., *Tokyo*
Prentice-Hall of Southeast Asia Pte. Ltd., *Singapore*
Whitehall Books, Ltd., *Wellington, New Zealand*



This publication is designed to provide accurate and authoritative information in regard to the subject matter covered. It is sold with the understanding that the publisher is not engaged in rendering legal, accounting or other professional service. If legal advice or other expert assistance is required, the services of a competent professional person should be sought.

—From a Declaration of Principles jointly adopted by a Committee of the American Bar Association and a Committee of Publishers and Associations.

**Library of Congress Cataloging in Publication Data**

Lucas, Paul D.
Accounting desk book for manufacturing companies.

Bibliography: p.
Includes index.
1. Accounting. 2. Financial statements.
I. Title.
HF5635.L9 657'.867 78-21655
ISBN 0-13-001701-9

Printed in the United States of America

This book is dedicated, as I am, to
Kay, Todd and Scott

**ALSO BY PAUL D. LUCAS**

*ACCOUNTING GUIDE FOR CONSTRUCTION CONTRACTORS*

# About the Author

Paul D. Lucas is a partner in the Certified Public Accounting firm of Boyd, Dehmel & Lucas. He is also an Associate Professor of Business Administration at Indiana Central University where he teaches accounting, auditing and federal income tax courses at both the graduate and undergraduate levels. He previously authored *Accounting Guide for Construction Contractors*.

For eight years Mr. Lucas was Treasurer and a Director of Grinding and Polishing Machinery Corporation. It was there that he developed much of the information for this book.

Paul Lucas is a member of the American Institute of Certified Public Accountants and the Indiana Association of Certified Public Accountants. He holds two degrees, a Bachelor of Science from Butler University and a Master of Business Administration from Indiana University.

# A Word from the Author

Up to now accounting books have paid little attention to the unique needs of specific industries. This lack of special attention has forced the accountant to use broad references and adapt them to his special needs—a genuine handicap. Thus came the idea for my first book, *Accounting Guide for Construction Contractors*, and now this one, *Accounting Desk Book for Manufacturing Companies*.

This book has been written to satisfy the needs of the professionals who work for manufacturers or have manufacturing clients. They will find this book easy to read, well illustrated, enlightening, thought provoking and reinforcing relative to their own ideas of accounting and its contributions to management. The manufacturer's financial statements and supporting schedules are presented at the beginning followed by a complete and efficient system to accumulate the accounting data necessary for acceptable accuracy and sufficient control.

Through the use of this efficient and adequately controlled system, the accountant can progress into many special areas where he or she can be of greater service to management. These areas include the handling and allocation of overhead, the use of algebraically proven variance formulas, special audits of marketing and purchasing, plus planning and forecasting to set more attainable goals.

Another very important area covered in this book, in which the accountant can be of help to the manufacturer, is in the selection of the best type of business organization—namely the proprietorship, partnership, regular corporation or small business corporation. There is also discussion and direction on how to best share responsibilities between the client and the auditor for maximum efficiency and mutual benefits plus ideas on presentations for capital procurement, things to look for in acquisitions and procedures for liquidations.

## HOW THIS BOOK IS ORGANIZED

*Accounting Desk Book for Manufacturing Companies* consolidates into a single volume numerous areas of accounting and relates them specifically to the manufacturing industry. However, to make these areas of accounting clearly understandable, they are covered in the traditional sequence. The financial statements are presented first, followed by a specially designed accounting system, and the book concludes with selected accounting topics as they relate to manufacturing.

The presentation of financial statements in Chapter 1 assumes that they will be available for external use and therefore prepared in accordance with generally accepted accounting principles. However, many of the reports developed later in this book are for internal use only, and depart from the generally accepted methods of presentation to emphasize specific financial aspects of managing a manufacturing company.

Chapter 2 develops the chart of accounts, discusses the terminology used in manufacturing accounting and sets up the general framework for the accounting system. It also discusses the various considerations in selecting a fiscal closing date.

Chapters 3, 4 and 5 present a full range of journals, ledgers, forms and a paperwork flow system—all designed especially for the manufacturing company. In addition these chapters emphasize methods of providing additional working capital, collecting accounts, purchasing procedures and objectives, and a very carefully controlled accounting system for labor costs.

Chapter 6 deals with the special problems of controlling and allocating overhead costs. Special attention is given to the cost-volume relationship of fixed overhead in product pricing and contract bidding.

Chapter 7 demonstrates the use of standard costs for products that are manufactured repetitively. The development of standard costs is illustrated to promote efficiency in product costing and as a means of analyzing actual costs of material, labor and overhead. Special variance formulas are developed and proven as a part of this cost analysis. Estimated costs and actual costs are also developed and compared for one-of-a-kind jobs.

Inventory costing alternatives are covered in Chapter 8. Costing methods are compared along with an analysis of the various inventory flow assumptions. The gross profit method for estimating inventories is illustrated as an alternative to perpetual records.

Chapter 9 wraps up the accounting process by illustrating end of period adjustments, controls and internal reports.

Plant and equipment, a major cost for the manufacturer, are studied and various aspects considered in Chapter 10. Attention is given to such decisions as leasing or buying, depreciation methods, and physical control. Also, the computations for return on investment, cash payback period, and the too often overlooked area of discounted cash flow are illustrated. Tax aspects of investments in plant and equipment are also discussed. A brief discussion of insurance coverage and prepaid insurance computations are also included in Chapter 10.

Chapter 11 puts together and explains the principles and steps involved in profit planning and forecasting. This process gives the manufacturer a sense of direction and develops guidelines for future operations.

Chapter 12 has been written to assist both the auditor and the manufacturer in a mutual effort to understand and conduct the audit. Areas of client assistance are suggested to both reduce audit costs and make the auditor's time more valuable.

Chapter 13 discusses the pros and cons of various forms of business organizations, namely the proprietorship, partnership, and the corporation. Special attention is given to the small business corporation along with the steps to incorporate and tax problems in incorporating.

Acquisitions, liquidations and capital procurement are covered in Chapter 14 with step-by-step liquidation procedures listed.

Having viewed the manufacturing industry from every angle, as public accountant, treasurer, director, auditor, advisor and writer, I have observed many worthwhile ideas and developed a number of my own. I wish to share these ideas to the greatest extent possible.

*Paul D. Lucas*

# CONTENTS

# Accounting Desk Book for Manufacturing Companies

# 1

# Presenting and Interpreting Financial Statements and Supplementary Schedules

## INITIAL CONSIDERATIONS AND USES OF FINANCIAL STATEMENTS

Traditionally, the financial statements have been the most widely used basis of analyzing the results of operations and the current financial position of the manufacturing company. When prepared for use outside the company, the financial statements must be included in an accountant's report that contains the following:

1. An opinion either unqualified, qualified, adverse or denied; if an audit has not been conducted, each page must be marked "unaudited."
2. The four principal financial statements:
   a. Income statement
   b. Statement of retained earnings
   c. Balance sheet
   d. Statement of changes in financial position
3. Adequate disclosure, which usually requires notes to financial statements to disclose information useful in analyzing operations or financial condition but not evident in the financial statements.

Often, other information is desirable for external reporting such as comparative financial statements, percentage analyses and supplementary schedules to present more details than are in the principal financial statements.

The requirements for internal reporting are not so rigid, but the accountant must restrict to internal use the use of reports that do not contain the required opinion, financial statements and disclosures. Internal reports, those reports for company management, may then be designed for specific purposes, contain certain studies and analyses, and depart from generally accepted accounting principles where information rather than compliance is the key element.

Extra care should be taken in the manner of presentation for all financial statements, reports and analyses. Considerably more time is required to accumulate the information through the accounting system than it takes to prepare reports for outsiders and management. Yet, the reports are the only accounting product seen by most users of financial information. All reports should be neatly prepared, pennies should be dropped, and the needs of the user should always be considered in determining the manner of presentation. Reports may be concise or thorough depending on how deeply the reader wishes to look into the information. Useless information should be omitted, as it detracts from the essential report elements. Too much information gets less than adequate attention, while too little information leaves important details unexplained. Reports are an accountant's finished product; he must give them his best effort.

The financial statements, schedules and analyses presented in this chapter are intended to be a general guide, and they may be expanded or contracted to meet the needs of a specific manufacturer.

## THE INCOME STATEMENT AND SUPPLEMENTARY SCHEDULES

The comparative income statements are supported by schedules of cost of goods manufactured and sold and schedules of general and administrative expenses. Supporting schedules facilitate the presentation of a concise, easy-to-read income statement by removing most of the analytical detail from the principal statement. Although these illustrations present separate costs and expenses for production and administration, it is desirable in large companies to analyze expenses for every department where meaningful allocations can be made. Expenses that cannot be allocated with reasonable accuracy should remain in an unallocated pool. Allocations are discussed further in Chapter 6.

**EXHIBIT A**

MACHINE MANUFACTURING CORPORATION

Comparative Income Statements
Years Ended March 31, 19X7 and 19X6

| | Year Ended March 31, | |
|---|---|---|
| | 19X7 | 19X6 |
| Net Sales | $880,000 | $790,000 |
| Cost of Goods Manufactured And Sold—schedule A-1 | 564,000 | 536,000 |
| Gross Profit | 316,000 | 254,000 |
| General And Administrative Expenses—schedule A-2 | 173,000 | 158,000 |
| Income From Operations Before Federal Income Tax | 143,000 | 96,000 |
| Federal Income Tax On Income From Operations | 55,000 | 32,000 |
| Net Income From Operations—exhibit D | 88,000 | 64,000 |
| Extraordinary Income—Gain On Sale Of Land | 10,000 | ---- |
| Federal Income Tax On Extraordinary Income | 3,000 | ---- |
| Net Extraordinary Income | 7,000 | ---- |
| Net Income—exhibit C | $ 95,000 | $ 64,000 |
| Earnings Per Share | | |
| Net Income from operations | $88 | $64 |
| Net extraordinary income | 7 | ---- |
| Net earnings per share | $95 | $64 |

**Figure 1-1**

**Schedule A-1**

MACHINE MANUFACTURING CORPORATION

Comparative Schedules of Cost of Goods Manufactured and Sold
Years Ended March 31, 19X7 and 19X6

| | Year Ended March 31, 19X7 | 19X6 |
|---|---|---|
| Finished goods inventory, beginning of year | $ 84,000 | $ 79,000 |
| Work in process, beginning of year | 76,000 | 70,000 |
| Materials | | |
| Inventory, beginning of year | 42,000 | 44,000 |
| Net purchases | 380,000 | 358,000 |
| Materials available | 422,000 | 402,000 |
| Less inventory, end of year | 46,000 | 42,000 |
| Materials issued to manufacturing | 376,000 | 360,000 |
| Direct labor | 118,000 | 112,000 |
| Manufacturing overhead | | |
| Indirect labor | 26,000 | 25,000 |
| Repairs | 4,000 | 4,000 |
| Depreciation | 18,000 | 17,000 |
| Factory supplies | 6,000 | 5,000 |
| Utilities | 3,000 | 3,000 |
| Insurance | 5,000 | 4,000 |
| Building maintenance | 1,000 | 1,000 |
| Payroll taxes | 9,000 | 8,000 |
| Property taxes | 2,000 | 2,000 |
| Retirement benefits | 3,000 | 2,000 |
| Cost variances | 1,000 | 2,000 |
| Miscellaneous | 2,000 | 2,000 |
| Total manufacturing overhead | 80,000 | 75,000 |
| Total goods in process | 650,000 | 617,000 |
| Less goods in process, end of year | 82,000 | 76,000 |
| Cost of goods manufactured | 568,000 | 541,000 |
| Total goods available | 652,000 | 620,000 |
| Less finished goods inventory, end of year | 88,000 | 84,000 |
| Cost of goods manufactured and sold—exhibit A | $564,000 | $536,000 |

**Figure 1-2**

**Schedule A-2**

MACHINE MANUFACTURING CORPORATION

Comparative Schedules of General and Administrative Expenses
Years Ended March 31, 19X7 and 19X6

| | Year Ended March 31, | |
|---|---|---|
| | 19X7 | 19X6 |
| Officers' salaries | $ 64,000 | $ 60,000 |
| Clerical salaries | 19,000 | 18,000 |
| Engineering salaries | 21,000 | 17,000 |
| Sales salaries | 30,000 | 27,000 |
| Repairs | 1,200 | 1,000 |
| Depreciation | 2,000 | 2,000 |
| Utilities | 1,300 | 900 |
| Telephone and telegraph | 2,700 | 2,100 |
| Insurance | 3,100 | 3,000 |
| Building maintenance | 1,000 | 800 |
| Payroll taxes | 6,000 | 7,000 |
| Property tax | 1,200 | 800 |
| State income tax | 3,000 | 1,900 |
| Travel and entertainment | 3,600 | 3,100 |
| Advertising | 1,900 | 2,400 |
| Office supplies | 1,500 | 1,200 |
| Dues and subscriptions | 900 | 800 |
| Professional services | 2,600 | 2,000 |
| Uncollectible accounts | 600 | 800 |
| Interest expense | 2,000 | 1,800 |
| Retirement benefits | 3,000 | 2,800 |
| Miscellaneous | 1,400 | 1,600 |
| Totals—exhibit A | $173,000 | $158,000 |

**Figure 1-3**

MACHINE MANUFACTURING CORPORATION

Comparative Percentage Analysis of Income Statements
Years Ended March 31, 19X7 and 19X6

| | Year Ended March 31, | |
|---|---|---|
| | 19X7 | 19X6 |
| Net Sales | 100.00% | 100.00% |
| Cost Of Goods Manufactured And Sold | 64.09 | 67.85 |
| Gross Profit | 35.91 | 32.15 |
| General And Administrative Expenses | 19.66 | 20.00 |
| Income From Operations Before Federal Income Tax | 16.25 | 12.15 |
| Federal Income Tax On Income From Operations | 6.25 | 4.05 |
| Net Income From Operations | 10.00 | 8.10 |
| Extraordinary Income—Gain On Sale Of Land | 1.14 | ---- |
| Federal Income Tax On Extraordinary Income | 0.34 | ---- |
| Net Extraordinary Income | 0.80 | ---- |
| Net Income | 10.80% | 8.10% |

**Figure 1-4**

MACHINE MANUFACTURING CORPORATION

Comparative Percentage Analysis of Cost of Goods Manufactured and Sold
Years Ended March 31, 19X7 and 19X6

| | Percent of Net Sales Year Ended March 31, | |
|---|---|---|
| | 19X7 | 19X6 |
| Finished goods inventory, beginning of year | 9.55% | 10.00% |
| Goods in process, beginning of year | 8.63 | 8.86 |
| Materials | | |
| Inventory, beginning of year | 4.77 | 5.57 |
| Net purchases | 43.18 | 45.32 |
| Materials available | 47.95 | 50.89 |
| Less inventory, end of year | 5.22 | 5.32 |
| Materials issued to manufacturing | 42.73 | 45.57 |
| Direct labor | 13.41 | 14.18 |
| Manufacturing overhead | | |
| Indirect labor | 2.96 | 3.17 |
| Repairs | 0.45 | 0.51 |
| Depreciation | 2.05 | 2.15 |
| Factory supplies | 0.68 | 0.63 |
| Utilities | 0.34 | 0.38 |
| Insurance | 0.57 | 0.51 |
| Building maintenance | 0.11 | 0.13 |
| Payroll taxes | 1.02 | 1.01 |
| Property taxes | 0.23 | 0.25 |
| Retirement benefits | 0.34 | 0.25 |
| Cost variances | 0.11 | 0.25 |
| Miscellaneous | 0.23 | 0.25 |
| Total manufacturing overhead | 9.09 | 9.49 |
| Total goods in process | 73.86 | 78.10 |
| Less goods in process, end of year | 9.32 | 9.62 |
| Cost of goods manufactured | 64.54 | 68.48 |
| Total goods available | 74.09 | 78.48 |
| Less finished goods inventory, end of year | 10.00 | 10.63 |
| Cost of goods manufactured and sold | 64.09% | 67.85% |

**Figure 1-5**

MACHINE MANUFACTURING CORPORATION

Comparative Percentage Analysis of General and Administrative Expenses
Years Ended March 31, 19X7 and 19X6

| | Percent of Net Sales Year Ended March 31, | |
|---|---|---|
| | 19X7 | 19X6 |
| Officers' salaries | 7.27% | 7.60% |
| Clerical salaries | 2.16 | 2.28 |
| Engineering salaries | 2.39 | 2.15 |
| Sales salaries | 3.41 | 3.42 |
| Repairs | 0.14 | 0.13 |
| Depreciation | 0.23 | 0.25 |
| Utilities | 0.15 | 0.12 |
| Telephone and telegraph | 0.31 | 0.27 |
| Insurance | 0.35 | 0.38 |
| Building maintenance | 0.11 | 0.10 |
| Payroll taxes | 0.68 | 0.89 |
| Property tax | 0.13 | 0.10 |
| State income tax | 0.34 | 0.24 |
| Travel and entertainment | 0.41 | 0.39 |
| Advertising | 0.22 | 0.30 |
| Office supplies | 0.17 | 0.15 |
| Dues and subscriptions | 0.10 | 0.10 |
| Professional services | 0.29 | 0.25 |
| Uncollectible accounts | 0.07 | 0.10 |
| Interest expense | 0.23 | 0.23 |
| Retirement benefits | 0.34 | 0.35 |
| Miscellaneous | 0.16 | 0.20 |
| Totals | 19.66% | 20.00% |

**Figure 1-6**

## INTERPRETING AND ANALYZING THE INCOME STATEMENT AND SUPPLEMENTARY SCHEDULES

The greatest amount of interest is usually centered in the income statement, Exhibit A (Figure 1-1), and its supporting schedules, A-1 and A-2 (Figures 1-2 and 1-3), with the most important single item being net income from operations. Favorable net income tends, over the long run, to cure financial condition and working capital problems. This is not to say that profits alone can substitute for sound financial management and proper utilization of financial resources. Profits that are squandered on assets or ventures that do not enhance future operating profits can rapidly wreck the current or overall financial position.

Growing enterprises also place added stress on financial, personnel and physical resources. Regardless of profitability, these increasing demands can diminish working capital faster than it can be provided by operations. The central point is that although net income from operations can be the most important single item in the financial statements, it is not a cure-all. The statements must be analyzed as a unit to adequately locate areas that need further investigation or attention.

The income statement indicates what appears to be a series of favorable trends when the current year is compared to the previous year. Total sales volume has increased $90,000 which represents an 11.4% increase in sales. The 11.4% sales increase is favorable, however, only because both gross profit and net income from operations increased as a result. Even here there is somewhat of an assumption that the increased volume was the cause of the increased profits. This assumption does seem to be supported by other evidence in the statements. Gross profit increased by $15,000 which is 24.4% over the previous year, and net income from operations increased by $24,000 or 36.9%. When profits increase at a higher rate than sales, it is an indication of favorable cost and expense control. These elements can best be analyzed by studying the comparative schedules of cost of goods manufactured and sold and general and administrative expenses and the related percentage analyses.

Extraordinary income from sale of land in the income statement and related federal income tax is presented separately from operating income because such a gain is considered to be nonrecurring. To include income that is not produced through normal operations in operating income distorts operating results and the comparability of the current period to the previous period.

Earnings per share is of primary importance to the owner-investors. Earnings per share is probably the most common measurement of return on investment used by investors and prospective investors. Again, net income from operations is the most important figure together with the related trend. For the Machine Manufacturing Corporation, net income from operations has increased from $64 per share to $88 per share. It would be of equal or greater interest to a current or prospective stockholder to see and evaluate management's forecast of earnings in future years.

Profitability is actually the product of just two elements, sales and total expenses. While increasing sales is almost always given attention, cost control, which is neither as glamorous nor popular with most personnel, is equally important. Certain costs and expenses are generated internally and therefore are more controllable than sales, all of which depend at least partially on external forces and conditions. It is difficult to train personnel, even management personnel, to place company profitability ahead of their own wants or desires for empire building. This problem necessitates that operating management constantly review costs and expenses and related trends. These costs and expenses for the Machine Manufacturing Corporation appear in Schedules A-1 and A-2. Here, the degree of analysis for internal purposes can be expanded or contracted as necessary in individual companies. Numerous methods of additional analyses are illustrated and discussed in subsequent chapters. The financial statements usually only suggest what has to be investigated rather than revealing the problem.

In the comparative percentage analysis of cost of goods manufactured and sold, Figure 1-5, materials, direct labor and manufacturing overhead have all decreased as a percent of sales with the greatest decrease being in materials issued. However, one cannot immediately assume greater production efficiency. A change in product mix to include greater portions of more profitable products could account for the decrease in cost percentages. Other possibilities would be increased selling prices, cheaper materials or labor, thinner spreading of fixed costs, volume purchases, bargain purchases, changes in product design or components, performing functions previously sublet, etc. The possibilities are endless—management should be aware or made aware of the reasons. Favorable trends are as valuable for planning as the discovery of unfavorable trends.

Figure 1-6, comparative percentage analysis of general and administrative expenses, is less revealing. Part of the reason for smaller differences is that general and administrative expenses simply represent a much smaller percentage of sales than do manufacturing costs. It would be interesting to know why engineering salaries increased as a percentage of sales while other salaries decreased. An increase isn't necessarily bad—perhaps the increased engineering salaries are related to the decreased production costs. Other changes in general and administrative expenses are nominal, but accounting still should be capable of determining the reasons for changes as needed by management.

## SETTING UP FOR THE BALANCE SHEET, STATEMENT OF RETAINED EARNINGS, STATEMENT OF CHANGES IN FINANCIAL POSITION, AND SUPPLEMENTARY SCHEDULE

Although all three of these financial statements are principal statements, their analysis must be linked together to determine the changes in the company's financial condition and the reasons for the changes.

The balance sheet should classify assets, liabilities and stockholders' equity items in a manner that clearly describes the content of each account. Assets and liabilities should also be classified as current or noncurrent under a caption that describes the general makeup of that group.

Current assets include those assets that will be converted into cash or used in the business within one year or the normal operating cycle if longer than one year. Examples of industries having a longer operating cycle are shipbuilding and distilleries.

Plant and equipment includes noncurrent, tangible assets used in the operation of the business. Other noncurrent assets such as intangibles, long-term investments, and miscellaneous items should be separately classified. Intent is often the determining factor in classifying an asset in the balance sheet. As an example, securities that are to be liquidated for future working capital would usually be current, while, if the intent is to hold them for an indefinite period, they would be classified as an investment.

In the balance sheet for the Machine Manufacturing Corporation, cash surrender value of officers' life insurance is classified as an other asset. Many accountants feel that this item represents an investment and would place it in an investment category between current assets and plant and equipment. Here again, intent and perhaps materiality could be a determining factor.

Generally, liabilities that are to be satisfied within one year are considered current. Current liabilities include the current installments payable on the principal of long-term installment obligations. However, to be current, a liability has to require the use of current assets. Therefore, a liability that is to be satisfied through the use of special funds set aside in noncurrent investments is not classified as a current liability.

**Exhibit B**

MACHINE MANUFACTURING CORPORATION

Comparative Balance Sheets at March 31, 19X7 and 19X6

ASSETS

| | March 31, 19X7 | March 31, 19X6 |
|---|---|---|
| Current Assets, | | |
| Cash in bank and on hand | $ 42,000 | $ 32,000 |
| Temporary investments—cost plus accrued interest | 10,400 | 5,100 |
| Accounts receivable—trade | 91,000 | 75,000 |
| Less allowance for uncollectible accounts | 3,000 | 2,000 |
| | 88,000 | 73,000 |
| Inventories—at lower of cost or market, first-in-first-out flow assumption | 216,000 | 202,000 |
| Prepaid expenses and advances | 2,600 | 1,900 |
| Total current assets | 359,000 | 314,000 |
| Plant And Equipment—at cost—schedule B-1 | 341,800 | 296,800 |
| Less accumulated depreciation | 76,000 | 56,000 |
| | 265,800 | 240,800 |
| Other Assets—Cash surrender value of officers' Life Insurance—face value $100,000 | 3,200 | 2,200 |
| | $628,000 | $557,000 |

**Figure 1–7**

**Exhibit B**

MACHINE MANUFACTURING CORPORATION

Comparative Balance Sheets at March 31, 19X7 and 19X6

LIABILITIES AND STOCKHOLDERS' EQUITY

| | March 31, 19X7 | March 31, 19X6 |
|---|---|---|
| Current Liabilities | | |
| Accounts payable—trade | $ 40,000 | $ 38,000 |
| Current portion of mortgage note payable | 6,000 | 4,000 |
| Accrued and withheld payroll taxes | 3,000 | 3,200 |
| Accrued salary and wages | 4,000 | 5,000 |
| Accrued federal income tax | 15,000 | 8,000 |
| Other accrued taxes and expenses | 8,000 | 11,800 |
| Total current liabilities | 76,000 | 70,000 |
| Long-Term Liability | | |
| Mortgage note payable | 200,000 | 180,000 |
| Less current portion shown above | 6,000 | 4,000 |
| | 194,000 | 176,000 |
| | 270,000 | 246,000 |
| Stockholders' Equity | | |
| Common stock, no par value, 10,000 shares authorized, 1,000 shares issued and outstanding | 60,000 | 60,000 |
| Retained earnings—exhibit C | 298,000 | 251,000 |
| | 358,000 | 311,000 |
| | $628,000 | $557,000 |

**Figure 1–7 (continued)**

**Exhibit C**

MACHINE MANUFACTURING CORPORATION

Comparative Statements of Retained Earnings
Years Ended March 31, 19X7 and 19X6

| | Year Ended March 31, | |
|---|---|---|
| | 19X7 | 19X6 |
| Retained Earnings, Beginning Of Year | $251,000 | $219,000 |
| Net Income—exhibit A | 95,000 | 64,000 |
| | 346,000 | 283,000 |
| Dividends Paid | 48,000 | 32,000 |
| Retained Earnings, End Of Year—exhibit B | $298,000 | $251,000 |

**Figure 1–8**

The statements of retained earnings can often be combined with the income statements. This combination may be desirable when the statements are brief, which is often the case with the statements of retained earnings. Starting with net income from the income statements the two may be combined as shown in Figure 1–9.

| | Year Ended March 31, | |
|---|---|---|
| | 19X7 | 19X6 |
| Net Income | $ 95,000 | $ 64,000 |
| Retained Earnings, Beginning Of Year | 251,000 | 219,000 |
| | 346,000 | 283,000 |
| Dividends Paid | 48,000 | 32,000 |
| Retained Earnings, End Of Year—exhibit B | $298,000 | $251,000 |

**Figure 1–9**

It may be noted that an objection to the above combination is the lack of emphasis given to net income by presenting the figures well up in the body of the statements rather than at the end.

**Schedule B-1**

MACHINE MANUFACTURING CORPORATION

Comparative Schedule of Plant and Equipment and Accumulated Depreciation
at March 31, 19X7 and 19X6

| | Cost | | | | Straight-line | Accumulated Depreciation | | | | Cost Less |
|---|---|---|---|---|---|---|---|---|---|---|
| Asset | March 31, 19X6 | Additions | Reductions | March31, 19X7 | Depreciation Rates | March 31, 19X6 | Additions | Reductions | March 31, 19X7 | Depreciation March 31, 19X7 |
| Office equipment | $ 9,000 | $ 2,000 | $ ---- | $ 11,000 | 10% | $ 3,000 | $ 1,000 | $ ---- | $ 4,000 | $ 7,000 |
| Autos and trucks | 13,800 | ---- | ---- | 13,800 | 25% | 7,000 | 3,450 | ---- | 10,450 | 3,350 |
| Machinery and equipment | 84,000 | 3,000 | ---- | 87,000 | 10% | 27,000 | 8,550 | ---- | 35,550 | 51,450 |
| Building | 150,000 | 50,000 | ---- | 200,000 | 4% | 19,000 | 7,000 | ---- | 26,000 | 174,000 |
| Land | 40,000 | ---- | 10,000 | 30,000 | | | | | | 30,000 |
| | $296,800 | $55,000 | $10,000 | $341,800 | | $56,000 | $20,000 | $ ---- | $76,000 | $265,800 |
| | | | | Exhibit B | | | Exhibit D | | Exhibit B | Exhibit B |

**Figure 1–10**

**Exhibit D**

MACHINE MANUFACTURING CORPORATION

Comparative Statements of Changes in Financial Position
Years Ended March 31, 19X7 and 19X6

| | Year Ended March 31, 19X7 | 19X6 |
|---|---|---|
| Working Capital Provided | | |
| Net income from operations—exhibit A | $ 88,000 | $ 64,000 |
| Add depreciation—included as expense in determining net income but not requiring funds—schedule B-1 | 20,000 | 19,000 |
| Working capital provided by operations | 108,000 | 83,000 |
| Extraordinary item—sale of land—net of applicable federal income tax | 17,000 | ---- |
| Total working capital provided | 125,000 | 83,000 |
| Working Capital Applied | | |
| Payment of Dividends | 48,000 | 32,000 |
| Purchase of equipment | 5,000 | 6,000 |
| Addition to building | 26,000 | ---- |
| Increase in cash surrender value of officers' life insurance | 1,000 | 1,000 |
| Decrease in long-term portion of mortgage note payable | 6,000 | 4,000 |
| Total working capital applied | 86,000 | 43,000 |
| Increase in Working Capital | $ 39,000 | $ 40,000 |

The long-term mortgage note payable was increased by $24,000 as partial financing of the building addition resulting in a financial transaction that did not affect working capital.

**Figure 1–11**

**Exhibit D**

MACHINE MANUFACTURING CORPORATION

Comparative Statements of Changes in Financial Position
Years Ended March 31, 19X7 and 19X6

| | Year Ended March 31, | |
|---|---|---|
| | 19X7 Increase (Decrease) | 19X6 Increase (Decrease) |
| Current Assets | | |
| Cash in bank and on hand | $ 10,000 | $ 9,000 |
| Temporary investments | 5,300 | 5,100 |
| Accounts receivable—net of allowance | 15,000 | 17,000 |
| Inventories | 14,000 | 12,000 |
| Prepaid expenses and advances | 700 | 900 |
| | 45,000 | 44,000 |
| Current Liabilities | | |
| Accounts payable—trade | 2,000 | 2,000 |
| Current portion of mortgage note payable | 2,000 | 1,000 |
| Accrued and withheld payroll taxes | ( 200) | 300 |
| Accrued salaries and wages | ( 1,000) | 1,000 |
| Accrued federal income tax | 7,000 | 4,000 |
| Other accrued taxes and expenses | ( 3,800) | ( 4,300) |
| | 6,000 | 4,000 |
| Increase in Working Capital | $ 39,000 | $ 40,000 |

**Figure 1–11 (continued)**

## MACHINE MANUFACTURING CORPORATION

### Comparative Percentage Analyses of Balance Sheets

### Assets

| | March 31, 19X7 | March 31, 19X6 |
|---|---|---|
| **Current Assets** | | |
| Cash in bank and on hand | 6.69% | 5.75% |
| Temporary investments—cost plus accrued interest | 1.66 | .91 |
| Accounts receivable—trade | 14.49 | 13.46 |
| Less allowance for uncollectible accounts | 0.48 | 0.36 |
| | 14.01 | 13.10 |
| Inventories—at lower of cost or market, first-in-first-out flow assumption | 34.39 | 36.27 |
| Prepaid expenses and advances | 0.42 | 0.34 |
| Total current assets | 57.17 | 56.37 |
| **Plant and Equipment—at cost** | 54.43 | 53.28 |
| Less accumulated depreciation | 12.11 | 10.05 |
| | 42.32 | 43.23 |
| **Other Assets—Cash surrender value of officers' life insurance—face value $100,000** | 0.51 | 0.40 |
| | 100.00% | 100.00% |

### Liabilities and Stockholders' Equity

| | 19X7 | 19X6 |
|---|---|---|
| **Current Liabilities** | | |
| Accounts payable—trade | 6.37% | 6.82% |
| Current portion of mortgage note payable | 0.96 | 0.72 |
| Accrued and withheld payroll taxes | 0.48 | 0.57 |
| Accrued salaries and wages | 0.64 | 0.90 |
| Accrued federal income tax | 2.38 | 1.44 |
| Other accrued taxes and expenses | 1.27 | 2.12 |
| Total current liabilities | 12.10 | 12.57 |
| **Long-Term Liability** | | |
| Mortgage note payable | 31.85 | 32.32 |
| Less current portion shown above | 0.96 | 0.72 |
| | 30.89 | 31.60 |
| | 42.99 | 44.17 |
| **Stockholders' Equity** | | |
| Common stock, no par value, 10,000 shares authorized, 1,000 shares issued and outstanding | 9.56 | 10.77 |
| Retained earnings | 47.45 | 45.06 |
| | 57.01 | 55.83 |
| | 100.00% | 100.00% |

**Figure 1-12**

## INTERPRETING AND ANALYZING THE BALANCE SHEET AND CHANGES IN FINANCIAL POSITION

The Machine Manufacturing Corporation is in a very strong financial position. The current ratio, current assets to current liabilities is 4.7 to 1, and working capital, current assets less current liabilities is $283,000. However, the quick current assets, cash, temporary investments and receivables are only $140,400. The company needs to be aware of inventory control procedures, with $216,000, 60% of its current assets, invested in inventories. In some cases it may be preferable to present inventories by stage of completion as:

| | | |
|---|---|---|
| Materials | $ 46,000 | |
| Goods in process | 82,000 | |
| Finished goods | 88,000 | |
| | | $216,000 |

Changes in plant and equipment items are presented in schedule B–1. Plant and equipment is mortgaged rather heavily in relation to the $265,800 book value. The balance sheet carries plant and equipment at cost less accumulated depreciation, the book value, which may be substantially different than the current appraisal value for mortgaging purposes.

The statement of changes in financial position indicates the reasons for the $39,000 increase in working capital, followed by an explanation of other financial transactions that did not affect working capital and changes in current assets and current liabilities, the working capital components.

The percentage analysis of the balance sheet indicates a stronger current position among the assets and a stronger stockholders' equity position; both tend to indicate increased strength in the overall financial position of the company.

## NOTES TO FINANCIAL STATEMENTS AND ADEQUATE DISCLOSURE

There are numerous items of relevant financial information that are necessary to fully understand the financial condition of a company and the results of operations for the period covered by the income statement that cannot be conveniently included in the face of the principal financial statements. Also, any event that may materially affect future operations or financial condition must be disclosed. The possible number and types of items and events that should be included in notes are almost endless; and in addition to the notes, each page of the report should be referenced as, "See accompanying notes to financial statements," to inform the readers that the notes are an integral part of the statements. Some of the more frequent items and events requiring notes to financial statements are as follows:

1. Summary of significant accounting policies—this should always be Note 1 and covers all areas having alternative generally accepted accounting principles for accounts presented in the income statement and the balance sheet. The more common areas of accounting policy disclosure for the manufacturing company include (a) Method of pricing inventory, cost or lower of cost or market, and inventory flow assumption, first-in-first-out, last-in-last-out, or one of the accepted averaging methods. (b) Plant and equipment, recorded at cost, the depreciation methods used and the amount of depreciation for the period. The use of the flow through or deferral method of accounting for investment tax credit should also be disclosed here. (c) Federal and state income tax, the use of deferrals where differing methods are used for financial statements and tax returns, disclosure of Subchapter S elections, consents and revocations. A note that net income is taxed directly to the proprietor or partners in those types of organizations should be included. (d) Any other areas of accepted accounting alternatives.

2. Liabilities and pledged assets—this note should disclose such information as the pledged assets and their book value, the interest rate and payment terms of the note, the use of and contents of any related escrow accounts, any restrictions imposed by the loan agreement, and other pertinent information.

3. Long-term leases—disclose length of lease, property leased, periodic payments, rights to sublease, option to renew, escalator clauses, expenses paid by lessee, restrictions imposed by lease, purchase options, and any other information about the lease that is of use to the reader of the financial statements.

4. Retirement plans—the important provisions of retirement plans should be noted with definite disclosure of liabilities imposed on the business by the plan. Plans that fund past service benefits must disclose the funding requirements, the method of amortizing the past service liability, and the amount of the past service liability. Retirement plans that have either defined contributions or defined benefits must disclose the funding method and liability. Profit sharing plans without fixed liabilities have a lesser impact on financial condition, but their existence and major provisions should be disclosed. Applications for plan qualifications and terminations should also be in notes to financial statements.

5. Contingencies include both possible assets and liabilities, the existence of or amount of which cannot be reasonably estimated or determined. Because the amount cannot be estimated with reasonable accuracy, it cannot be presented as an amount in the financial statements. This uncertainty necessitates disclosure in a note along with disclosure of other financially pertinent information. Outside

verification of contingencies, such as an attorney's letter, should be sought when there is litigation or other need for legal opinion. Care must also be exercised in the disclosure of dollar amounts that might be damaging to the company being reported upon, if obtained by plaintiffs, defendants or other third parties.

6. Buy and sell agreements that pose a possible liability or significant change in ownership must be disclosed. The amount of the potential liability must be disclosed along with significant payment terms and interest rates. Funding, such as life insurance, that covers all or part of the potential liabilities should be noted, along with the requirements for funding.
7. Employee stock options with details of number of shares, issue price, option dates, type of stock, dilution effect, and expiration dates must be disclosed.
8. Deferred compensation plans and their potential liabilities must be disclosed.
9. Post statement events—those events occurring between the statement date and completion date of the report must be noted if they have a potential, significant financial impact on future operations. Such events can include, but are not limited to, changes in ownership or management, major transactions, catastrophes, changes in policies or operations, etc.

## FREQUENCY OF FINANCIAL STATEMENT PRESENTATION

Unless there are a limited number of deliveries to customers that would make monthly reporting meaningless, and that may be an erroneous assumption, financial statements should be prepared for the manufacturer each month. Monthly statements, however, are usually aimed primarily at company management and probably need not go to the extent to meet the disclosure requirements as do external reports. Also, additional reports may be prepared for management on a monthly or more frequent basis that are not presented to outsiders. These reports are primarily for management controls and are presented and discussed in Chapter 9.

As a minimum, financial statements should be prepared quarterly. In many situations lending institutions or other third parties may request quarterly reports.

Equally important to the frequency of presentation of financial statements and reports, is the punctuality of financial reporting. Monthly financial statements and reports should be completed within 3 to 10 days after the end of the month. This punctuality requires that accounting procedures be current at the end of every month which takes no more total time and effort than being constantly behind. Quarterly and annual reports which require additional verifications and disclosures may take additional time to prepare. However, ancient reports lose their punch for management decision making, their most important aspect.

**SUMMARY**

The four principal financial statements, the income statement, statement of retained earnings, balance sheet, and statement of changes in financial position are more useful when compared to statements from similar accounting periods. Statements should be concise with many details presented in schedules to supplement financial information in the principal statements. Percentage analyses are also very useful in relation to income, cost and expense items and in analyzing shifts in financial condition.

In addition to the principal statements and supplementary schedules, every report prepared by an independent accountant must include an opinion or denial of an opinion. Also, every report for external use must have the necessary notes to financial statements for adequate disclosure. Incomplete reports must be restricted to internal use.

Financial reports in almost all circumstances should be prepared every month for the manufacturer. Although quarterly and annual reports for external use may require slightly longer to verify and prepare, monthly reports for management should be prepared shortly after the month-end to be of greatest use to management.

# 2

# Framework of a Modern Manufacturing Accounting System

## PRESENTATION AND USE OF A FLEXIBLE CHART OF ACCOUNTS

The chart of accounts should be constructed in such a way that it provides all the accounts necessary to record current transactions and leaves enough space in the numbering system to add additional accounts over a period of years. The accounts should be arranged in a numerical sequence that follows the five major categories of accounts: assets, liabilities, stockholders' equity or capital, income, and costs and expenses. Subgroups are necessary under these major categories to further classify items within the primary areas.

The following model chart of accounts can be altered as necessary to meet the needs of individual manufacturing companies.

**Figure 2–1**

**MANUFACTURING COMPANY**
**CHART OF ACCOUNTS**

ASSETS—100

| Account Number | Account |
|---|---|
| 101 | Petty cash |
| 102 | Cash in bank |
| 110 | Temporary investments |
| 115 | Accounts receivable—trade |
| 119 | Allowance for uncollectible accounts |
| 120 | Accounts receivable—employees |
| 121 | Accounts receivable—affiliates |
| 124 | Travel advances |
| 134 | Prepaid insurance |
| 140 | Materials inventory |
| 141 | Goods in process inventory |
| 142 | Finished goods inventory |
| 143 | Goods on consignment—out |
| 150 | Office furniture and equipment |
| 151 | Machinery and equipment |
| 152 | Vehicles |
| 153 | Patterns |
| 154 | Dies and fixtures |
| 155 | Buildings |
| 156 | Land |
| 160 | Accumulated depreciation—office furniture and equipment |
| 161 | Accumulated depreciation—machinery and equipment |
| 162 | Accumulated depreciation—vehicles |
| 163 | Accumulated depreciation—patterns |
| 164 | Accumulated depreciation—dies and fixtures |
| 165 | Accumulated depreciation—buildings |
| 170 | Organization costs |
| 171 | Patents |
| 172 | Goodwill |
| 180 | Cash surrender value of officers' life insurance |
| 181 | Special funds |
| 182 | Long-term investments |
| 190 | Utility deposits |

LIABILITIES—200

| Account Number | Account |
|---|---|
| 201 | Accounts payable—trade |
| 205 | Notes payable—short-term |
| 210 | Accrued payroll |
| 211 | Accrued commissions |
| 212 | Accrued royalties |
| 213 | Accrued retirement funds |
| 214 | Accrued expenses |
| 220 | Sales tax payable |
| 221 | Accrued property tax |
| 222 | Accrued state income tax |
| 223 | Accrued federal income tax |
| 230 | Accrued state unemployment tax |
| 231 | Accrued federal unemployment tax |
| 232 | Accrued employer F.I.C.A. tax |
| 233 | Withheld F.I.C.A. tax |
| 234 | Withheld federal income tax |
| 235 | Withheld state income tax |
| 236 | Withheld county or city tax |
| 237 | Withheld union dues |
| 238 | Withheld—other |
| 251 | Dividends payable |
| 260 | Mortgage note payable |
| 261 | Bonds payable |
| 262 | Premium or discount on bonds payable. |

STOCKHOLDERS' EQUITY—300

| Account Number | Account |
|---|---|
| 301 | Common stock |
| 310 | Preferred stock |
| 320 | Additional paid-in capital |
| 330 | Treasury stock |
| 340 | Retained earnings |
| 341 | Appropriated retained earnings |
| 350 | Dividends on common stock |
| 351 | Dividends on preferred stock |

## SALES AND OTHER INCOME—400

## RETURNED SALES—500

## COST OF SALES—600

| ACCOUNT | ACCOUNT NUMBER Sales | Returned Sales | Cost of Sales |
|---|---|---|---|
| Machine 1 | 401 | 501 | 601 |
| Machine 2 | 402 | 502 | 602 |
| Machine 3 | 403 | 503 | 603 |
| Custom machines | 410 | 510 | 610 |
| Repair parts | 420 | 520 | 620 |
| Service | 430 | 530 | 630 |
| Interest income | 490 | | |
| Miscellaneous income | 491 | | |
| Extraordinary gains | 495 | | |

## FACTORY EXPENSES—700

| Account Number | Account |
|---|---|
| 701 | Direct labor |
| 702 | Direct labor applied |
| 703 | Supervisory salaries |
| 704 | Factory repairs and services |
| 705 | Factory equipment rental |
| 706 | Factory supplies |
| 707 | Factory maintenance |
| 708 | Shipping and receiving labor |
| 761 | Depreciation—machinery and equipment |
| 763 | Depreciation—patterns |
| 764 | Depreciation—dies and fixtures |
| 770 | Miscellaneous factory expense |
| 780 | Materials variances |
| 781 | Direct labor variances |
| 782 | Factory overhead variances |
| 799 | Factory expense applied |

## GENERAL AND ADMINISTRATIVE EXPENSES—800

| Account Number | Account |
|---|---|
| 801 | Officers' salaries |
| 802 | Engineering salaries |
| 803 | Clerical salaries |
| 811 | Commission expense |
| 812 | Royalty expense |
| 813 | Retirement benefits |
| 814 | Interest expense |
| 819 | Uncollectible accounts |
| 821 | Property tax |
| 822 | State income tax |
| 823 | Federal income tax |
| 824 | Travel and entertainment |
| 830 | State unemployment tax |
| 831 | Federal unemployment tax |
| 832 | F.I.C.A. tax |
| 834 | Insurance |
| 840 | Heat |
| 841 | Electricity |
| 842 | Water |
| 843 | Telephone and telegraph |
| 844 | Repairs |
| 845 | Maintenance |
| 850 | Freight out |
| 851 | Advertising |
| 852 | Office supplies |
| 853 | Dues and subscriptions |
| 854 | Professional services |
| 855 | Discounts lost |
| 860 | Depreciation—office furniture and equipment |
| 862 | Depreciation—vehicles |
| 865 | Depreciation—buildings |
| 869 | Vehicle expense |
| 870 | Amortization of organization costs |
| 871 | Amortization of patents |
| 872 | Amortization of goodwill |
| 880 | Officers' life insurance |
| 890 | Miscellaneous |
| 895 | Extraordinary losses |
| 899 | Factory overhead applied |

This chart of accounts can be classified into categories within the five major types of accounts as follows:

| | |
|---|---|
| ASSETS—100 | |
| Current assets | 101 to 149 |
| Plant and equipment | 150 to 169 |
| Intangible assets | 170 to 179 |
| Investments | 180 to 189 |
| Other assets | 190 to 199 |
| LIABILITIES—200 | |
| Current liabilities | 201 to 259 |
| Long-term liabilities | 260 to 269 |
| Deferrals | 270 to 279 |
| STOCKHOLDERS' EQUITY—300 | |
| Paid-in capital | 301 to 329 |
| Treasury stock | 330 to 339 |
| Retained earnings | 340 to 349 |
| Dividends | 350 to 359 |
| SALES | 401 to 489 |
| OTHER INCOME | 491 to 499 |
| RETURNED SALES | 501 to 589 |
| COST OF SALES | 601 to 689 |
| FACTORY EXPENSES | 701 to 799 |
| GENERAL AND ADMINISTRATIVE EXPENSES | 801 to 899 |

**Figure 2-2**

Also, there is an asset-expense, liability-expense tie-in of account numbers for related accounts—examples:

| | |
|---|---|
| Allowance for uncollectible accounts | — 119 |
| Uncollectible accounts expense | — 819 |
| Accrued commissions | — 211 |
| Commissions expense | — 811 |

This tie-in of account numbers makes memorizing easier and saves time in looking up account numbers.

Expense accounts have not been fragmented between factory expenses and general and administrative expenses except where a natural division exists, as in the case of depreciation expense on various assets; example: depreciation of machinery and equipment, factory expense; depreciation of office furniture and equipment, general and administrative expense.

Many of the accounts in the 800 series contain elements of both factory expense and general and administrative expense. Expenses are allocated to inventory costs through credits to contra accounts 702, direct labor; 799, factory expense; and 899, factory overhead in general and administrative expenses. This procedure allows all expense accounts to remain intact for simpler analysis and convenient comparisons. It necessitates worksheet allocation of those 800 series accounts that contain both factory and general and administrative expenses. These procedures are explained in subsequent chapters on allocations, cost systems and end of period adjustments.

## MANUFACTURING TERMINOLOGY

Certain terminology is somewhat unique to manufacturing and should be discussed at this point for easier reading and future reference.

*Materials*—often called raw materials, but the term raw materials really refers to unprocessed natural resources as distinguished from other materials used by the manufacturer. Materials include all items purchased which become a part of the finished product. Materials inventory is transferred to goods in process once the materials enter the manufacturing process. Components may be finished goods for one manufacturer and materials to the buying manufacturer.

*Direct labor*—is that labor which is used to produce or handle the products manufactured. Production labor, such as supervisory labor that does not work directly on the product becomes a part of factory expense.

*Factory expense*—also called manufacturing expense, factory overhead, manufacturing overhead or just overhead, represents all expenses other than materials and direct labor which are necessary to the production process, the maintenance of inventories, and the handling of goods. Factory expenses also include those expenses, such as payroll taxes and fringe benefits, allocable to all factory labor. Expenses related to the space used for production are also a part of factory expenses.

*Standard costs*—are the costs of products produced for sale to customers—or what the product should cost under normal production conditions. The standard cost of a product includes the normal quantity of materials, direct labor and factory expense.

*Variances*—this is the amount by which the actual costs of a product differ from the predetermined standard costs. Variances are usually actual cost differences from standard cost for the elements of both price and quantity.

*Variable costs*—also called direct costs, are those costs directly related to the quantity produced, as materials, direct labor and variable overhead.

*Fixed costs*—are costs that remain relatively unchanged in total amount within the normal production range; examples: depreciation and property taxes on real estate, insurance on building and contents, and utilities to some extent.

*Goods in process*—inventory in the conversion process from materials to which a portion of the direct labor and factory expenses have been added.

*Finished goods*—inventory which is ready for sale to customers.

## ACCUMULATION AND CONTROL OF FINANCIAL DATA

Every accounting system centers around the general ledger, of which the framework is the chart of accounts. The general ledger summarizes all the transactions recorded in the various journals on a day to day basis. The transactions are classified by the various accounts in the journals and posted in total to the general ledger at the end of each month. Each month a trial balance of the general ledger must be prepared, but the trial balance proves nothing except that total debits equal total credits. The genuine accuracy proof of the general ledger is the use of controls, primarily a control account system, for every balance sheet account, and a reliable system for accumulating data for income statement accounts.

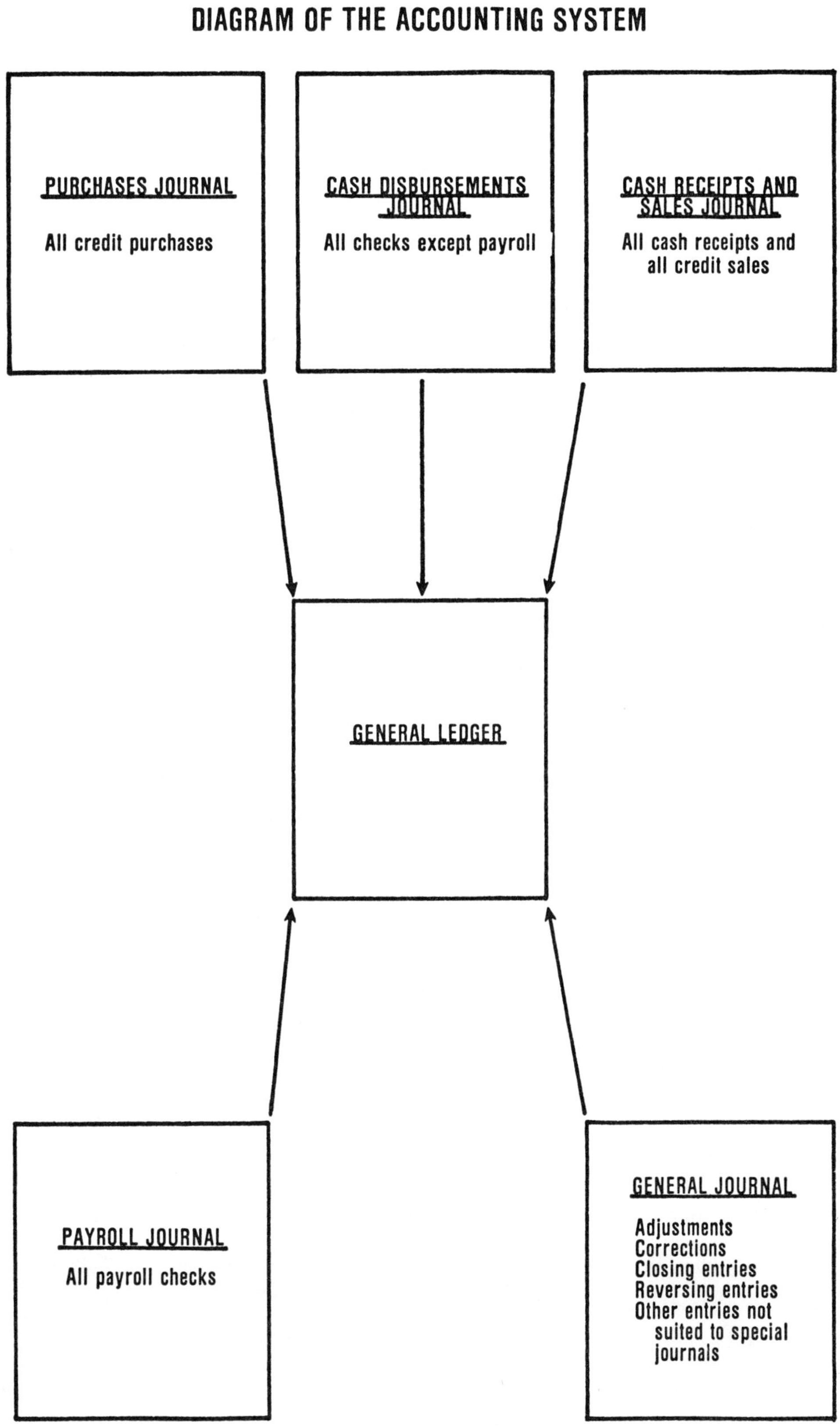
DIAGRAM OF THE ACCOUNTING SYSTEM
PURCHASES JOURNAL
All credit purchases
CASH DISBURSEMENTS JOURNAL
All checks except payroll
CASH RECEIPTS AND SALES JOURNAL
All cash receipts and all credit sales
GENERAL LEDGER
PAYROLL JOURNAL
All payroll checks
GENERAL JOURNAL
Adjustments
Corrections
Closing entries
Reversing entries
Other entries not suited to special journals

Figure 2-3

Control features for general ledger accounts on a monthly basis are as follows:

Petty cash—count and reconcile to impress balance.

Cash in bank—reconcile balance per bank to balance per books.

Temporary investments—subsidiary ledger or list, compute interest receivable.

Accounts receivable trade—subsidiary ledger.

Allowance for uncollectible accounts—monthly, estimate for reasonableness or add 1/12 of estimated annual write-off; quarterly or annually, compute per predetermined formula or judgment based on analysis of accounts receivable or sales volume.

Accounts receivable—employees—subsidiary ledger.

Accounts receivable—affiliates—subsidiary ledger or tie-in of intercompany accounts.

Travel advances—subsidiary ledger.

Prepaid insurance—monthly estimate of prepaid or expense, quarterly or annual schedule for computation.

Inventories—perpetual records or gross profit estimate monthly, annual physical count.

Plant and equipment and accumulated depreciation—monthly estimate of 1/12 annual depreciation, subsidiary of assets and accumulated depreciation, recomputed quarterly or annually, or computation schedule, annual physical verification.

Organization costs—monthly amortization.

Patents—subsidiary ledger for patents and amortization; amortize monthly at 1/12 estimated annual amortization; compute quarterly or annually.

Goodwill—monthly amortization.

Cash surrender value of life insurance—monthly increase of 1/12 of annual increase; verify with insurance schedule quarterly or annually.

Special funds—reconcile balances, subsidiary ledgers, add accrued interest, etc., depending on contents of funds.

Long-term investments—subsidiary ledger or schedule, compute accrued interest and set up other receivables as due or declared.

Utility deposits—subsidiary ledger or note in general ledger.

Accounts payable—trade—subsidiary ledger (usually unnecessary), total unpaid invoices or vouchers monthly.

Notes payable—short-term—subsidiary ledger or schedule.

Accrued payroll—monthly computation.

Accrued commissions—monthly computation, perhaps a subsidiary ledger.

Accrued retirement funds—monthly computation, past service amortization at 1/12 annual amount, or accrue 1/12 annual amount each month depending on funding requirements; verify estimates or computations quarterly or annually.

Accrued expenses—compute monthly.

Sales tax payable—verify to return prepared or amount collected.

Accrued property tax—estimate at 1/12 annual each month, compute annually based on assessment and tax rate.

Accrued state income tax—compute monthly based on rate and annualized income less deposits.

Accrued federal income tax—compute monthly based on rates and annualized income less deposits.

Accrued state and federal unemployment taxes—compute monthly based on taxable payroll and applicable rates.

Accrued employer F.I.C.A. tax—match monthly withholding, compute quarterly less deposits.

Withholdings—amount withheld less deposits and payments.

Dividends payable—declared but unpaid at dividend rate times number of shares outstanding.

Mortgage note payable—per amortization schedule, reclassify next 12 principal payments as current liability.

Bonds payable—per subsidiary ledger of bond holders, alphabetically, numerically or both.

Premium or discount on bonds payable—per amortization schedule, amortization becomes decrease or increase of interest expense.

Deferred items—per computations.

Common stock—per subsidiary ledger by stockholders alphabetically and by certificate numbers.

Preferred stock—per subsidiary ledger by stockholders alphabetically and by certificate numbers.

Additional paid-in capital—record of accumulation by source, separate general ledger accounts by source may be kept.

Treasury stock—subsidiary ledger by certificate numbers.

Retained earnings—record of accumulated net income and net loss since inception less dividends declared since inception and current appropriations.

Appropriated retained earnings—current authorizations.

Dividends on common stock—those declared during the current year.

Dividends on preferred stock—those declared during the current year.

All income and expense accounts—current year's accumulations through various journals, each item supported by transaction, source documents or computations.

## TRACING THE FLOW OF MATERIALS, LABOR AND MANUFACTURING OVERHEAD THROUGH THE ACCOUNTING SYSTEM

All production costs move through the accounting system in the form of inventories and ultimately become a part of cost of goods manufactured and sold as shipments are made to customers. The amount of materials, labor and overhead processed through the system varies slightly depending on whether standard costs or actual costs of production are used. We will assume the use of standard costs which are usually more practical for repetitive products or processes.

Assume that 1,000 units of product SEL are to be produced with the standard cost per unit as follows:

| | |
|---|---|
| Materials—2 lbs. at $1.50 | = $ 3.00 |
| Direct labor—3 hours at $5.00 | = 15.00 |
| Manufacturing overhead—<br>$3.00 per direct labor hour—<br>3 hours at $3.00 | = 9.00 |
| Total standard cost per unit | $27.00 |

The "T" accounts in Figure 2-4 illustrate the flow of costs through the system.

| Materials | |
|---|---|
| A. 10,000 | D. 3,000 |

| Accounts Payable, etc. | |
|---|---|
| | A. 10,000 |
| | C. 9,500 |

| Direct Labor | |
|---|---|
| B. 15,000 | |

| Cash and withholdings or accrued wages | |
|---|---|
| | B. 15,000 |

| Manufacturing Expenses | |
|---|---|
| C. 9,500 | |

| Direct Labor Applied | |
|---|---|
| | E. 15,000 |

| Goods in Process | |
|---|---|
| D. 3,000 | G. 27,000 |
| E. 15,000 | |
| F. 9,000 | |

| Manufacturing Expenses Applied | |
|---|---|
| | F. 9,000 |

| Finished Goods | |
|---|---|
| G. 27,000 | H. 27,000 |

| Cost of Goods Sold | |
|---|---|
| H. 27,000 | |

**Figure 2-4**

The "T" accounts in Figure 2-4 can be journalized and explained as follows:

| | Debit | Credit |
|---|---|---|
| A. Materials | 10,000 | |
| Accounts payable | | 10,000 |
| Purchase of materials | | |
| B. Direct labor | 15,000 | |
| Cash and withholdings or accrued wages | | 15,000 |
| Cost of direct labor | | |
| C. Manufacturing expenses | 9,500 | |
| Accounts payable, etc. | | 9,500 |
| Cost of manufacturing expenses—the costs would actually be charged to various expense accounts | | |
| D. Goods in process | 3,000 | |
| Materials | | 3,000 |
| Materials issued to manufacturing for 1,000 units of product SEL | | |

| | | Debit | Credit |
|---|---|---|---|
| E. Goods in process | | 15,000 | |
| Direct labor applied | | | 15,000 |
| Direct labor for 1,000 units of product SEL | | | |
| F. Goods in process | | 9,000 | |
| Manufacturing expenses applied | | | 9,000 |
| \$3.00 × 3,000 direct labor hours | | | |
| G. Finished goods | | 27,000 | |
| Goods in process | | | 27,000 |
| Transfer of completed goods from goods in process to finished goods—cost elements as follows: | | | |
| Materials | \$ 3,000 | | |
| Direct labor | 15,000 | | |
| Manufacturing expenses | 9,000 | | |
| Total | \$27,000 | | |
| H. Cost of goods sold | | 27,000 | |
| Finished goods | | | 27,000 |
| Transfer inventory cost to cost of goods sold on sale to customer | | | |

The preceding example will be expanded to illustrate the handling of variances (differences between standard and actual costs) in Chapter 7.

A simplified diagram of the physical flow of the elements appears in Figure 2-5.

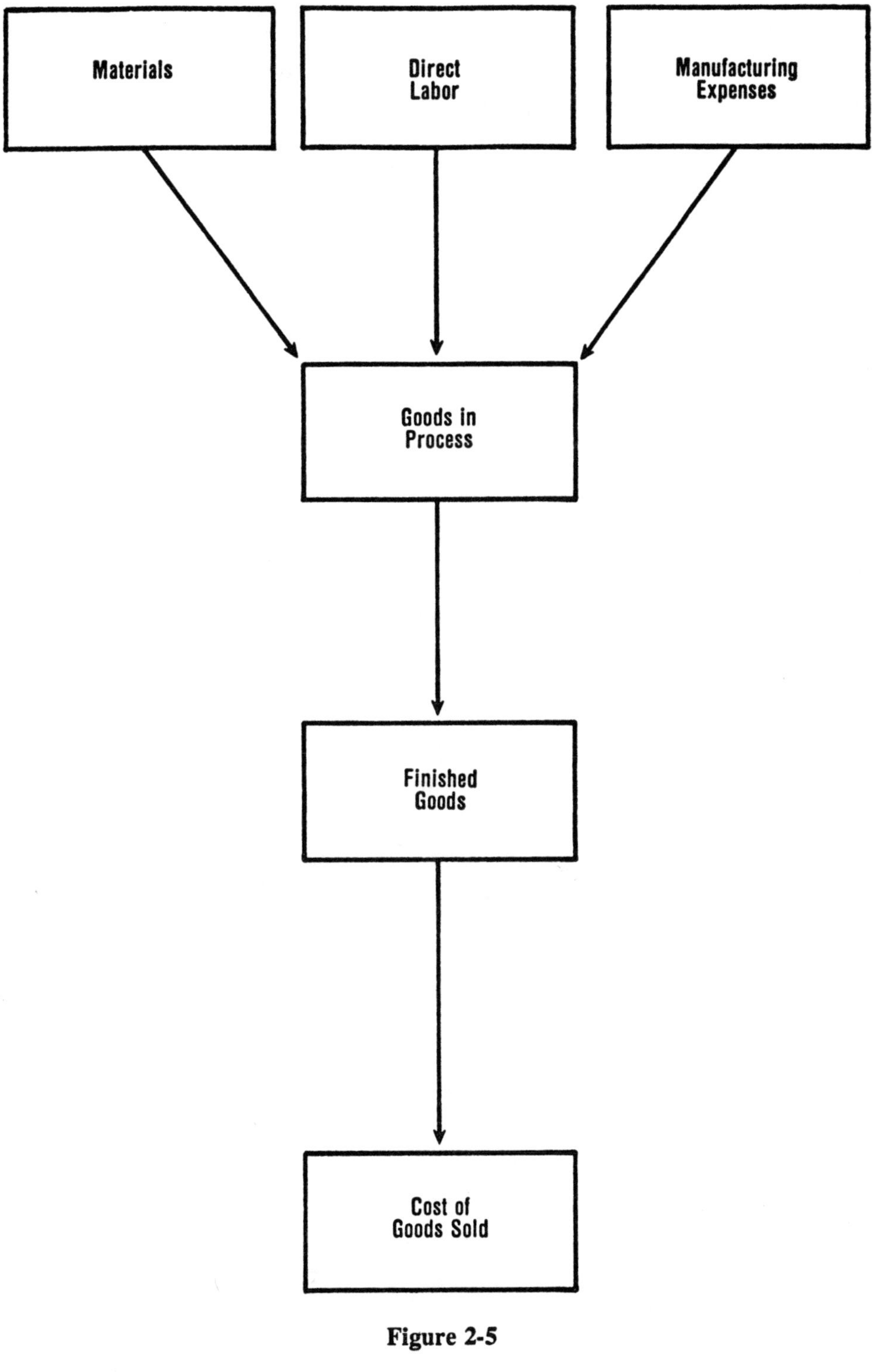
Materials
Direct Labor
Manufacturing Expenses
Goods in Process
Finished Goods
Cost of Goods Sold

**Figure 2-5**

## POINTS TO CONSIDER IN SELECTING MONTHLY AND FISCAL CLOSING DATES

Choosing a closing date for each month during the fiscal year has only to consider the practical aspects. It is sometimes more convenient to close each month on a particular day of the week rather than the last day of the month. Also, for comparative purposes related to periodic financial statements and reports, more useful information can sometimes be obtained by dividing the year into 13 four-week periods. Another possibility for greater balance in periodic reporting is to divide the year into periods each of which has an equal number of working days.

There are also disadvantages in selecting a closing date other than month-end. Most taxes must be remitted based on payroll, sales, etc., for calendar months or quarters. These requirements do not make other closing dates unworkable; they do complicate reporting for tax purposes slightly in that the tax figures do not coincide exactly with the general ledger postings. Another disadvantage is that most customers, suppliers, banks, etc., will be operating on a calendar month. This conflict in closing dates complicates reconciliation of bank accounts, unpaid invoices to statements and other items where dates overlap. The accountant, the manufacturer, and other management personnel must consider the advantages and disadvantages to decide individual cases on interim accounting periods and closing dates.

Selecting a year-end date also involves the auditor and is restricted by the Internal Revenue Code. A corporation may close its first fiscal year on the last day of any calendar month providing that the year does not contain more than 12 months. There is also available a 52–53 week year that may close on a specific day of the week that immediately precedes the end of the month or the day on which the day of the week falls nearest the end of the calendar month. In every situation it is important to select a fiscal year-end that will provide for the greatest simplicity in closing the records and performing the audit. Usually, this date should be at the low point of the operating cycle, should avoid December 31 because of the holidays and auditor's workload at that date, and should also be at a date when the closing will not conflict with vacations, especially those of accounting personnel.

A regular corporation, as opposed to a Subchapter S corporation, may change its fiscal year by filing a short period return on which the tax computation is annualized. Prior permission of the Commissioner of Internal Revenue is required unless certain tests are met.

A partnership must use the same fiscal year as its principal partners unless permission is obtained, usually for an acceptable business reason.

Rarely, because of various complications, does a proprietorship use other than a calendar year.

**SUMMARY**

The chart of accounts should be designed with accounts listed in the approximate sequence in which they will appear on the balance sheet and income statement. A numbering system must be used that will allow the addition of new accounts in each category. Every chart of accounts should be adapted to the needs of the individual manufacturing company or group of companies. It is improper to subordinate the information needed in the firm to a so-called standard chart of accounts.

The accounting system used by the manufacturer must accumulate financial transactions efficiently and accurately. These transactions must be evidenced by documents or computations, recorded in the journals and summarized in the ledgers. It is essential to build controls into the system for every general ledger account. These controls must be used repetitively as a part of the monthly closing routine.

Materials, direct labor and various manufacturing expenses flow through production as material is processed, converted into finished goods inventory, and sold to customers. It is accounting's function to maintain records of the cost elements as they flow through the production and storage facilities.

Careful consideration must be given to both interim and fiscal closing dates. The advantages to the company, the company personnel, and the auditor must be considered in selecting these dates.

# 3

# Streamlining Sales Orders, Billings, Accounts Receivable and Cash Receipts— Squeezing Working Capital Liquidity

## HOW TO MAKE EFFICIENT USE OF MULTIPURPOSE AND MULTICOPY SALES ORDERS AND SALES INVOICE FORMS

The most convenient handling of sales orders can be accomplished through the use of multicopy, snap-out carbon forms specially printed for each manufacturing company. Substantial time can be saved by reducing typing to an absolute minimum through putting essential information on the forms only once. Most electric typewriters can cut many legible copies through light weight, throw away carbon and light weight paper. The following is an example of combining the same sales order-invoice forms into multiform packages of ten and seven copies each. The ten copy forms are used for manufactured products and the seven copy forms for stock shipments. See Figure 3-1.

Ten Part Form

| Copy Number | Color | Destination | Purpose |
|---|---|---|---|
| 1 | White | Customer | Invoice |
| 2 | White | Customer | Duplicate invoice |
| 3 | Yellow | Shipping | Packing slip |
| 4 | Green | Accounting | Recording and alphabetical file |
| 5 | Salmon | Accounting | Numerical file |
| 6 | Blue | Shipping | Shipping notice |
| 7 | Pink | Engineering | Drawings |
| 8 | Orange | Purchasing | Ordering components |
| 9 | Green | Manufacturing | Assembly or processing |
| 10 | White | Customer | Acknowledgment |

Each of the above forms is identical except for color and identification, such as 9, Manufacturing, etc., and copy 10 is marked "Acknowledgment, will ship on or about (date) ". Copies 7, 8 and 9 can usually be eliminated for shipments of certain stock items.

Procedures for form preparation and flow are as follows:

a. All information except shipping date, carrier, prices, extensions, and total billing is typed on the forms when the customer's order is received. The carrier may be typed at the time the order is received if specified by the customer or the sales department.

b. Copies are distributed to the various departments as: Copies 1, 2, 4 and 5 are assembled with the customer's order and filed alphabetically by customer name in accounting. Other departments may have access to this file as advisable, but accounting should maintain control. This file becomes an open order file and should be reviewed periodically, at least weekly, to detect orders that need positive action. Perhaps an open order listing should be prepared by accounting and presented to one individual responsible for customer service.

c. Copies 3 and 6, the packing slip and shipping notice, are sent immediately to shipping. Shipping pulls the goods from stock or awaits the delivery from manufacturing depending on the type of items on the order. Copies 3 and 6 are marked with the shipping date, quantities shipped and back ordered, carrier, and shipping charges if applicable. Copy 3 goes with the goods to the customer. A copy of the bill of lading is attached to copy 6 which is returned to accounting on the same day that the shipment is made. This shipping notice is used to pull the order from the open order file. The invoices are completed (copies 1, 2, 3 and 5).

d. Copies 1 and 2, along with additional invoice copies if requested, and a copy of the bill of lading, when used, are sent to the customer immediately. Back orders

**GRINDING & POLISHING MACHINERY CORP.**
P. O. Box 19039 – 2801 Tobey Drive
Indianapolis, Indiana 46219
Phone: 317–898-0750

**INVOICE NO.** ______________
**TERMS:** Net 30 days
FOB Indianapolis, Ind.

SHIP TO (SAME AS SOLD TO UNLESS SPECIFIED)

SOLD TO

MARK: ______________

| ORDER DATE | PUR ORDER NO | DATE SHIPPED | INVOICE DATE | SHIP VIA |
|---|---|---|---|---|
| | | | | |

| QUANTITY | | PART NUMBER AND DESCRIPTION | PRICING |
|---|---|---|---|
| SHIPPED | BACK ORDERED | | |
| | | | |
| SHIPPING CHARGES | | | |
| TOTAL | | | |

WE HEREBY CERTIFY THAT THESE GOODS WERE PRODUCED IN COMPLIANCE WITH ALL APPLICABLE REQUIREMENTS OF SECTIONS 6, 7 AND 12 OF THE FAIR LABOR STANDARDS ACT, AS AMENDED, AND OF REGULATIONS AND ORDERS OF THE UNITED STATES DEPARTMENT OF LABOR ISSUED UNDER SECTION 14 THEREOF.

2 DUPLICATE INVOICE

**Figure 3-1**

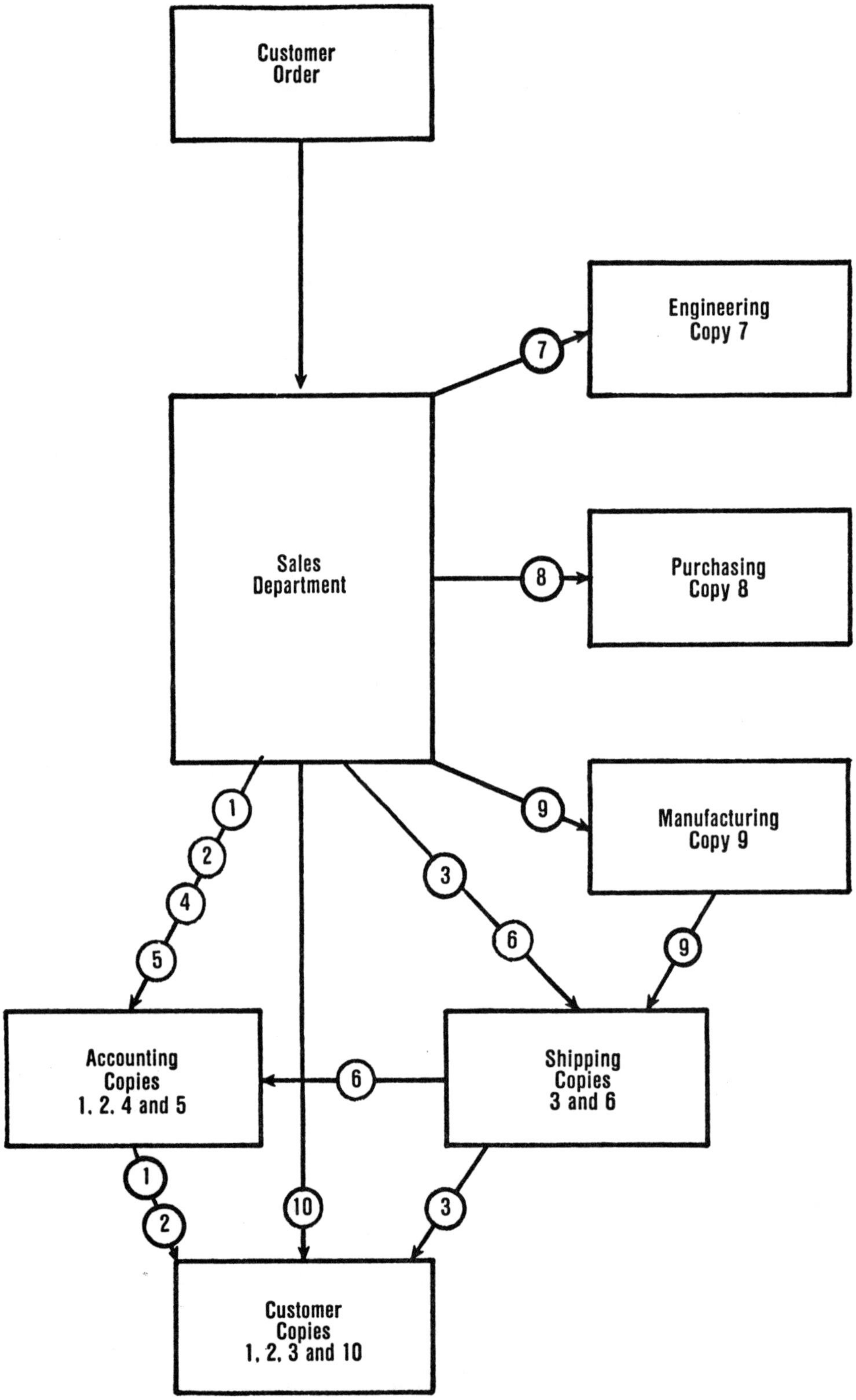


**Sales Order—Invoice Multicopy Forms — Flow Diagram**

**Figure 3-2**

initiate the same order-invoice process over again. The shipping notice, customer order, etc., are attached to copy 4 and filed alphabetically by customer. Copy 5 goes to a numerical invoice file.

e. If the item is manufactured, copy 9 from manufacturing goes with the item to shipping for identification and is then destroyed.

f. Copies 7 and 8 go to engineering and purchasing respectively to trigger drawings, blue prints, and purchase orders as necessary. These copies may then be destroyed.

When ordering these multicopy forms, more than one quote and the vendor's advice should be obtained. It is important to remember that the manufacturer's customer receives these forms, and that they are a possible means of advertising through the company logo, trademark and overall appearance. Also, in ordering the forms, the copies can be spot glued to tear apart easily where desirable. Another time saver is to order extra single invoice copies that can be inserted with extra carbon when customers request more than two invoice copies.

The process and flow of forms is diagramed in Figure 3-2.

## SPECIAL JOURNALS FOR SALES, COST OF SALES, ACCOUNTS RECEIVABLE AND CASH RECEIPTS

It is equally important that the journals and ledgers used in recording and summarizing financial transactions be designed to fit the needs of the manufacturer. There are two principal considerations in designing accounting journals and ledgers—efficiency and information. These two guides were also followed in selecting the chart of accounts in Chapter 2. That chart of accounts is the framework for the journals, ledgers and transactions presented in this and following chapters.

It is often convenient to record both sales and cash receipts in the same journal. These two sources represent both sides of practically all accounts receivable entries. In the system presented here the accounts receivable ledger card is a direct overlay of the journal for simultaneous recording and posting. This procedure saves time and increases accuracy by eliminating the need to post from the sales and cash receipts journal to the accounts receivable ledger. When the accounts receivable card is used as an overlay of the journal, the figures are transferred by carbon or other copy paper rather than being rewritten—one less writing, one less chance for error. The following journal and ledger card illustrate a system that can easily be modified to meet the needs of the individual manufacturer.

MACHINE MANUFACTURING CORPORATION

Page 173

| | | | 115 — Accounts Receivable | | | 102 | Sales | | | | | |
|---|---|---|---|---|---|---|---|---|---|---|---|---|
| | | | | | | | 401 | 402 | 403 | 410 | 420 | 430 |
| | | Invoice | | | | | Machine | Machine | Machine | | Repair | |
| Date | Customer | Number | Debit | Credit | Balance | Cash | 1 | 2 | 3 | Custom | Parts | Service |
| 7- 1- | XYZ | 101 | 1,000.00 | | 11,000.00 | | 950.00 | | | | | |
| 7- 2- | XYZ | CR | | 5,000.00 | 6,000.00 | 5,000.00 | | | | | | |
| 7- 3- | XYZ | CM 201 | | 100.00 | 5,900.00 | | | | | | | |

**Figure 3-3**

Accounts Receivable

Customer XYZ — Card # 2

Address 107 West 3rd. Street, Indianapolis, IN 46200

| | | | 115—Accounts Receivable | | |
|---|---|---|---|---|---|
| | | Invoice | | | |
| Date | Customer | Number | Debit | Credit | Balance |
| 7- 1- | XYZ | 101 | 1,000.00 | | 11,000.00 |
| 7- 2- | XYZ | CR | | 5,000.00 | 6,000.00 |
| 7- 3- | XYZ | CM 201 | | 100.00 | 5,900.00 |

**Figure 3-4**

SALES AND CASH RECEIPTS JOURNAL

Month of May , 19

| 601 Machine 1 | 602 Machine 2 | 603 Machine 3 | 610 Custom | 620 Repair Parts | 630 Service | 142 Finished Goods | 220 Sales Tax | 850 Freight Out | 500 Returns Account | 500 Returns Amount | Miscellaneous Account | Miscellaneous Debit | Miscellaneous Credit | All other accounts, such as Sales, Discounts, etc. |
|---|---|---|---|---|---|---|---|---|---|---|---|---|---|---|
| 600.00 | | | | | | 600.00 | 19.00 | 31.00 | | | | | | |
| | | | | (50.00) | | | | | # 520 | 100.00 | # 140 | 50.00 | | |

**Figure 3–3 (continued)**

## THE MARKETING AUDIT

Marketing consists of considerably more than salesmanship. The scope of marketing also includes distribution, product selection, advertising, and pricing. The ability to create adequate markets is usually the most critical problem facing the manufacturer when considering long-run profitability. As we look at achieving maximum profits, the usual limitation is total sales volume. We can also visualize how sales volume hinges on the proper mix of salesmanship, the ultimate in distribution, proper product selection, the best use of advertising dollars and the most advantageous pricing policies for each product.

Other factors that can limit profits such as personnel resources, financial resources and production capacity tend to be short-run in most situations and can be remedied with even moderate profits produced by less than desirable sales volume. Thus, in all but the rare situations, marketing becomes the limiting factor and places comparable limits on other functions and profits. From this reasoning, which is usually the fact, comes what marketing people call "The Marketing Concept."

The marketing concept has different meanings to different people. With the accountant's emphasis on maximum long-run profit and his knowledge that sales volume is the most common factor in limiting profit, it would seem that marketing should get primary emphasis within the firm and all other functions would be subordinated. To accept this concept one must go back to the total functions of marketing, as mentioned earlier, coupled with the wants, or sometimes needs, of the customer.

Once we have accepted the marketing concept, or at least determined that the firm should be marketing oriented, we can begin to visualize the importance or practicality of the marketing audit. Here the word audit must be defined broadly, for the accountant is inclined to think of only one audit, "The Audit." A marketing audit cannot be as precise as our usual audit of the financial statements. It is extremely difficult to determine the ultimate marketing plan or results.

The marketing audit should be performed by an individual who has much the same independence and competence as the financial auditor. He should have a thorough understanding of marketing, evidence gathering and report writing. A team with complimentary abilities could also accomplish a useful marketing audit. Certainly, a financial auditor and management services technician could be of substantial aid.

The marketing audit becomes an outside, expert appraisal or evaluation of the firm's marketing policies and functions. Marketing policies are determined by actions, not just words. In defining policies it is first necessary to determine the manufacturing company's actual goals. We speak freely of maximizing long-run profits, but how about the sole proprietor who is going to disolve his business inside of five years? How about the manufacturer who controls his business personally and doesn't want it to grow beyond that size? Success has been achieved within these limits. The rate of growth must be within the bounds established for risk by the owners, right or wrong. Therefore, goals from one manufacturer to the next may differ widely, and the success of each measured against the achievement of those goals. Several goals (objectives) are acceptable as:

1. Maximum long-run profits
2. Maximum short-run profits
3. Constant, controllable profit growth
4. Maximum return on limited investment
5. Maximum security for owners and/or management
6. Maximum distributions to stockholders
7. Maximum growth for stock values
8. Combinations of the above—but not an attempt to do everything for everybody

Thus, the marketing audit should determine the overall goal of the manufacturing firm and how well the goal fits actual and planned performance. Planning within the marketing department must be tailored toward achieving the overall company objectives. Here, we might have a basic conflict if we assume that the company should have accepted the marketing concept. Does the company organization place the proper emphasis on marketing to let volume lead the way for the other resource requirements? Perhaps not, and if not, there may be a conflict between marketing policy and company policy that must be resolved to attain a coordinated effort and better results.

Next, there should be a look at marketing strategy. Is the marketing department going after a certain segment of the market? Are different products being developed? Or are competitors being met head-on? Maybe service should be more complete to satisfy the customers' total needs with one package. Will the current or planned strategy best attain the established goals?

Then day-to-day tactics must be in support of the designed strategy. Are the products and markets being developed daily to augment the strategic methods selected to pursue the established goals?

Personnel performance should be evaluated as a part of the marketing audit. Performance and ways to achieve performance should be considered in view of each individual's assigned functions within the total marketing function.

Finally, there should be a review of the grooving of the market function with the other functions, namely production, finance, personnel and housekeeping.

The marketing audit should always be beneficial to the manufacturer. But, as every other function, its estimated worth must be evaluated in relation to its cost. The return in relation to cost is determined by agreement between management and the marketing auditor on the scope of the review—how far to dig in various areas. This decision may depend on the ability, either innate or gained by experience, of the auditor or management to know when they are onto something worthwhile. In the total investigation of the functions that marketing is expected to perform, each should be examined, keeping in mind the previously mentioned guides to a successful operating plan.

## GUIDELINES ON CREDIT PROCEDURES, BILLINGS, STATEMENTS, AND FOLLOW UPS

At least half of the job of creating adequate current operating funds is tied to billings and collections. Here, good habits and speed are the keys to providing the most favorable inflow of cash. The fastest possible collection on every receivable, however, may be in conflict with the marketing concept and the primary goals of the manufacturing company. For instance a profitable sale that results in a 45 day, 60 day or 90 day collection is usually preferable to no sale; but the dealer or customer should never be given the idea that slow payments will be continually tolerated.

In granting credit the gathering of evidence on the prospective buyer should be the principal guide. Most buyers are known, and previous credit experience is often adequate evidence on which to make a decision. An unusually large order from an existing customer merits additional investigation similar to that of a new customer. In fact, the amount of dollars in any order is of primary consideration as to the extensiveness of credit investigation.

The possible sources of information regarding a customer's payment reliability are numerous. Credit ratings, such as Dun & Bradstreet, are often immediately available if the manufacturer has sufficient need to subscribe to the service. This rating alone, combined with personal judgment, may be all the credit information that is necessary for many orders. The same source can usually provide more detailed information when desirable.

References furnished by the potential buyer can be written or called depending on the urgency or convenience in each situation. References should be asked about the length of time they have been selling to the customer, amount of credit granted at any one time, speed of payment, and any other comments.

The credit department of the manufacturer's bank can contact the customer's bank to obtain information. This source can be helpful, particularly when the buyer is aware that the bank is to be questioned as a credit reference. The buyer may feel a certain obligation to the banker who recommended him, and the banker may also feel an obligation to assist in collections where he has given a favorable recommendation. The author has found bankers to be candid, reliable, and accommodating in obtaining credit information.

Credit terms should be stated on the invoice, on quotations, and when otherwise requested by the buyer. Care must be taken when accepting a customer's purchase order. Occasionally, credit terms are stated on a purchase order that do not agree with the terms of the seller. Traditionally, the seller has always stated the payment terms. Stating other than the normal terms on a purchase order without previous discussion with the seller is out of order with normal business routine; especially, the taking of discounts is apt to be overlooked by the seller in accepting the order, which interferes with the flow of paper work and goods and services and often leads to disputes after the shipment is made.

Terms granted by the seller, although stated on the invoices, should not be completely inflexible when other than normal terms will result in less risk or a more reasonable set of transactions in a specific situation. No credit should be extended where collection is doubtful unless the amount of the credit is small enough that the loss will be insignificant. Also, precaution must be taken to prevent the granting of additional credit on risky customers simply because a limited amount has been shipped on open account. His credit file, which may be just his accounts receivable card, should be flagged until additional experience is obtained.

Shyness should never be a factor in discussing credit terms. The exchange of cash is probably the most important element in the complete round of transactions included in a sale and purchase. When special terms are preferable, they should be openly proposed. Cash on delivery is often the best procedure when credit cannot be extended on standard products. The greatest loss with C.O.D. shipments usually includes only shipping and possibly storage charges. Buyer permission for C.O.D. terms should be obtained prior to shipment.

Where payment for or acceptance of custom products is doubtful, an amount equal to one-half the estimated costs may be requested with the order, the other one-half of the estimated cost on delivery, and the balance in perhaps 60 to 90 days. These procedures give both the seller and buyer a degree of protection and somewhat of an equal break on terms. The buyer should not be informed that the terms are based on cost, however, unless it is a cost-plus agreement.

Cash discounts, such as a percentage discount if paid in 10 days, etc., are partially price concessions rather than totally affordable awards for early payment. Usually, payment discounts are dictated by competition rather than being affordable methods of improving cash flow. However, the importance of more rapid collections, the amount of the discount and alternative returns on the money collected must be considered. As an example a 2%/10 days/net 30 discount is equal to approximately a 36% simple interest rate computed as follows:

R = rate
$100 = amount
20 days = length of discount period

$$\frac{100}{1} \times \frac{R}{1} \times \frac{20}{360} = \$\ 2$$

$$\frac{2000\,R}{360} = \$\ 2$$

$$2000\,R = \$720$$

$$R = 36\%$$

If terms of 2/10/n30 are granted, they must be a price concession, the seller must have to pay 36% for money or have other means of obtaining funds. It follows that 1/10/n30 terms equals an 18% simple interest rate, etc.

One of the most common procedures for analyzing the needs for follow-up measures on accounts receivable is the aging schedule. This schedule is a trial balance of accounts receivable with invoices listed for each customer by number of days past due. A common way to set up aging schedule columns is illustrated in Figure 3-5. Except where management needs to evaluate the credit department or when used to analyze the uncollectible account allowance, an accounts receivable aging is largely a waste of time—as is sending a monthly statement to every customer. Neither procedure should be used unless done mechanically on machine spare time, as a periodic management review or an audit procedure.

An equally effective, more efficient collection procedure is to have a typist or clerk pull only past due accounts, type detailed statements on them and give the statements to the credit manager. This procedure can sometimes be shortcut by simply shooting a picture of the accounts receivable card and letting the picture serve as a statement. A rubber stamp can be used to identify the sender and that it is a statement of account.

The credit manager can often write collection notes directly on the statements. Statements on past due accounts should be sent twice a month instead of once on about the 5th and 20th of the month. These dates get the statements to the customers just ahead of normal payment dates. Phone calls should be made on large and local accounts over 60 days old. The call should always be made to an officer in the customer's office to avoid wasting the call by talking to someone who does not have the authority to make a definite promise. Small past due accounts on which reasonable collection efforts have been made should be given to a collection agency. More extensive efforts should be made on larger account balances before turning them over to an agency. Notes should be made on accounts turned over to an agency to prevent further credit and as a reminder to check on the agency's efforts. Small amounts that have been paid around by a customer should not be given to an agency until extensive effort has been made to determine what the problem is.

MACHINE MANUFACTURING CORPORATION

Accounts Receivable Aging Schedule—June 30, 19X7

| Customer | Total Balance | Month of Billing: June | May | April | Prior: Month | Amount |
|---|---|---|---|---|---|---|
| ABC CO. | $10,000 | $ 8,000 | $1,000 | $500 | 8-X6 | $500 |
| XYZ CORP. | 9,000 | 9,000 | | | | |
| Totals | $19,000 | $17,000 | $1,000 | $500 | | $500 |

**Figure 3-5**

Various measurements are used to determine the effectiveness of credit procedures. The most common are accounts receivable turnover and number of days sales in accounts receivable. Accounts receivable turnover is determined by dividing annual sales by average accounts receivable and is computed thusly:

| | Accounts Receivable Balance |
|---|---|
| January | $ 30,000 |
| February | 36,000 |
| March | 39,000 |
| April | 41,000 |
| May | 48,000 |
| June | 54,000 |
| July | 50,000 |
| August | 43,000 |
| September | 42,000 |
| October | 37,000 |
| November | 36,000 |
| December | 35,000 |
| | $491,000 |

$491,000 / 12 = $40,917 Average accounts receivable

Annual sales $310,000 / 40,917 = Turnover of 7.6 times per year

Occasionally, it is suggested that the beginning and ending balance of accounts receivable when added together and divided by two will give a reasonable average. Most businesses are somewhat seasonal, and beginning and ending yearly balances are actually from the same date within the year and not at all an average balance.

The other measure is number of days sales in accounts receivable and is computed as follows:

Accounts receivable balance: $35,000

Annual sales: 310,000 / 365 = $849 average daily sales

35,000 / 849 = 41—number of days sales in accounts receivable

These analyses of accounts receivable must all be viewed with deeper insight. A rapid turnover or short collection period is only desirable as long as profitable sales are not turned away in the process. There is no substitute for good judgment augmented by as much information as can be obtained with reasonable effort on which to make credit and collection decisions.

## EXAMINING WORKING CAPITAL VERSUS WORKING CAPITAL LIQUIDITY AND CASH FLOW

The amount of working capital that a company has (current assets less current liabilities) is in itself somewhat meaningless. Two examples follow for discussion purposes:

| | Company One | Company Two |
|---|---|---|
| Current assets | $105,000 | $10,000 |
| Current liabilities | 100,000 | 5,000 |
| Working capital | $ 5,000 | $ 5,000 |

As is evident, both companies one and two have the same amount of working capital. In most situations it would be a reasonable assumption that company two is in the better working capital position. This comparison leads to a second measure of working capital, the working capital ratio. The ratio is equal to current assets divided by current liabilities. Thus, company one has a working capital ratio of 1.05 to 1, and company two has a ratio of 2 to 1, much stronger than company one, even though each has $5,000 of working capital. Probably, company one is the larger company, and larger companies usually need more working capital to meet day-to-day operating requirements.

Neither the amount of working capital nor the working capital ratio adequately depict the true working capital position. A firm's actual position can be determined only by examining the makeup of current assets and current liabilities. Here, it is necessary to look for working capital liquidity. How quickly can current assets be converted into cash? How quickly must current liabilities be paid? If company one's current assets of $105,000 are all cash, it can easily satisfy the $100,000 in current obligations. If company two's current assets are all inventory, it may take months and additional costs to process the inventory and convert it into cash. The $5,000 of obligations may have to be paid before any cash is available. Liquidity is the key to a sound current position. Rapid conversion of other current assets to cash, deferral of payment of obligations, such as monthly rather than annual insurance payments, all help to squeeze the most out of working capital by improving liquidity.

## CONTROLLING CASH RECEIPTS

Every company regardless of size needs to exercise control over cash beginning with cash receipts. Large companies can work out an elaborate system of cross verification that is also practical because duties can be separated for each function of handling cash and receivables and balance verifications. Smaller companies also need to control cash receipts, to a reasonable degree, even if there is only one bookkeeper. Control examples include:

1. More than one person present when mail is opened.
2. One individual runs a tape of daily checks received and reports the amount each day in a daily report to management—see Chapter 9.
3. Another individual prepares the deposit slip and mails the deposit to the bank. This person would usually be the bookkeeper and would record and post in the records.
4. When the deposit slip (a duplicate) is returned by the bank, it is compared to the daily report.
5. Ideally, another employee or officer would reconcile the bank statement each month.

Additional controls for purchases and cash disbursements are discussed in Chapter 4.

## SUMMARY

Multicopy sales orders and invoice forms with zip-out carbon can be designed to eliminate duplicate typing of similar information needed for various departments and functions. Color codes are also helpful in identifying those forms going to various departments and assisting in identification for paper flow purposes.

Every company can utilize special cash receipts and sales journals with an exact overlay for accounts receivable to save time and increase accuracy. Often standard systems can be used or modified to fit a company's specific needs.

Marketing consists of a wide range of functions and should be serviced by the other major functions within the firm. A manufacturer's potential is usually limited by the sales he can create for his product. Therefore, marketing should be the central focus, with other departments aimed at satisfying the needs of marketing. An excellent method of testing this concept is the marketing audit. Although not an exact science, the marketing audit can assist in putting all functions on the track as set forth by original or revised management policy.

Success in handling customer credit requires an efficient means of policing past due accounts, a set credit policy and excellent judgment based on the most reliable information available for granting credit. Also, a knowledge of what represents the overall best interests of the firm is necessary in determining when to vary from set credit policies, either to the stringent or lenient side.

Liquidity must be considered when analyzing working capital position. Working capital that will not be available for some time to satisfy current obligations may lead one into a false security on current position.

Cash receipts must be controlled to the degree practical. At least limited control through some division duties must be exercised in every firm.

# 4

# Controlling Purchases, Cash Disbursements, and Petty Cash

## PRIMARY PURCHASING OBJECTIVES

Purchasing is the other end of the profit picture from sales and deserves equal attention. Not as glamorous, subordinated as a supporting function, and dependent on the results of marketing efforts, purchasing is likely to be shunned or delegated without adequate management consideration. How the money is spent has a substantial impact on how much revenue can be retained as profit. Therefore, purchasing objectives must be clearly defined and the correct emphasis put on the preferable objective in each situation. The objectives of purchasing should be:

1. *Selecting the best vendor based on price, service and quality.* Each of these determinates can be of the greatest importance as the circumstances dictate. Price is the first consideration when service and quality related to the item being purchased are adequate to prevent shortages, meet customer expectations, and conform to the general quality of the manufactured product for both appearance and durability.

In many situations there is no difference in prices and no detectable difference in quality. Service then becomes the predominate consideration. Service includes making deliveries on schedule or stocking for the manufacturer's use and providing technical assistance as necessary. Occasionally, there is a need for an extended effort by a vendor to help the manufacturer out of a tight situation. A vendor who is oriented to serving the needs of his customers will put forth a maximum effort to get his customer out of a jam even when there is no possibility of making a profit on that specific transaction. Other vendors will not. Enough said.

The quality of a vendor's product must be considered from two standpoints. What effect does it have on production time and how does it affect long run customer satisfaction. Products that cause waste, rework, production stoppages, or slower production rates are undesirable unless proper materials or supplies aren't available, or the low quality is compensated for by price differences.

None of the three vendor offerings, price, service or quality take a clear-cut precedence in every situation. Judgment must be exercised for each acquisition to determine which characteristic is most important.

2. *Proper scheduling of deliveries.* Although sometimes related to the reliability of the vendor, the proper scheduling of deliveries depends most strongly on planning as a part of the purchasing function. Both early and late deliveries tie up cash. In the case of early deliveries the tie-up is caused simply because cash is invested in inventory longer than necessary. Late deliveries tie up cash by delaying the whole conversion-turnover process. Other components, direct labor and overhead costs are sometimes held in inventory because of the lack of one or more parts necessary for completion and shipment. Such a delay caused by a late delivery can tie up cash and profit equal to many times the cost of the awaited item.

   Three elements must be considered in scheduling deliveries—units on hand, usage, and lead time. A minimum stocking quantity should be planned for every item used repetitively. The number of units kept in stock is likewise a product of usage and lead time plus a satisfactory reserve. The number of units in stock and the ordering point can be determined by perpetual inventory quantities recorded on a computer and the order triggered through the same process when the minimum stock quantity is reached. Where perpetual records and the use of a computer are not practical, a periodic physical count of key items should be made. A list of key items should be prepared with new items added and obsolete items deleted as changes occur. As often as necessary, on a regular day of the week, month, etc., the physical check of minimum stock quantities should be made. This procedure is not a time-consuming process and becomes faster as it is repeated. If perpetual records are not maintained, there is no other way to prevent out-of-stock situations.

Material usage figures can be prepared by accounting. Accounting, to determine cost of sales, must record the sale of each unit of finished products and replacement parts. This history over a period of time, plus a reasonable forecast are the best indicators of future usage. Mere estimates are usually insufficiently accurate and heavily influenced by what has happened in the immediate past.

Lead time must be determined based on prior experience with the vendors plus a current knowledge of the market situation and processing time for some parts. Vendor acknowledgments of delivery dates should be requested on every order. These acknowledgments should be compared to the required delivery dates and orders expedited as needed. Open order files should be reviewed regularly for past due items and follow-ups made.

Lead time is often elusive and difficult to plan. An example was a special motor that went from eight weeks to sixteen months because of motor demand. In that particular case a way was found to make a substitute product that used a standard motor. Many events, which purchasing should attempt to be aware of, can influence lead time. Maintaining or searching for an alternative product or source is a useful hedge.

3. *Determining order quantities.* The first guide to order quantities is the amount necessary for a reasonable restocking quantity based primarily on usage. Quantity discounts should also be considered to reduce the cost per unit providing the discount does not require placing an unreasonable amount of inventory in stock. The author can recall a situation where a five-year supply of a specific part was ordered. The product had not changed for years and there was no future change anticipated. If run in sufficient quantity, the part could be purchased from a vendor who used an automatic machining process at a fraction of the present cost. Through the use of a high return, discounted cash flow computation, the purchase appeared to be an excellent investment. Time proved the computation correct. However, ordinarily, excessive quantities should not be put in stock.

   Sometimes, a blanket order can be used to obtain a discount with deliveries scheduled to meet the stock requirements. Blanket orders insure stocking requirements are met, reduce the number of units actually required to be on the shelf, and gain a better price.

Selecting vendors, proper scheduling of deliveries, and determining order quantities are extremely important to the manufacturer and should be given adequate emphasis with decisions based on compiled historical data, reliable usage forecasts, and accurate computations.

## PURCHASING PROCEDURES

Every purchase must be documented by a purchase order issued by the purchasing department or a certain individual responsible for buying. Orders should go through a central control to prevent duplications and maintain control over open orders, follow-ups, etc. Also, central purchasing can simply do a better job of achieving the three previously discussed objectives because of the knowledge acquired through practice and specialization. Suggestions on new sources, new products and quantities should be given to purchasing and welcomed by them to utilize the combined knowledge of the buyer and other personnel, but the actual buying function must be centralized.

Many purchase orders are not originated by the purchasing department and will be preceded by a requisition or parts list. The purpose for which the goods are purchased should be documented by attaching the requisition to the purchase order or marking the destination of each item on the retained copy of the purchase order.

Purchase order forms should be purchased in multicopy, zip-out carbon sets with as many copies as necessary to meet the requirements of the manufacturing company. Forms should be prenumbered for easy reference and accountability. Standard, inexpensive forms are often satisfactory and can be ordered with the amount of listing space ordinarily required. The form copies may be distributed as follows when required:

| Copy Number | Destination |
|---|---|
| 1 | Vendor |
| 2 | Vendor acknowledgment (optional) |
| 3 | Retained in purchasing |
| 4 | Accounting |
| 5 | Receiving (optional) |
| 6 | Requisitioner (optional) |

As a practical matter, it is not necessary to send purchase orders to most vendors when orders are phoned in. Orders that are mailed after being phoned in should be marked "confirming."

As goods are received, the packing slip should flow from receiving through purchasing to accounting. Purchasing should attach its copy of the purchase order to the packing slip if the order is complete. If the order is only partially received, purchasing should mark the items received on its copy of the purchase order and immediately send the packing slip on to accounting. Accounting should match the purchase order, the packing slip, and the vendor's invoice before vouching for payment. The entire purchasing process can be diagramed as shown in Figure 4–1.

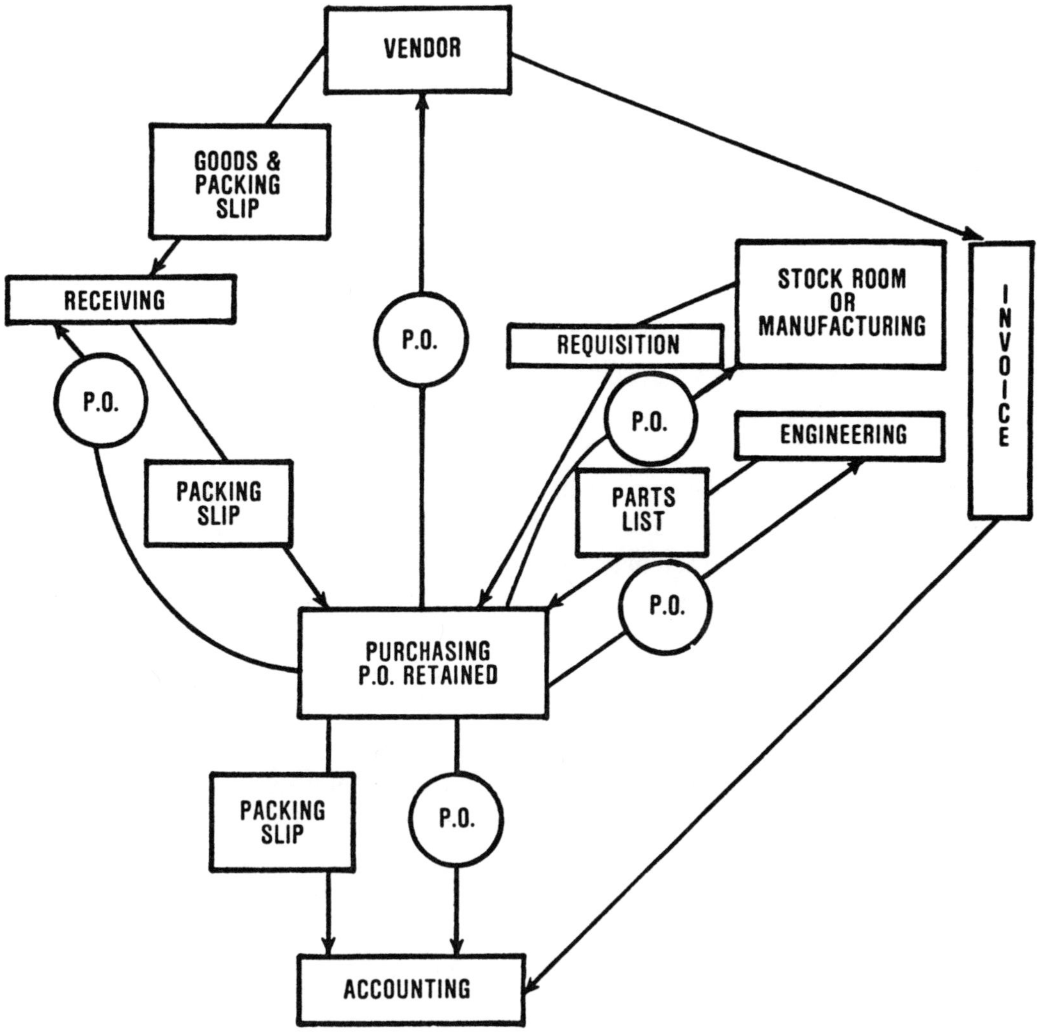


**Diagram of the Purchasing Process**

**Figure 4–1**

If materials are on hand as a result of buying in excess of actual requirements, they should be returned to the vendor unless a foreseeable use is apparent. Permission should be obtained from the vendor before making the return. Also, the name of the individual who approved the return should be mentioned on the paper work evidencing the return. A copy of the paper work including date of return, date of purchase, purchase order number, vendor invoice number, price, units, and description should accompany the return and kept on file to await the credit memo. The file should be checked periodically and the vendor reminded if the credit memo is not received in a reasonable length of time. Credit memos are often slow because of the need for batch computer runs or a lack of enthusiasm for credit memos by many vendors.

## SPECIAL PURCHASES JOURNAL AND USE OF MULTICOPY CHECKS AND REMITTANCE ADVICES FOR EFFICIENT, SIMULTANEOUS RECORDING

Purchasing and cash disbursements in payment of accounts payable constitute a related cycle of financial transactions, and should be planned as one continuous function. As vendors' invoices are received and matched with purchase orders and packing slips, payment dates should be determined according to available discounts or other payment terms. The payment date should be marked on the invoices before they are given to the bookkeeper for recording. It is often possible to meet vendors' terms by paying only on certain days of the month as the 10th and 25th. Checks are more efficiently prepared and fewer in number by grouping invoices in this way.

The illustrations of a special purchases journal and a multicopy check and remittance advice (Figure 4–2 and 4–3) have several advantages:

1. Invoices are entered on the remittance advices and in the purchases journal simultaneously—providing greater efficiency.
2. Invoices are grouped to minimize the number of checks written.
3. Discount terms are spelled out.
4. The need for a separate accounts payable subsidiary ledger is eliminated.

Short-run cash disbursements can also be planned by totaling the remittance advices and adding payroll requirement and expected direct cash payments.

The multicopy check in Figure 4-3 will be completed on the payment date with the discount (only in total) and the net amount, dated and the check completed, signed and mailed. All invoices will already be entered on the remittance advice and the purchases journal and the check has been addressed to cut the work load on the payment date. A copy of the check and remittance advice can be attached as a cover for the paid invoices; a second copy can be kept with all copies summarized on a cover sheet each month as a short cut cash disbursements journal, as illustrated in Figure 4-4. Copies should be printed nonnegotiable and separated before the checks are signed.

The same multicopy checks can be used to pay items that do not go through accounts payable, simply by filling in the account to be charged on the remittance advice. All other checks with no number in the account column are charged to accounts payable when the monthly summary of disbursements is made.

The file of remittance advices that have been entered in the purchases journal, but not paid, become a subsidiary of accounts payable and may be totaled at month-end to verify the balance in account 201, the accounts payable general ledger account.

## SPECIAL CASH DISBURSEMENTS JOURNAL

If the checks written each month are too numerous to be conveniently summarized from a check copy as a cash disbursements journal, a special journal should be used. The same procedures as previously described may be used for the purchases journal except that the remittance advice and the checks are purchased separately and only in duplicate. The vendor's name is entered on the remittance advice with the check to be written later when payment is due.

These checks are an exact overlay of the cash disbursements journal for simultaneous entries. As the checks are written, the original copy of the remittance advice is attached and mailed to the vendor with the check. The duplicate copy of the check and remittance advice are attached as a cover for the paid invoices. Figures 4-5 and 4-6 illustrate the special check and cash disbursements journal. Special window envelopes should be utilized to prevent rewriting the names and addresses already on checks.

MACHINE MANUFACTURING CORPORATION

PURCHASE JOURNAL

Page 101 | Month of June, 19X7

| Date | Invoice # | Ref. | 201 Accounts Payable | Vendor | 140 Materials | 706 Factory Supplies | 852 Office Supplies | Other accounts with repetitive entries | Miscellaneous | | |
|---|---|---|---|---|---|---|---|---|---|---|---|
| | | | | | | | | | Account | Debit | Credit |
| 6-1-x7 | 101 | | 300.00 | ABC Co. | 300.00 | | | | | | |
| 6-5-x7 | CM102 | | (50.00) | ABC Co. | (50.00) | | | | | | |

**Figure 4-2**

Machine Manufacturing Corporation
Indianapolis, IN 46200

Bank
Code

To: National Bank
Indianapolis, IN
No. 1101

Date____________________

Pay________________________________________ Dollars $_____

To the
Order of ABC Co.
101 A Road
Indianapolis, IN 46200

Account code

Remittance Advice

| Date | Invoice # | Account | Amount | Discount | Net |
|---|---|---|---|---|---|
| 6-1-x7 | 101 | | 300.00 | | |
| 6-5-x7 | CM102 | | (50.00) | | |
| | | | | | |
| | | | | | |
| | | | | | |
| | | | | | |
| | | | | | |
| | | | | | |

Detach Before Depositing — Machine Manufacturing Corporation, Indianapolis, IN 46200

**Figure 4-3**

MACHINE MANUFACTURING CORPORATION

Summary of Cash Disbursements from Check Copies
Month of July 19X7

| 102 Cash | 201 Accounts Payable | 124 Travel Advances | 220 Sales Tax Payable | 232 Accrued FICA Tax | 233 Withheld FICA Tax |
|---|---|---|---|---|---|
| (38,529.00) | 32,600.00 | SS 200.00 | 50.00 | 600.00 | 600.00 |
| per tape | per tape | BS 150.00 | | | |
| | | JB 200.00 | | | |
| | | 550.00 | | | |

| 234 Withheld Federal Tax | 235 Withheld State Tax | 236 Withheld County Tax | 237 Withheld Union Dues | 260 Mortgage Note Payable | 814 Interest Expenses |
|---|---|---|---|---|---|
| 1,400.00 | 150.00 | 50.00 | 120.00 | 187.00 | 313.00 |

| 824 Travel and Entertainment | 834 Insurance | 840 Heat | 841 Electricity | 842 Water | 843 Telephone and Telegraph |
|---|---|---|---|---|---|
| 76.00 | 280.00 | 100.00 | 270.00 | 60.00 | 120.00 |
| 40.00 | 70.00 | | | | 6.00 |
| 10.00 | 350.00 | | | | 3.00 |
| 126.00 | | | | | 129.00 |

| 850 Freight Out | 851 Advertising |
|---|---|
| 17.40 | 460.00 |
| 18.20 | 87.00 |
| 36.10 | |
| 79.30 | 547.00 |
| 8.00 | |
| 6.00 | |
| 5.00 | |
| 50.00 | |
| 87.10 | |
| 19.90 | |
| 327.00 | |

**Figure 4-4**

MACHINE MANUFACTURING CORPORATION

Page 201 | Cash Disbursements Journal | Month of July 19x7

| Date | Payee | 102 Cash | Check Number | 201 Accounts Payable | Other Accounts with frequent entries | Miscellaneous | | |
|---|---|---|---|---|---|---|---|---|
| | | | | | | Account | Debit | Credit |
| 7-1-x7 | ABC Co. | 100.00 | 1101 | 100.0 | | | | |

**Figure 4-5**

Machine Manufacturing Corporation

Indianapolis, IN 46200

Bank Code

To: National Bank
Indianapolis, IN

No. 1101

Pay: One hundred & no/100------------------Dollars

| Date | Pay to order of: | Amount |
|---|---|---|
| 7-1-x7 | ABC Co. | $100.00 |

101 A Road
Indianapolis, IN 46200

Account Code

Figure 4-6

## HOW TO HANDLE PURCHASE DISCOUNT TRANSACTIONS

Purchase discounts allowed by vendors for paying within 10 days usually should be taken if the discount is 1% (equivalent of 18% annual interest) or more. Recent accounting has properly tended to treat these discounts as a reduction in the cost of the item purchased. The conclusion is that the discounts actually represent price concessions on the purchase rather than financial income. This conclusion is generally correct.

The accounting for purchase discounts has failed to provide the needed information for management when recorded as in example A.

Example A

| | Amount of Invoice | Percent Discount | Amount of Discount | |
|---|---|---|---|---|
| 1. | $1,000 | 2% | $20 | Discount taken |
| 2. | 3,000 | 1% | 30 | Discount passed |

Entry on receipt of invoices: (gross method)

| | | |
|---|---|---|
| Inventory | 4,000 | |
| Accounts payable—1 | | 1,000 |
| Accounts payable—2 | | 3,000 |

Entry on payment of invoices:

| | | |
|---|---|---|
| Accounts payable—1 | 1,000 | |
| Accounts payable—2 | 3,000 | |
| Discounts earned | | 20 |
| Cash in bank | | 3,980 |

Note that example A discloses the discounts earned, but not the discounts lost.

Example B

| | Amount of Invoice | Percent Discount | Amount of Discount | |
|---|---|---|---|---|
| 1. | $1,000 | 2% | $20 | Discount taken |
| 2. | 3,000 | 1% | 30 | Discount passed |

Entry on receipt of invoices: (net method)

| | | |
|---|---|---|
| Inventory | 3,950 | |
| Accounts payable—1 | | 980 |
| Accounts payable—2 | | 2,970 |

Entry on payment of invoices:

| | | |
|---|---|---|
| Accounts payable—1 | 980 | |
| Accounts payable—2 | 2,970 | |
| Discounts lost | 30 | |
| Cash in bank | | 3,980 |

Note that example B discloses discounts lost, and the reason for passing the discount should be determined for the manufacturer.

## PURCHASING AUDIT PROCEDURE

The purchasing audit should be conducted by an individual or team of individuals with a knowledge of purchasing objectives and procedures plus an understanding of auditing or investigative techniques.

Purchasing, because it is a supporting function, must align itself to the overall objectives of the manufacturer through satisfying the needs of marketing and production. However, purchasing can contribute greatly to the success of the enterprise by suggesting to or assisting marketing and production in the selection of materials that meet the most desirable combined criteria for price, quality and service.

What has been mentioned thus far largely establishes the boundaries for a purchasing audit. The purchasing auditor should build his review around the following procedures:

1. Determine the primary goal or goals of the manufacturing company.
2. Review the coordination of marketing, production, purchasing, engineering, finance, and accounting toward the achievement of the company goals, and specifically determine that purchasing is on target.
3. Review purchasing objectives with those previously discussed in this chapter in mind.
4. Chart and list purchasing procedures to determine that the complete function is being performed; determine if any unnecessary procedures can be eliminated.

The purchasing auditor should keep the best communications open with the purchasing department, related functions, and management to arrive at recommendations that will be useful to the manufacturer. Verbal discussions should precede written reports to avoid recommendations that may not be workable for the particular manufacturing company.

## CHOOSING BETWEEN AN IMPREST OR FLUCTUATING PETTY CASH SYSTEM

Petty cash should be and is used for a minimal number and size of transactions when the rest of the purchasing and receipts and disbursements sytems are operated effectively. However, there are always situations, because of urgency, convenience or size of transaction, that require the use of cash.

One individual must be responsible for petty cash transactions. The cash and current transactions should be kept in a lock box. Petty cash tickets (Figure 4-7) are prenumbered and prepared for each transaction in ink to prevent alterations. Supporting documents, as cash register tapes, etc., are stapled to the petty cash ticket.

The petty cash custodian must be required to make regular accountings for petty cash. These accountings should be made when the fund falls below or exceeds predetermined amounts and just before the end of each month. At the time of the accounting the petty cash ticket numbers should be accounted for and the tickets cancelled to prevent their being presented for payment again.

Machine Manufacturing Corporation—Petty Cash Ticket 101

Date 7-17, 19X7

Cash — Paid to [X] / Received from [ ]

Name Owen Corp.

For Nuts & bolts

Amount $ 4.12

Charge or ~~Credit~~

Account 706

Signed Ima Custodian

**Figure 4-7**

Most accountants would prefer to operate petty cash as an imprest system. Under an imprest system the petty cash fund is opened for a specific amount that will meet the needs for cash without undue risk, say $100. At each accounting a check is written or deposit made to adjust the fund balance to exactly $100. No entry is made to petty cash since the $100 is already the general ledger petty cash balance. Instead, the check or deposit is charged and credited directly to the appropriate income and expense accounts. The check should always be payable to the petty cash custodian, not cash or petty cash, to emphasize responsibility and prevent misuse.

Sometimes a fluctuating system, which lacks the control of an imprest system, can be more convenient by saving some trips to the bank. With a fluctuating system there is no need to reimburse the fund to make an accounting, as the balance can change. Unless cash is needed in the fund, it can be adjusted to the actual cash on hand rather than writing a check. This type of adjustment to an imprest system usually requires a later reversing entry.

Figure 4-8 illustrates a summary of petty cash transactions from which the amount of the check or adjustment to the fund is determined.

MACHINE MANUFACTURING CORPORATION

Summary of Petty Cash Transactions
Month of July 19x7

| Ticket # | 101 Petty Cash | 706 Factory Supplies | 844 Repairs | 852 Office Supplies |
|---|---|---|---|---|
| 101 | 4.12 | 4.12 | | |
| 102 | 7.61 | | 7.61 | |
| 103 | 5.27 | 5.27 | | |
| 104 | 1.04 | | | 1.04 |
| | 18.04 | 9.39 | 7.61 | 1.04 |
| | 81.96 | Cash count | | |
| | 100.00 | Fund amount | | |

**Figure 4-8**

If a reimbursement check is written, the following entry is made from the check through cash disbursements:

| | | | |
|---|---|---|---|
| Factory supplies | 706 | 9.39 | |
| Repairs | 844 | 7.61 | |
| Office supplies | 852 | 1.04 | |
| Cash in bank | 102 | | 18.04 |

If no reimbursement is made, the following general journal entry is made:

| | | | |
|---|---|---|---|
| Factory supplies | 706 | 9.39 | |
| Repairs | 844 | 7.61 | |
| Office supplies | 852 | 1.04 | |
| Petty cash | 101 | | 18.04 |

When the accounting is made, the cancelled tickets and the summary of petty cash transactions are filed in an envelope marked "petty cash transactions" month of July, 19x7.

**SUMMARY**

The purchasing function should be run with the primary objectives in mind and under a set of definite, applied procedures. Specially selected or designed forms and journals should be used to accommodate purchasing and accounting for purchases. The purchases journal can be tied in with the cash disbursements function as a continuous set of procedures to simplify and make the accounting more efficient and accurate.

Multicopy checks may be used with attached or detached remittance advices. The remittance advices have the vendors' invoices entered on them simultaneously with the purchases journal. Check copies may be summarized as a cash disbursements journal or a separate journal recorded simultaneously with the writing of detached checks. In either procedure a check copy can be used as a cover for paid invoices.

Purchase discounts should be treated as a reduction of the cost of the item purchased and accounted for in a manner that flags discounts lost.

An audit or review may be conducted of purchases to determine that the objectives and procedures used by purchasing are sound and in line with the overall goals of the manufacturing company.

Petty cash procedures should be specified and followed. An imprest system provides more reliable control while a fluctuating system may be more convenient.

# 5

# Accounting for Labor and Payroll Taxes

## SPECIAL PAYROLL JOURNAL, EARNINGS CARDS, AND CHECKS FOR SIMULTANEOUS RECORDING

The payroll records for the manufacturing company should be selected as a unit and the gross to net pay for each employee written only once. In the following examples the payroll journal, earnings card, and payroll check are exact overlays and may all be recorded simultaneously by the use of carbon or treated paper.

| Date | Hours | Rate | Regular Pay | Over-Time | Gross Pay | Federal Tax | FICA Tax | State Tax | City Tax | Other | Net Pay | Name |
|---|---|---|---|---|---|---|---|---|---|---|---|---|
| 7-31-x7 | 40 | 5.00 | 200.00 | | 200.00 | 40.00 | 11.70 | 4.00 | 1.00 | | 143.30 | J. Jones |

Machine Manufacturing Corporation, Indianapolis, Indiana 46200

Machine Manufacturing Corporation
Indianapolis, Indiana 46200

Bank
Code

TO: National Bank
Indianapolis, Indiana

Pay One hundred forty three and 30/100——————Dollars No. 147

To the Order of | Joe Jones | 7-31-x7 | $143.30 |

Sample Pay Check

Account Code

**Figure 5-1**

Year 19x7
Name Joe Jones
Street 123 B Street
City Indianapolis, IN 46200

Soc. Sec. #
Exemptions
Married ______ Single

| Date | Rate |
|---|---|
| 9-1-x6 | 5.00 |

| Date | Hours | Rate | Regular Pay | Over-time | Gross Pay | Federal Tax | FICA Tax | State Tax | City Tax | Other | Net Pay | Name |
|---|---|---|---|---|---|---|---|---|---|---|---|---|
| 7- 3-x7 | 41 | 5.00 | 200.00 | 7.50 | 207.50 | 42.00 | 12.14 | 4.00 | 1.00 | | 148.36 | J. Jones |
| 7-10-x7 | 40 | 5.00 | 200.00 | | 200.00 | 40.00 | 11.70 | 4.00 | 1.00 | | 143.30 | J. Jones |
| 7-17-x7 | 42 | 5.00 | 200.00 | 15.00 | 215.00 | 44.00 | 12.58 | 4.00 | 1.00 | | 153.42 | J. Jones |
| 7-24-x7 | 45 | 5.00 | 200.00 | 37.50 | 237.50 | 50.00 | 13.89 | 5.00 | 1.00 | | 167.61 | J. Jones |
| 7-31-x7 | 40 | 5.00 | 200.00 | | 200.00 | 40.00 | 11.70 | 4.00 | 1.00 | | 143.30 | J. Jones |
| | | | | | | | | | | | | Quarter |
| | | | | | | | | | | | | Year-to-date |
| | | | | | | | | | | | | |
| | | | | | | | | | | | | Quarter |
| | | | | | | | | | | | | Year-to-date |

**Employee Earnings Card**

**Figure 5-2**

## MACHINE MANUFACTURING CORPORATION

### Payroll Journal

**Period Ended 7-29-x7**

| Date | Hours | Rate | Regular Pay | Over-time | Gross Pay | Federal Tax | FICA Tax | State Tax | City Tax | Other | Net Pay | Name | Check # | 701 Direct Labor | 703 Super-visory | 801 Officer's Salaries | 802 Engin-eering | 803 Cler-ical |
|---|---|---|---|---|---|---|---|---|---|---|---|---|---|---|---|---|---|---|
| 7-31-x7 | 41 | 5.00 | 200.00 | 7.50 | 207.50 | 42.00 | 12.14 | 4.00 | 1.00 | | 148.36 | J. Jones | 147 | 207.50 | | | | |
| 7-31-x7 | 40 | 5.00 | 200.00 | | 200.00 | 40.00 | 11.70 | 4.00 | 1.00 | | 143.30 | B. Brown | 148 | 200.00 | | | | |
| 7-31-x7 | 40 | 6.00 | 240.00 | | 240.00 | 50.00 | 14.04 | 5.00 | 1.50 | | 169.46 | J. Baker | 149 | 240.00 | | | | |
| 7-31-x7 | | | 300.00 | | 300.00 | 60.00 | 17.55 | 6.00 | 2.00 | | 214.45 | B. Shively | 150 | | 300.00 | | | |
| 7-31-x7 | 40 | | 500.00 | | 500.00 | 100.00 | 29.25 | 9.00 | 3.00 | | 358.75 | L. Pritchett | 151 | | | 500.00 | | |
| 7-31-x7 | 40 | 4.00 | 160.00 | | 160.00 | 20.00 | 9.36 | 3.00 | 1.00 | | 126.64 | S. Schrowe | 152 | | | | | 160.00 |
| 7-31-x7 | 40 | 5.10 | 204.00 | | 204.00 | 40.00 | 11.93 | 4.00 | 1.00 | | 147.07 | R. Reiman | 153 | | | | 204.00 | |
| | | | 1,804.00 | 7.50 | 1,811.50 | 352.00 | 105.97 | 35.00 | 10.50 | | 1,308.03 | Total | | 647.50 | 300.00 | 500.00 | 204.00 | 160.00 |
| 7-03-x7 | | | 1,900.00 | 10.00 | 1,910.00 | 400.00 | 111.74 | 40.00 | 12.00 | | 1,346.26 | Forward | | 710.00 | 300.00 | 500.00 | 240.00 | 160.00 |
| 7-10-x7 | | | 1,800.00 | 20.00 | 1,820.00 | 360.00 | 106.47 | 40.00 | 10.00 | | 1,303.53 | Forward | | 650.00 | 300.00 | 500.00 | 210.00 | 160.00 |
| 7-17-x7 | | | 1,800.00 | 40.00 | 1,840.00 | 370.00 | 100.00 | 40.00 | 10.00 | | 1,320.00 | Forward | | 660.00 | 300.00 | 500.00 | 220.00 | 160.00 |
| 7-24-x7 | | | 2,000.00 | 100.00 | 2,100.00 | 420.00 | 120.00 | 50.00 | 15.00 | | 1,495.00 | Forward | | 900.00 | 300.00 | 500.00 | 230.00 | 170.00 |
| | | | 9,304.00 | 177.50 | 9,481.50 | 1,902.00 | 544.18 | 205.00 | 57.50 | | 6,772.82 | Summary | | 3,567.50 | 1,500.00 | 2,500.00 | 1,104.00 | 810.00 |

**Figure 5-3**

## SUMMARIZING AND CLASSIFYING THE PAYROLL

The payroll can be summarized for each month and posted to the general ledger by carrying totals for each weekly payroll to the last payroll journal page as illustrated in Figure 5-3. It should be emphasized that the payroll journal is a record of original entry equal to other journals and there is no necessity in taking the additional step of entering the payroll in either a voucher register or the general journal prior to posting to the general ledger.

Dates related to the payroll are often confusing and often handled incorrectly. Part of this fault lies with the companies that print the payroll forms and journals who continually use the words "period ending" on the earning cards, checks and payroll journals. Payrolls should be entered in the records on the date the checks are issued. This is the same rule that applies to all cash disbursements, of which payroll is simply a classification. Also, the word "ending" does not indicate that the period for which the payroll was written has already passed. Payrolls are almost always written after they have been earned by the employees and the correct terminology is "period ended."

As an example, assume that the week ended July 29, 19x7, and that the checks were issued August 1, 19x7. The payroll should not have been entered in the payroll journal or on the employees earnings cards until August 1, 19x7, the day the checks were issued. The payroll would be summarized with the remaining August payrolls and posted to the general ledger on August 31. An accrual entry would have been made on July 31, 19x7, to pick up the unpaid payroll, and a reversing entry made on August 1, 19x7. A disbursement for the net pay and the withholdings had not been made at July 31, 19x7; therefore, it would have been incorrect to have entered the gross to net payroll in July. Also, as will be presented in the discussion of payroll taxes, payroll tax deposits become a liability only after the withholdings are actually made and the payroll actually paid.

## THE WEEKLY TIME CARD

All hourly paid employees should punch the clock each time they report for or leave work, including lunch hours and personal time used for errands. The weekly time card, presented in Figure 5-4, should be reviewed for accuracy and signed by the foreman before being sent to accounting. In accounting the weekly time cards become the source for determining the number of hours for which each hourly employee is to be paid and the amount of overtime for which the hourly employee is to receive overtime pay.

## THE DAILY TIME CARD

All production personnel must keep a daily time card that accounts for the same number of hours reported on that day on the weekly time card. The hours recorded on the daily time card become accounting's input for accumulating costs on products costed at actual costs or the input for the comparison of actual to standard costs on products having standard costs. The hours recorded on the daily time cards may also become the basis for billing for service orders and a guide for billing customers on other orders. The daily time card is illustrated in Figure 5-5 and can be enlarged or modified to furnish the information needed by individual manufacturing companies.

| Name | J. Jones | | |
|---|---|---|---|
| Date | Hours | Time | |
| 7-25-x7 | | In | 7.00 |
| 7-25-x7 | | Out | 12.00 |
| 7-25-x7 | | In | 13.00 |
| 7-25-x7 | 8 | Out | 16.00 |
| 7-26-x7 | | In | 7.00 |
| 7-26-x7 | | Out | 12.00 |
| 7-26-x7 | | In | 13.00 |
| 7-26-x7 | 8 | Out | 16.00 |
| 7-27-x7 | | In | 7.00 |
| 7-27-x7 | | Out | 12.00 |
| 7-27-x7 | | In | 13.00 |
| 7-27-x7 | 8 | Out | 16.00 |
| 7-28-x7 | | In | 7.00 |
| 7-28-x7 | | Out | 12.00 |
| 7-28-x7 | | In | 13.00 |
| 7-28-x7 | 8 | Out | 16.00 |
| 7-29-x7 | | In | 7.00 |
| 7-29-x7 | | Out | 12.00 |
| 7-29-x7 | | In | 13.00 |
| 7-29-x7 | 9 | Out | 17.00 |
| | | In | |
| | | Out | |
| | | In | |
| | 41 | Out | |
| A. Foreman | | | |

**Weekly Time Card—For Computing Payroll**

**Figure 5-4**

| Name | | J. Jones | | |
|---|---|---|---|---|
| Date | | 7-25-x7 | | |
| Job # | Units | Function | Time | |
| Mach<br>1 | 3 | Assembly | In<br>Out | 7.00<br>11.50 |
| Mach<br>3 | | | In<br>Out | 11.50<br>12.00 |
| | 4 | | In<br>Out | 13.00<br>16.00 |
| | | | In<br>Out | |
| | | | In<br>Out | |
| | | | In<br>Out | |
| | | | In<br>Out | |
| | | | In<br>Out | |
| | | | In<br>Out | |
| | | | In<br>Out | |
| | | | In<br>Out | |
| | | | In<br>Out | |
| | | | In<br>Out | |
| | | | In<br>Out | |
| | | | In<br>Out | |
| A. Foreman | | | | |

**Daily Time Card—For Reporting Daily Performance**

**Figure 5-5**

**HOW TO ACCRUE END OF PERIOD PAYROLL**

Almost every month one payroll period will overlap the end of the old month and the beginning of the new month. The entire payroll will be paid in and charged to the new month through the payroll journal. This procedure is correct, but the amount of labor charged to each month is incorrect because part of the services were performed in the preceding month and, therefore, have to be pushed back into that month through an accrual entry. Procedures are illustrated in the following example.

Assume that the payroll period ended on Friday, August 1, and that the checks were written and entered on Monday, August 4, for a five day week as follows:

| | | | |
|---|---|---|---|
| 8-4-x7 | Direct labor | 2,000 | |
| | Supervisory salaries | 300 | |
| | Officers' salaries | 500 | |
| | Engineering salaries | 400 | |
| | Clerical salaries | 150 | |
| | Various withholdings | | 900 |
| | Cash | | 2,450 |

To determine the exact amount of payroll chargeable to July, an analysis would have to be made of the weekly time cards to determine the number of hours worked through July 31. However, the following method of estimating is usually sufficiently accurate.

| 4/5 | | | | 1/5 |
|---|---|---|---|---|
| Monday | Tuesday | Wednesday | Thursday | Friday |
| 7-28 | 7-29 | 7-30 | 7-31 | 8-1 |

The July 31, 19x7, accrual could be entered as follows:

| | | | |
|---|---|---|---|
| 7-31-x7 | Direct labor (2000 × 4/5) | 1,600 | |
| | Supervisory salaries (300 × 4/5) | 240 | |
| | Officers' salaries (500 × 4/5) | 400 | |
| | Engineering salaries (400 × 4/5) | 320 | |
| | Clerical salaries (150× 4/5) | 120 | |
| | Accrued payroll (900 + 2,450 × 4/5) | | 2,680 |
| | To accrue payroll at 7-31-x7 | | |

The 8-1-x7 reversal could be entered as follows:

| | | |
|---|---|---|
| 8-1-x7 Accrued payroll | 1,680 | |
| Direct labor | | 1,600 |
| Supervisory salaries | | 240 |
| Officers' salaries | | 400 |
| Engineering salaries | | 320 |
| Clerical salaries | | 120 |
| To reverse the 7-31-x7 Payroll accrual | | |

The results, partially illustrated by "T" accounts are as follows:

**Accrued Payroll**

| Debit | | Credit | |
|---|---|---|---|
| | | 7-31-x7 | 2,680 |
| 8- 1-x7 | 2,680 | | |

**Direct Labor**

| Debit | | Credit | |
|---|---|---|---|
| 7-31-x7 | 1,600 | | |
| | | 8- 1x7 | 1,600 |
| 8- 4-x7 | 2,000 | | |
| Balance | 2,000 | | |

The above accounts illustrate that the accrued payroll balance is $2,680 at 7-31-x7 and zero after the reversing entry on 8- 1-x7. A total of $2,000 is charged to direct labor, $1,600 or 4/5 in July and a net of $400 or 1/5 in August.

## THE ADVANTAGES AND DISADVANTAGES OF SPECIAL PAYROLL BANK ACCOUNTS

Many manufacturers prefer to set up a separate bank account to be used only for payroll checks. Most banks offer this service at no additional charge to customers whose general checking accounts they have on deposit. However, a special payroll bank account offers both advantages and disadvantages which must be weighed before the account is opened.

One consideration deals strictly with mechanics. Each week a check is written on the general account equal to the total net payroll and deposited in the payroll account. The balance kept in the payroll account may be zero unless it is necessary to keep a minimum balance in the account to cover payoffs between regular pay days. Either way, a zero balance or a minimum balance, reconciling the payroll account is quite simple—but it is an additional account to reconcile.

Duties, such as check signing and bank reconciliations, can be divided by establishing a separate payroll account. The type of verification necessary in signing payroll checks differs from other disbursements, and management may be able to delegate one or the other by requiring dual signatures of responsible employees along with adequate documentation.

A very favorable consideration for a special payroll bank account is the ability to keep payroll records confidential by isolating the payroll. In this way the total payroll, or perhaps just the executive payroll, can be kept by management or a trusted employee to prevent pay rates from becoming general knowledge.

Regardless of whether payroll is run through the general bank account or a special payroll bank account, the paychecks should be so marked and a different color from the general checks. This makes paycheck identification considerably easier and is an absolute must, along with a different numbering sequence, where the paychecks are handled through a separate bank account.

## PAYROLL TAX EXPENSE, ACCRUALS AND DEPOSITS

Payroll taxes represent a significant amount of expense and require detailed records on the earnings of every employee. The amount of payroll taxes per employee has continued to increase over the years, led by increases in F.I.C.A. tax. State and federal unemployment taxes can also be sufficiently high as to merit attention. A combination of the three taxes can exceed $1,200 per employee per year at the time this book is being written.

The principal means of minimizing payroll taxes is avoiding layoffs and employee turnover. All three payroll taxes have maximum amounts of individual employees' earnings per calendar year to which the taxes apply. However, each employee starts with zero with a new employer on the date he begins his employment. Therefore, employees who are on the payroll for an entire year are apt to have significantly more wages exempt from payroll taxes than are employees hired during the year.

State unemployment tax rates are dependent on what is commonly referred to as an experience rating. In general this rating is affected by both the amount of unemployment tax that has been paid to the state and the amount of unemployment claims against the employer.

Careful attention should be given to the following in an effort to minimize unemployment taxes:

1. Level work load planning—in the long-run it may also be preferable to use regular employees on overtime, at least temporarily, than to hire new employees who will be dismissed later. Seasonal businesses may find it less expensive to maintain a level work force and store inventory than to hire large numbers of temporary personnel in peak seasons. There are two sides to this approach, and in some cases a level work load is impracticable, if not impossible.

2. Selecting employees should be accomplished with great care. Hiring is a difficult and sometimes a less than pleasant task, particularly when there are other matters that need attention. Patience is probably a key to selecting new personnel. Several applicants usually have to be screened to find one suitable for the particular job. Even with great care some mistakes will still occur.

Payroll tax accruals are widely misunderstood. The liability for payroll taxes occurs when the paychecks are issued—as of that day, not at the end of the period when the salaries and wages are earned. There are no accrued payroll taxes on accrued payrolls.

There are usually three payroll taxes to accrue—the same ones that become expenses to the manufacturer, namely, state and federal unemployment taxes, which are paid entirely by the employer, and F.I.C.A. tax paid one half by the employer with the other half withheld from the employee.

Monthly accruals may be made for state and federal unemployment taxes by analyzing the employees' earnings cards for taxable wages, multiplying the taxable wages by the appropriate percent, and deducting previous payments. Assume that the rates are 2.7% for state unemployment tax and 0.5% for federal unemployment tax. Further assume that the maximum taxable wage per employee is $4,200 and that employees have been paid gross wages as follows through July 31, 19X7.

| | Seven Months Ended July 31, 19x7 | |
|---|---|---|
| Employee | Gross Wages | Taxable Wages |
| A | $ 3,600 | $ 3,600 |
| B | 4,100 | 4,100 |
| C | 6,000 | 4,200 |
| D | 4,800 | 4,200 |
| E | 10,000 | 4,200 |
| F | 12,000 | 4,200 |
| G | 4,000 | 4,000 |
| H | 16,000 | 4,200 |
| | $60,500 | $32,700 |

| | State Unemployment Tax | Federal Unemployment Tax |
|---|---|---|
| Taxable wages | $32,700.00 | $32,700.00 |
| Tax rate | .027 | .005 |
| Tax for seven months | 882.90 | 163.50 |
| Payments: | | |
| April, 19x7 | 540.00 | 100.00 |
| July, 19x7 | 297.00 | — |
| Total payments | 837.00 | 100.00 |
| Accrued, July 31, 19x7 | $ 45.90 | $ 63.50 |

Assuming there was no balance in the accrued tax accounts, the accrual entry would be made as follows:

| | | | |
|---|---|---|---|
| 7-31-x7 | State unemployment tax | 45.90 | |
| | Federal unemployment tax | 63.50 | |
| | Accrued state unemployment tax | | 45.90 |
| | Accrued federal unemployment tax | | 63.50 |

Generally, state unemployment tax is payable by the end of the calendar month following the end of a calendar quarter and is paid with the state unemployment tax return. Federal unemployment tax must be deposited at a depository bank by the end of the month following the end of each calendar quarter if the accrued liability exceeds $100. This deposit is made on deposit card Form 508. The federal return, Form 940, is due for the calendar year ended December 31, 19x7, by January 31, 19x8.

The accrual problem for employer F.I.C.A. tax is simplified by the fact that half of the tax is withheld from the employees. And, except for the rounding of pennies or errors, the employer's share of the tax equals what has been withheld. Therefore, the accrual entry for the first two months of each calendar quarter can be equal to the amount withheld for each of those two months. The calculation for the final month of the quarter should agree with the payroll tax return, Form 941. The calculation may be illustrated as follows:

| | F.I.C.A. Tax | | |
|---|---|---|---|
| | Withheld | Accrued | |
| April, 19x7 | $1,200 | $1,200 | |
| May, 19x7 | 1,205 | 1,205 | |
| June, 19x7 | 1,220 | 1,224 | (1) |
| Quarter totals | $3,625 | $3,629 | |

| | | |
|---|---|---|
| (1) Taxable payroll for the quarter per Form 941 | | $62,000 |
| Combined employee/employer rate | | .1117 |
| Total F.I.C.A. tax for the quarter | | $ 7,254 |
| Withheld | $ 3,625 | |
| Accrued—April | 1,200 | |
| —May | 1,205 | |
| | | 6,030 |
| July 31, 19x7 accrual | | $ 1,224 |

The accrual entry would be made as follows:

| | | | |
|---|---|---|---|
| 7-31-x7 | F.I.C.A. tax expense | 1,224 | |
| | Accrued F.I.C.A. tax | | 1,224 |

F.I.C.A. tax and withheld federal income tax on employees are required to be deposited periodically at depository banks unless the total taxes, including withholdings and the employer's portion of the F.I.C.A. tax, is less than $200 for a calendar quarter. This low limitation makes it necessary for practically all manufacturers to make periodic deposits by using deposit card—Form 501.

When the amount of the federal income tax withheld plus the employee-employer F.I.C.A. tax exceeds $200, but is less than $2,000, the combined taxes must be deposited by the 15th day of the following month, except for the last month of the quarter, when the deposit is not due until the end of the month following the end of the quarter. Tax deposit requirements are illustrated in the following table:

| Month | Combined Taxes | Deposit Required and Date |
|---|---|---|
| January | $180 | None |
| February | 170 | $350 by March 15 |
| March | 190 | Paid with return by April 30 |
| April | 210 | $210 by May 15 |
| May | 190 | None |
| June | 180 | $370 by July 31 |
| July | 250 | $250 by August 15 |
| August | 190 | None |
| September | 200 | $390 by October 31 |
| October | 70 | None |
| November | 60 | None |
| December | 50 | $180 with return by January 31 |

When the amount of the combined taxes exceed $2,000, the deposit must be made within three working days, illustrated as follows:

| Date Paid | Combined Taxes | Deposit Required and Date |
|---|---|---|
| January 7 | $ 400 | None |
| January 14 | 500 | None |
| January 21 | 400 | None |
| January 28 | 600 | $1,900 by February 15 |
| February 4 | 1,000 | None |
| February 11 | 900 | None |
| February 18 | 700 | $2,600 by February 21 |
| February 25 | 700 | None |
| March 3 | 700 | None |
| March 10 | 700 | $2,100 by March 13 |
| March 17 | 2,100 | $2,100 by March 20 |
| March 24 | 800 | None |
| March 31 | 1,000 | $1,800 by April 30* |

*Had this amount exceeded $2,000, the deposit would have been due by April 3.

## A BLUEPRINT FOR ABSOLUTE ACCURACY IN ALL PAYROLL TRANSACTIONS

Materially correct may be acceptable in many areas of accounting, but not with the payroll. Errors in computing the payroll or in paying payroll taxes cause problems that are time consuming and difficult to correct. Short an employee on pay day—the employee will let you know about it. Overpay an employee and then ask that the money be returned. Make an error in reporting to a taxing authority or in making a deposit and go through the rigamarole of straightening it out. Pay a penalty plus interest because of an error. Try to find your own error according to an additional assessment notice from the tax authority. Estimate how long it will take and how many hours will be spent understanding and explaining a real foul-up on payroll taxes to the Internal Revenue Service.

Accuracy verifications are available and should be used. Some procedures to test the accuracy of the payroll and payroll taxes are as follows:

1. Always crossfoot the total debits and credits of the payroll journal before issuing any pay checks.
2. Determine at the beginning of the year the maximum amount of F.I.C.A. tax to be withheld from any employee. Do not forget and over-withhold.
3. Always determine that the employer's portion of the F.I.C.A. tax is approximately the same as the F.I.C.A. tax withheld. If not, locate the error and correct it before filing Form 941.
4. Prove the total wages reported on the payroll tax returns to the salaries and wages expense accounts in the general ledger. Since salaries and wages are reported on a cash basis for payroll taxes, the amount in the general ledger expense accounts will have to be adjusted for beginning and ending accruals.
5. Foot the total taxes withheld on the earnings cards and tie to the general ledger withholding accounts.
6. After computing the taxable payroll for F.I.C.A. tax and state and federal unemployment taxes, verify the amount on the returns by footing the taxable payroll from the earnings cards.
7. At the end of the calendar year, tie the amounts reported on the W-2's to the quarterly payroll tax returns and tie gross salaries and wages to the general ledger expense accounts.
8. If a special payroll bank account is used, tie the disbursements to the net pay each quarter and for the calendar year.

## SUMMARY

The manufacturing company's payroll records should be selected as one unit to include the journal, earnings cards, checks, and daily and weekly time cards. The system should be adapted to the manufacturer's needs rather than the manufacturer adapting to the system. There are many standard, inexpensive systems that can be used with, perhaps, small modifications.

The payroll can be summarized and classified in the payroll journal at the end of each month, immediately after the last pay day of the month, and posted directly from the payroll journal. This journal is a record of original entry and may be a direct source for posting to the general ledger.

End of period payrolls may be accrued by taking the fraction of the unpaid days at the end of the month to the total days in the week that overlaps the end of the old month and the beginning of the new month. If the payday lags a week or more behind the pay period, it is likely that a week or more will have to be accrued at the end of the month.

Salaries and wages expense accounts should be kept intact with distributions or allocations made by crediting a contra-account. The need to analyze salaries and wages is constant and too difficult if the expenses are fragmented and scattered.

Special payroll bank accounts are available—advantages and disadvantages should be carefully analyzed by the accountant before opening the account. The advantages don't automatically outweigh the disadvantages.

There are at least four taxes related to payrolls, and more in most locations. They are complicated, there are many dates to remember, and they are expensive. The employer pays one half of the employee's F.I.C.A. tax, and the state and federal unemployment taxes. Controlling employee turnover and layoffs are the two most important factors in reducing payroll taxes.

Payrolls and payroll taxes must be recorded and reported accurately. Accuracy verifications prior to issuing checks and filing tax returns can save significant time and penalties later.

# 6

# Cost Control and Allocation of Manufacturing Overhead Costs

## THE COST ELEMENTS OF OVERHEAD

Overhead is a term that can be defined very broadly as all costs that are not a visible part of the finished product—namely, every cost except the materials and the workmanship in the manufactured product. Other costs and expenses are overhead, but some overhead is a necessary part of production while other overhead is incurred for various functions such as administration, marketing, etc. That portion of overhead related to production becomes a part of the total product cost, while other overhead is simply expensed during the appropriate accounting period. The difference occurs when part or all of current production is not sold and becomes inventory at the end of the current period. This causes the manufacturing overhead included in the cost of the inventory to be deferred until the following periods when that inventory is sold and becomes a part of cost of goods sold. This deferral can be illustrated as follows:

| Production Costs—19x7 | | |
|---|---|---|
| Materials | | $18,000 |
| Direct Labor | | $12,000 |
| Manufacturing overhead | | $20,000 |
| Total production costs | | $50,000 |

| Other Costs—19x7 | | |
|---|---|---|
| Administrative | | $10,000 |
| Marketing | | $15,000 |
| Total other costs | | $25,000 |

| Income Statement—19x7 | | |
|---|---|---|
| Sales 75% of production | | $72,000 |
| Cost of Sales: | | |
| Production costs | $50,000 | |
| Less ending inventory—25% of production | $12,500 | |
| | | $37,500 |
| Gross Profit | | $34,500 |
| Administrative costs | $10,000 | |
| Marketing costs | $15,000 | |
| | | $25,000 |
| Net income | | $ 9,500 |

Note that the costs deferred through the ending inventory, $12,500, include manufacturing overhead of $5,000 (20,000/50,000 × 12,500). Of course, this overhead will not become expense until the inventory is sold in the following period, while the $25,000 of administrative and marketing costs were expensed during the current period.

## METHODS OF CHARGING MANUFACTURING OVERHEAD

By referring to the chart of accounts in Chapter 2, the expenses in the 700 and 800 series of accounts that are a part of manufacturing overhead may be categorized as shown in Figure 6-1.

It is difficult to achieve all things through the chart of accounts, and those accounts in Figure 6-1 that are partially manufacturing overhead and partially other overhead (those accounts in the 800 series) illustrate this difficulty. There are three methods that can be used to sort out the charges to these accounts between manufacturing and other costs.

*One*—separate accounts, one for the portion of each expense that pertains to manufacturing and one or more accounts for the remaining portion or portions that pertain to administration, marketing, etc. Then each entry can be analyzed and charged partially to manufacturing and partially elsewhere. This procedure is not preferable because it necessitates making the same computation several times that can be done only in total on a periodic basis.

*Two*—as the computations are made periodically on a worksheet, an entry can be made to transfer a portion of the expense from the account where originally recorded, such as account 832, F.I.C.A. tax to account 732, F.I.C.A. tax manufacturing. This procedure is more efficient and probably more accurate than number one because fewer computations are necessary.

*Three*—the worksheet computation can be made to determine the portion of each expense account that should be allocated to manufacturing. One transfer entry is made to goods in process each month based on a predetermined rate and direct labor hours. These amounts, as computed on the worksheet, are compared with the total overhead transferred to goods in process by use of a contra account, 899, Factory Overhead Applied. This method achieves the same results by worksheet comparisons, requires less bookkeeping, leaves a simpler audit trail, and allows better expense comparisons in total between periods because accounts are not fragmented.

| Account Number | Account | Manufacturing Overhead Totally | Manufacturing Overhead Partially |
|---|---|---|---|
| 703 | Supervisory salaries | X | |
| 704 | Factory repairs and services | X | |
| 705 | Factory equipment rental | X | |
| 706 | Factory supplies | X | |
| 707 | Factory maintenance | X | |
| 708 | Shipping and receiving labor | X | |
| 761 | Depreciation—machinery and equipment | X | |
| 763 | Depreciation—patterns | X | |
| 764 | Depreciation—dies and fixtures | X | |
| 770 | Miscellaneous factory expense | X | |
| 813 | Retirement benefits | | X |
| 821 | Property tax | | X |
| 830 | State unemployment tax | | X |
| 831 | Federal unemployment tax | | X |
| 832 | F.I.C.A. tax | | X |
| 834 | Insurance | | X |
| 840 | Heat | | X |
| 841 | Electricity | | X |
| 842 | Water | | X |
| 862 | Depreciation—vehicles | | X |
| 865 | Depreciation—buildings | | X |
| 869 | Vehicle expense | | X |

**Figure 6-1**

## DIFFERENCE BETWEEN VARIABLE, SEMIVARIABLE, AND FIXED OVERHEAD

Production volume can be the key to profitability—yes, sometimes, because of the different ways in which costs and expenses, both manufacturing and general, behave in relation to volume. There is a reasonable range within which one can determine with acceptable accuracy how each expense will behave. In so doing, we divide expenses into three categories: variable, semivariable and fixed. These categories can be described as follows:

*Variable Expenses* so named becuase they vary in direct proportion to production volume—the number of units of the product produced. Variable expenses (or costs) include direct material and labor plus part of overhead. Probably the best examples of variable overhead are factory supplies and payroll taxes on direct labor. Both tend to follow production volume closely.

*Semivariable Expenses* could just as easily be called semifixed as they contain elements of both variable and fixed expenses. Semivariable expenses tend to increase at certain levels of production and remain constant until another higher level of production is reached. The classic example here is supervisory labor. One man can supervise so many employees—at a specific number of employees a second, third, etc., supervisor has to be added.

*Fixed Expenses* do not change in total as long as production volume remains within a relative range. Examples of fixed expenses include depreciation (if computed based on annual rates), property taxes, certain insurance coverages, etc. It is a very important concept to note that fixed costs per unit of production decrease as volume increases.

Generally, semivariable expenses are classified either as variable or fixed depending on which they more closely resemble—and most of the time they are fixed within a certain production range. Referring to the same manufacturing overhead expenses is Figure 6-1; they can be classified as variable or fixed as illustrated in Figure 6-2.

Some of the expenses in Figure 6-2 might be classified differently under different circumstances. Supervisory salaries could be variable for supervisors who are also production personnel. Factory equipment rental could be fixed where a specific piece of equipment is rented continuously, etc.

Some expense classifications contain both variable and fixed elements—retirement benefits for supervisors are fixed but for direct labor and shipping and receiving labor they are variable. Payroll taxes follow the same pattern. Certain insurance such as liability, product liability, and fire and extended coverage on building and contents tend to be fixed while part of workmen's compensation and employee benefits insurance are variable.

| Account Number | Account | Manufacturing Overhead Variable | Manufacturing Overhead Fixed |
|---|---|---|---|
| 703 | Supervisory salaries | | X |
| 704 | Factory repairs and services | X | |
| 705 | Factory equipment rental | X | |
| 706 | Factory supplies | X | |
| 707 | Factory maintenance | X | |
| 708 | Shipping and receiving labor | X | |
| 761 | Depreciation—machinery and equipment | | X |
| 763 | Depreciation—patterns | | X |
| 764 | Depreciation—dies and fixtures | | X |
| 770 | Miscellaneous factory expenses | X | |
| 813 | Retirement benefits | X | X |
| 821 | Property tax | | X |
| 830 | State unemployment tax | X | X |
| 831 | Federal unemployment tax | X | X |
| 832 | F.I.C.A. tax | X | X |
| 834 | Insurance | X | X |
| 840 | Heat | | X |
| 841 | Electricity | X | |
| 842 | Water | X | |
| 862 | Depreciation—vehicles | | X |
| 865 | Depreciation—buildings | | X |
| 869 | Vehicle expense | X | |

**Figure 6-2**

## COMPUTING PREDETERMINED OVERHEAD RATES

Manufacturing overhead costs and expenses have to be absorbed in the cost of the products, and this absorption process requires that a reasonable basis be determined for costing the correct amount of overhead to each unit of production. Since overhead costs are incurred either because of the passage of time, as fixed costs that amount to a specific dollar amount per year, or because of production as variable costs, the most logical basis on which to establish rates is direct labor hour. Direct labor dollars may also be a reasonable basis for overhead rates except as distorted by overtime pay. Overhead usually does not occur at the time and one half rate, perhaps with the exception of payroll taxes and retirement benefits based on total compensation. Overhead rates per direct labor hour should also be broken down into variable and fixed rates for analytical purposes. An example of predetermining factory overhead rates is presented in Figure 6-3.

Computation of Overhead Rates per Direct Labor Hour

Factory Expenses—Year Ending March 31, 19x8

(Estimated 50,000 Direct Labor Hours)

| Account Number | Account | Total | Variable Per Hour | Variable Amount | Fixed |
|---|---|---|---|---|---|
| 703 | Supervisory salaries | $ 50,000 | $ | $ | $50,000 |
| 704 | Factory repairs and services | 25,000 | .50 | 25,000 | |
| 705 | Factory equipment rental | 5,000 | .10 | 5,000 | |
| 706 | Factory supplies | 35,000 | .70 | 35,000 | |
| 707 | Factory maintenance | 20,000 | .40 | 20,000 | |
| 708 | Shipping and receiving labor | 30,000 | .60 | 30,000 | |
| 761 | Depreciation—machinery and equipment | 20,000 | | | 20,000 |
| 763 | Depreciation—patterns | 5,000 | | | 5,000 |
| 764 | Depreciation—dies and fixtures | 4,000 | | | 4,000 |
| 770 | Miscellaneous factory expense | 10,000 | .20 | 10,000 | |
| | | $204,000 | $2.50 | $125,000 | $79,000 |

**Figure 6-3**

Based on the 50,000 estimated direct labor hours, the total overhead rate for factory expenses is:

$$\text{Variable: } \frac{\$125{,}000}{50{,}000 \text{ hours}} = \$2.50$$

$$\text{Fixed: } \frac{\$\ 79{,}000}{50{,}000 \text{ hours}} = \underline{1.58}$$

$$\text{Total: } \frac{\$204{,}000}{50{,}000 \text{ hours}} = \underline{\underline{\$4.08}}$$

In addition to the factory overhead in the above accounts there is additional factory overhead in certain 800 series accounts. These accounts contain both factory overhead and general and administrative expenses. Therefore, a proper allocation must be made between the two types of expenses. Such allocations might be determined as follows:

*Retirement Benefits*—expected contribution for employees in various wage and salary expense classifications; may follow compensation; must know basis for computing contribution allocation between various employees.

*Property Tax*—allocate based on valuation of assessed property used in manufacturing plus inventory versus other property; square footage may be useful in determining the allocation of property tax on real estate.

*Payroll Taxes*—follows salaries and wages; must consider maximum taxable compensation per employeé in making allocation.

*Insurance*—must be broken down into various types and each fairly allocated between factory costs and other expenses. Also, insurance is partially a variable cost and partially fixed. Workmen's compensation and the related liability insurance is variable or fixed depending on the related wages and can be allocated based on the rate per labor dollar used to compute the premium. Property damage insurance can be allocated based on the value of the factory assets and inventory insured versus other assets insured. General liability, product liability and liability umbrella tend to be fixed, but must be partially allocated to factory costs based on a percentage of liability it is estimated that the factory creates. Health insurance, group life and indemnity tend to follow the number of eligible employees and are variable or fixed depending on whether the employees' wages are variable or fixed. Insurance on vehicles tends to be semivariable, but more closely resembles a fixed cost within a normal operating range and can be allocated to factory overhead based on the vehicles used for factory purposes, such as handling materials. Most other insurance, such as surety bonds, etc. is an administrative cost.

*Utilities*—unless utilities are separately metered, the allocation between factory and other overhead becomes somewhat arbitrary. However, electricity usage can be estimated reasonably closely based on kilowatt-hour ratings, heat per square foot and exposure, and water on estimated usage. Electricity and water tend to vary with production, while heat may be fixed because it is required regardless of total production time.

*Depreciation of Vehicles*—it is a fixed cost based on vehicles used for production purposes.

*Depreciation of Building*—is a fixed cost and may have to be allocated based on costs per square foot of factory and administrative space if the same building houses both functions.

*Vehicle Expense*—varies with the amount of use given factory vehicles and is more of a variable than fixed expense.

Predetermined rates for these expenses may be computed as in Figure 6-4.

Based on 50,000 estimated direct labor hours, the total factory overhead rate for expenses in the mixed accounts is as follows:

$$\text{Variable: } \frac{\$43{,}000}{50{,}000 \text{ hours}} = \$\ .86$$

$$\text{Fixed: } \frac{\$49{,}500}{50{,}000 \text{ hours}} = \underline{.99}$$

$$\text{Total: } \frac{\$92{,}500}{50{,}000 \text{ hours}} = \underline{\underline{\$1.85}}$$

COMPUTATION OF OVERHEAD RATE PER DIRECT LABOR HOUR

Mixed Expenses—Year Ending March 31, 19x8

(Estimated 50,000 Direct Labor Hours)

| Account Number | Account | Total | Administrative | Factory[1] | Variable Per Hour | Variable Amount | Fixed |
|---|---|---|---|---|---|---|---|
| 813 | Retirement benefits | $ 7,000 | $ 3,000 | $ 4,000 | $.05 | $ 2,500 | $ 1,500 |
| 821 | Property tax | 8,000 | 2,000 | 6,000 | | | 6,000 |
| 830 | State unemployment tax | 2,900 | 600 | 2,300 | .04 | 2,000 | 300 |
| 831 | Federal unemployment tax | 800 | 200 | 600 | .01 | 500 | 100 |
| 832 | F.I.C.A. tax | 21,600 | 5,000 | 16,600 | .28 | 14,000 | 2,600 |
| 834 | Insurance | 30,000 | 10,000 | 20,000 | .20 | 10,000 | 10,000 |
| 840 | Heat | 20,000 | 5,000 | 15,000 | | | 15,000 |
| 841 | Electricity | 13,000 | 4,000 | 9,000 | .18 | 9,000 | |
| 842 | Water | 4,000 | 1,000 | 3,000 | .06 | 3,000 | |
| 862 | Depreciation—vehicles | 4,000 | 2,000 | 2,000 | | | 2,000 |
| 865 | Depreciation—building | 16,000 | 4,000 | 12,000 | | | 12,000 |
| 869 | Vehicle expense | 4,000 | 2,000 | 2,000 | .04 | 2,000 | |
| | | $131,300 | $38,800 | $92,500 | $.86 | $43,000 | $49,500 |

[1]See narrative on bases for allocation between administrative and factory.

**Figure 6-4**

The total predetermined factory overhead rate for the year ending March 31, 19x8 is summarized as in Figure 6-5.

| | | Total | Variable | Fixed |
|---|---|---|---|---|
| 700's | Factory expense accounts | $4.08 | $2.50 | $1.58 |
| 800's | Mixed expense accounts | 1.85 | .86 | .99 |
| | Predetermined overhead rates | $5.93 | $3.36 | $2.57 |

**Figure 6-5**

## ALLOCATING OVERHEAD TO MANUFACTURING COSTS

Once the rates of factory overhead are determined, the allocation to goods in process becomes a routine record keeping procedure. The allocation is made by applying overhead to goods in process on a computation of direct labor hours, usually as standard for repetitive products, multiplied by the predetermined rates. Such a computation for April, 19x8 might be as illustrated in Figure 6-6.

| Product | Direct Labor Hours | |
|---|---|---|
| Machine 1 | 762 | standard |
| Machine 2 | 629 | standard |
| Machine 3 | 897 | standard |
| Custom machines | 479 | actual |
| Parts | 901 | standard |
| Service | 400 | actual |
| Total | 4,068 | |

**Figure 6-6**

Since it is impractical to establish standard direct labor hours for custom machinery and customer service, these items are recorded at actual direct labor hours. The accounting entries to transfer overhead costs to goods in process are made using the predetermined rates established in Figure 6-5.

| | | | |
|---|---|---|---|
| Goods in process | 141 | 24,123.24 | |
| Factory expense applied | 799 | | 16,597.44 |
| Factory overhead applied | 899 | | 7,525.80 |

| | | |
|---|---|---|
| 799 | 4,068 × 4.08 = | $16,597.44 |
| 899 | 4,068 × 1.85 = | 7,525.80 |
| Total | 4,068 × 5.93 = | $24,123.24 |

| | | |
|---|---|---|
| Machine 1 | 762 × 5.93 = | $ 4,518.66 |
| Machine 2 | 629 × 5.93 = | 3,729.97 |
| Machine 3 | 897 × 5.93 = | 5,319.21 |
| Custom machines | 479 × 5.93 = | 2,840.47 |
| Parts | 901 × 5.93 = | 5,342.93 |
| Service | 400 × 5.93 = | 2,372.00 |
| Total | | $24,123.24 |

## OVERAPPLIED AND UNDERAPPLIED OVERHEAD COSTS

Each month, as a normal control routine, the actual factory expense and overhead incurred for the year-to-date should be compared to the amounts applied through accounts 799 and 899. The aim is to be evenly applied at year-end. High or low volume during individual months or unusual expenses during certain parts of the year will result in temporary over or under application. These possibilities are to be expected and accepted, for this is one of the purposes of predetermined rates—to level the amount applied per direct labor hour throughout the year. However, the reason for over or under application must be evident and expected to be within reasonable limits for the entire year. If not, rate corrections and reallocations for the year-to-date must be made.

## FLEXIBLE OVERHEAD RATES AND ADJUSTMENTS FOR REALLOCATION

Fixed costs per direct labor hour change as the level of production increases or decreases. It is beneficial to know what overhead rates are at various levels of production for planning purposes as an aid to marketing in pricing the products. Figure 6-7 illustrates the effect of production level on the overhead rates.

| | Variable | Fixed | Total |
|---|---|---|---|
| 700 accounts: | | | |
| | $112,500 | $59,250 | $171,750 |
| 800 accounts: | | | |
| | 38,700 | 37,125 | 75,825 |
| Totals | $151,200 | $96,375 | $247,575 |

Figure 6-7 clearly illustrates that fixed costs per direct labor hour tend to decline as volume increases. This is the result of spreading a fixed amount of costs over more units of input, direct labor hours, and will ultimately produce a product, output, at a lower unit cost. A change in anticipated volume is the most common cause of over or underapplied overhead.

Assume that the predetermined overhead rate was established at $5.93 per direct labor hour based on an estimated 50,000 direct labor hours. Further assume that nine months operation have been completed and, because of a significant increase in sales, 45,000 hours of direct labor have already been used. The remainder of the year will continue at the average rate for the first nine months and will result in a total of 60,000 direct labor hours. If our actual overhead projections were accurate, variable manufacturing overhead incurred would amount to ($3.36 × 45,000 direct labor hours) or $151,200. Fixed overhead would stay at $128,500 and the combined total of actual overhead would be as follows: (Refer to Figure 6-3 and 6-4 for 45,000 direct labor hours for variable costs and expenses and ¾ of a year for fixed costs and expenses).

| | Direct Labor Hours | | | | | | |
|---|---|---|---|---|---|---|---|
| | 35,000 | 40,000 | 45,000 | 50,000 | 55,000 | 60,000 | 65,000 |
| Variable overhead ($3.36 per hour) | $117,600 | $134,400 | $151,200 | $168,000 | $184,800 | $201,600 | $218,400 |
| Fixed overhead ($79,000 +$49,500) | 128,500 | 128,500 | 128,500 | 128,500 | 128,500 | 128,500 | 128,500 |
| Total overhead | $246,100 | $262,900 | $279,700 | $296,500 | $313,300 | $330,100 | $346,900 |
| Rates: | | | | | | | |
| Variable | $3.36 | $3.36 | $3.36 | $3.36 | $3.36 | $3.36 | $3.36 |
| Fixed | 3.67 | 3.21 | 2.86 | 2.57 | 2.34 | 2.14 | 1.98 |
| Total | $7.03 | $6.57 | $6.22 | $5.93 | $5.70 | $5.50 | $5.34 |

**Figure 6-7**

Manufacturing overhead would have been applied, based on 45,000 direct labor hours as follows:

| | | |
|---|---|---|
| 700 accounts | $4.08 × 45,000 = | $183,600 |
| 800 accounts | $1.85 × 45,000 = | 83,250 |
| Total | $5.93 × 45,000 = | $266,850 |

The amount of overapplied manufacturing overhead is $266,850 applied less $247,575 actual for the first nine months of $19,275. The normal production level would have been 37,500 direct labor hours (¾ × 50,000 annual). Actual production hours exceeded the normal hours by 7,500 (45,000 less 37,500). Manufacturing overhead has been overapplied by 7,500 hours times the combined fixed overhead rates of $1.58 for the 700 accounts plus $.99 for the 800 accounts (7,500 × 1.58 + 7,500 × .99) = $11,850 + $7,425 or a total of $19,275 as previously stated. In the general ledger the total credits to account 799, Factory Expense Applied, exceed actual manufacturing expenses by $11,850. Likewise, the total credits to account 899, Factory Overhead Applied, exceed actual manufacturing overhead expenses by $7,425. Because the overapplied overhead is significant, there needs to be a reallocation. This reallocation should be based on the number of direct labor hours from current production, a total of 45,000 hours, that are in the various cost of sales, finished goods, goods in process, and goods on consignment categories. Assume the following direct labor hours for the reallocation entry:

| | Direct Labor Hours | Rate Changes[1] | Adjustments |
|---|---|---|---|
| Goods in process | 6,600 | $0.4283 | $2,827 |
| Finished goods | 12,000 | 0.4283 | 5,140 |
| Goods on consignment—out | 600 | 0.4283 | 257 |
| Cost of sales—machine 1 | 7,200 | 0.4283 | 3,084 |
| Cost of sales—machine 2 | 6,000 | 0.4283 | 2,570 |
| Cost of sales—machine 3 | 4,800 | 0.4283 | 2,056 |
| Cost of sales—custom machines | 4,200 | 0.4283 | 1,799 |
| Cost of sales—repair parts | 2,400 | 0.4283 | 1,028 |
| Cost of sales—service | 1,200 | 0.4283 | 514 |
| Total | 45,000 | $0.4283 | $19,275 |

| | |
|---|---|
| [1]at 50,000 | $5.9300 |
| at 60,000 | 5.5017 |
| Combined | $0.4283 |

The adjusting entry would be made as follows:

| | Account Number | | |
|---|---|---|---|
| Factory expense applied | 799 | 11,850 | |
| Factory overhead applied | 899 | 7,425 | |
| Goods in process | 141 | | 2,827 |
| Finished goods | 142 | | 5,140 |
| Goods on consignment—out | 143 | | 257 |
| Cost of sales—machine 1 | 601 | | 3,084 |
| Cost of sales—machine 2 | 602 | | 2,570 |
| Cost of sales—machine 3 | 603 | | 2,056 |
| Cost of sales—custom machines | 610 | | 1,799 |
| Cost of sales—repair parts | 620 | | 1,028 |
| Cost of sales—service | 630 | | 514 |

In the remaining three months of the year the overhead rates would be corrected to the 60,000 direct labor hour level, or for the 799 factory expense:

| | | |
|---|---|---|
| Variable: | | $2.500 |
| Fixed: | $\frac{\$79{,}000}{60{,}000}$ = | 1.317 |
| | Total rate | $3.817 |

For applied factory overhead:

| | | |
|---|---|---|
| Variable: | | $ .860 |
| Fixed: | $\frac{\$49{,}500}{60{,}000}$ = | .825 |
| | Total rate | $1.685 |

## COMPUTING THE BREAKEVEN POINT AND TARGET PROFIT

The key to computing the breakeven point is knowing the total fixed costs and the percent of variable costs in sales dollars. These fixed and variable costs must include those previously discussed as manufacturing costs plus the fixed and variable elements of general and administrative expenses, marketing expenses and other functional breakdowns of expenses. To illustrate, let's do a percentage analysis of an income statement, with net sales equal to 100 percent, followed by the percentages for all variable costs and expenses and the dollar amounts of fixed costs and expenses.

| | | |
|---|---|---|
| Net Sales | | 100% |
| Variable Costs and Expenses: | | |
| Materials | 25% | |
| Direct labor | 20 | |
| Variable overhead | 20 | |
| Variable general and administrative expenses | 8 | |
| Variable selling expenses | 7 | |
| Total variable costs and expenses | | 80% |
| Variable Profit | | 20% |
| Fixed Costs and Expenses: | | |
| Fixed overhead | $128,500 | |
| Fixed general and administrative expenses | 40,000 | |
| Fixed marketing expenses | 24,500 | |
| Total fixed costs and expenses | | $193,000 |

The breakeven point (no profit or loss) is determined by dividing total fixed costs and expenses by the variable profit percent. Thus:

$$\text{Breakeven} = \frac{\$193{,}000}{.20} = \$965{,}000$$

This breakeven sales figure can be proved by reconstructing the previously presented income statement in dollars.

| | |
|---|---|
| Net Sales | $965,000 |
| Total Variable Costs and Expenses—80% of sales | 772,000 |
| Variable Profit | 193,000 |
| Total Fixed Costs and Expenses | 193,000 |
| Net Income or Loss | –0– |

To compute the amount of sales necessary to reach a desired profit before federal income tax, the same formula is used with the desired profit, say $100,000, added to the total fixed costs and expenses as follows:

$$\frac{\$193{,}000 + \$100{,}000}{.20} = \$1{,}465{,}000$$

This sales figure can be proved as presented below:

| | |
|---|---|
| Net Sales | $1,465,000 |
| Total Variable Costs and Expenses—80% of sales | 1,172,000 |
| Variable Profit | 293,000 |
| Total Fixed Costs and Expenses | 193,000 |
| Net Profit before Federal Income Tax | $ 100,000 |

The previous proofs of breakeven and target profit should be used to verify the calculations; an error could be critical. Also, the breakeven point as computed is based on average variable profit. If there is a substantial difference in markup on various products, any material change in the mix of products sold will change the breakeven or target profit point, and a new calculation must be made.

## CONSIDERATIONS ON BIDDING AND THE EFFECT OF FIXED OVERHEAD ON COST-VOLUME RELATIONSHIP

Stated simply, the cost-volume relationship theory is that if an additional sale can be made in a contract that covers all variable costs and expenses plus any markup, it will increase profits. This theory is substantiated by the fact that the fixed costs and expenses must be incurred anyway. Care must be exercised that such a sale does not decrease or replace other, more profitable sales by any noticeable amount. This increase in profit can be illustrated by adding a new contract of $100,000 with variable costs and expenses of $90,000 to the previous income statement at the breakeven point. Note that at the breakeven point fixed costs and expenses were 20 percent of sales.

| | Breakeven Point | New Contract | Combined Total |
|---|---|---|---|
| Net Sales | $965,000 | $100,000 | $1,065,000 |
| Variable Costs and Expenses | 772,000 | 90,000 | 862,000 |
| Variable Profit | 193,000 | 10,000 | 203,000 |
| Fixed Costs and Expenses | 193,000 | -0- | 193,000 |
| Net profit before Federal Income Tax | $ -0- | $ 10,000 | $ 10,000 |

The result of the new contract, a marginal one returning only half the average profit, is to lower the total fixed costs and expenses to sales from 20 percent to 18.1 percent. The fact that profit can be made fairly rapidly once sales pass the breakeven point is also an important, recognizable business concept.

## SUMMARY

The overhead costs of most importance to a manufacturer are those related to producing the product, although administrative and other expenses, sometimes also called overhead, must be controlled to the extent possible. The primary difference in accounting for the two types of overhead is that manufacturing overhead becomes a cost of the inventory produced and is partially deferred to a later period through the ending inventory. Administrative and other overhead not related directly to manufacturing is expensed in the period incurred.

Manufacturing overhead is made up of all costs of manufacturing besides materials and direct labor. Generally, these costs are allocated to manufacturing as a rate per direct labor hour.

There are two principal types of overhead, variable, that is directly related to production volume, and fixed, which stays constant in total within a normal operating range of volume.

Manufacturing overhead rates should be predetermined based on estimated total direct labor hours for the year. This procedure prevents penalizing low points during the year with an unreasonable rate and facilitates the use of standard product costs.

Manufacturing overhead is then allocated to the various products produced based on standard direct labor hours or actual direct labor hours for special products and services that do not have standard costs.

Cumulative totals of actual manufacturing overhead costs and expenses should be compared each month to the cumulative totals applied. If overhead is expected to be significantly over or underapplied for the year because of a change in volume, etc., the rates should be corrected and the year-to-date allocation corrected by a reallocation based on direct labor hours in goods in process, finished goods and cost of sales.

Every manufacturer should know his approximate breakeven point, determined by dividing total fixed costs and expenses, by the variable profit percent. This same theory also carries over to the computation of profit in a marginal bid contract, as any sale price that recovers all variable costs does make a contribution towards increased profits.

# 7

# Cost Information Systems for Convenience and Efficiency

## ACCUMULATING ACTUAL COSTS FOR ONE-OF-A-KIND PRODUCTS

Every product that is manufactured on a repetitive basis can have a standard cost established. Other products which are special, custom or one-of-a-kind must be costed out at actual costs; there is no basis on which to establish what is standard.

Actual costing reverts to an accumulation of material and direct labor costs with allocations of factory expense and factory overhead to complete the cost of the custom product. If parts are used on the custom product that are also used on standard products, these particular parts will already have a standard cost established, and they can be costed at standard even though the rest of the custom item will be costed at actual.

Actual costing requires detailed record keeping on each specific product. This record keeping starts with a parts list for the product as presented in Figure 7-1. Generally, the part numbers assigned to the various parts are derived from the print numbers assigned by the designer. These print numbers should be kept in sequence, but those parts that are standard on other machines may keep the standard part number. Other components will be purchased and may use the part number assigned by the manufacturer or distributor.

The assembly print number may be used by the assemblers to record their time on the daily time cards. Time should be recorded by individual part numbers for machining operations, welding the frame, etc. Accurate costs by individual parts is extremely important as a guide for quoting replacements as necessary. Also, the very best method of filing the cost completed parts list is necessary, perhaps alphabetical, with a cross reference by serial number of the machine.

MACHINE MANUFACTURING CORPORATION

Parts List    Assembly No. C101    Serial No. G 7676    Date 8-9x8

Customer KTS Corp.    Machine KTS Custom Belt Grinder

| Part No. | Description | Units | Type Material | Unit Cost Material | Unit Cost Labor | Unit Cost Overhead | Total Cost Material | Total Cost Labor | Total Cost Overhead | Total Cost |
|---|---|---|---|---|---|---|---|---|---|---|
| C 102 | Frame | 1 | S ½" HR | 327.00 | 200.00 | 150.00 | 327.00 | 200.00 | 150.00 | 677.00 |
| C 103 | Guards | 2 | S 16 ga. | 24.00 | 80.00 | 60.00 | 48.00 | 160.00 | 120.00 | 328.00 |
| M 470 | Pulleys | 4 | Cast A | 12.00 | 16.00 | 12.00 | 48.00 | 64.00 | 48.00 | 160.00 |
| C 105 | Shafts | 2 | S 1" CR | 8.00 | 28.00 | 21.00 | 16.00 | 56.00 | 42.00 | 114.00 |
| PW 14 | Bearings | 4 | Purchase | 3.00 | | | 12.00 | | | 12.00 |
| AR 17 | Sheave | 2 | Purchase | 4.00 | | | 8.00 | | | 8.00 |
| V 726 | Belts | 2 | Purchase | 6.00 | | | 12.00 | | | 12.00 |
| C 101 | Assembly | 1 | — | | 280.00 | 210.00 | | 280.00 | 210.00 | 490.00 |
| | | | | | | | 471.00 | 760.00 | 570.00 | 1,801.00 |

**Figure 7-1**

## COMPARISON OF ACTUAL COSTS TO ESTIMATED COSTS

In order to quote any custom product, estimates must be detailed based on the material to be used, labor costs of machining, fabricating and assembling, plus the normal load for overhead. These estimated costs must then be compared to actual costs to measure performance and to improve estimating techniques. A short cut method would be to make a copy of the actual costs as recorded on the parts list and jot in the corresponding estimated costs in a different color. Where the estimates vary substantially from actual, the reason should be determined to improve quoting accuracy on subsequent products.

## DEVELOPING STANDARD COSTS FOR REPETITIVE PRODUCTS

A standard cost for a product must be developed in somewhat the same way actual costs are compiled with the ingredient of judgment added to what actual costing has revealed. Standards should be established or revised based on the combined knowledge of cost accounting, production, purchasing and engineering. Recorded costs for various parts and functions are then just the starting point in establishing the standard. The more experience and the more times actual costs have been recorded, the more reliable the information becomes as a guide to what should be standard.

Standard costs must be determined by arriving at a separate cost for each part of the product plus the cost of assembling or otherwise putting all these parts together into a complete, finished, ready-to-sell product. This working part by part toward a finished product means the more complex the product the more complex the process of developing the standard.

The starting point is the parts list similar to the one illustrated in Figure 7-1. Engineering drawings must be read to determine the actual measurements of many of the pieces that are to be fabricated or processed from purchased materials. In this type of fabrication, there is usually scrap created that has no other use because materials are often not available in the exact measurements required. Therefore, the material cost will include the size of the entire unit of material, only part of which actually becomes a part of the finished product. Other materials or components will not be altered or receive further processing prior to assembly and therefore have no waste.

Purchasing is often aware of a better source for certain materials and components or may be able to obtain quantity discounts once the product goes into full production, and must be consulted regarding the costs recorded versus what will become standard. Production and engineering may also be aware of changes that can be made in the materials used to improve the product or reduce the costs and, likewise, must be consulted in establishing what will become standard. Production and engineering can also usually foresee reasons why the labor time or rates will change as the product is manufactured repetitively and can add to the refinement of the original standard cost.

Except for changes in processing centers, etc., overhead allocation is primarily a function of accounting once the material and labor standards are established. Also, at least on initial runs, accounting should evaluate the standards in detail against actual performance to either determine that the standards are reasonable or should be revised. The same detailed analysis should be made from time to time on later dates to continually reevaluate the standards.

In summary, accounting should develop standard costs for material, labor and overhead for each part plus the processing or assembly of the final product. The cost accountant should have available the actual costs and his preliminary standard costs plus supporting details on sources of materials, print numbers from which details have been developed, and the labor time cards to establish who performed the various functions and when they were accomplished. All of this should be available and reviewed individually or jointly with purchasing, engineering and production to evaluate and revise the preliminary standards based on the combined knowledge of the four departments. Following this, the standards should be carefully evaluated and reviewed on initial production runs before being adopted.

## THE PRIMARY BENEFITS OF STANDARD COSTS

Although there is some additional work required to establish standard costs, even this is minimal because determining the actual costs as a basis for the standards is the biggest part of the job; the time saved in costing inventory, transfer of inventory and costing sales outweighs the time spent in establishing the standard many times. It is easy to visualize the transfer of materials, labor and overhead through the production process to finished goods and cost of sales at standard, just a set of accounting entries to transfer the various elements at predetermined costs versus separate computations for each part and element if actual costs were computed and used for inventory record keeping.

The physical inventory of finished goods and materials is also very simple to cost at standard. The physical inventory of goods in process is somewhat more difficult to cost, but still easier at standard than at actual. At times it is necessary to refer to parts lists on goods in process and build up a standard for individual items based on parts in process, stage of completion, etc. This information is all available from the buildup of the original or revised standards. Sometimes, for goods in process, it is easier to start with the finished goods standard cost and deduct functions and parts not completed and the related overhead.

The time saved by costing products at standard may be sufficient reason alone to establish standard costs for each standard product. However, more value as a management tool in manufacturing comes from the ability to measure actual performance against what should have been accomplished, the standard of performance.

## COMPARISON OF ACTUAL COSTS AND STANDARD COSTS

The differences between actual costs and standard costs, usually called variances, are broken down and analyzed according to the cost elements of material, labor and overhead. These variances serve to evaluate performance and the standards continuously. When actual costs are less than the standard costs the variances are described as favorable—when actual costs are greater than standard costs the variances are conversely called unfavorable. The choice of favorable and unfavorable as a means of describing variances is perhaps unfortunate. Whether a variance is truly favorable or unfavorable cannot be determined by simply comparing actual to standard. One must know the reason for the variance. As an example, an overtime premium would probably cause an unfavorable labor rate variance—but if the overtime is the result of an additional profitable order, is the variance truly unfavorable?

Materials variances are the result of a difference between the price paid for the material and the price used as standard and the amount of materials used versus the standard usage. The price variance is fairly easy to determine; the usage variance requires detailed records of actual materials used and is therefore not as easily determined.

The materials price variance can be measured at the time of purchase or as materials are used in production. Each point has advantages and disadvantages. If it is assumed that the price of materials is entirely the function of purchasing, the point of acquisition is the proper point at which the variance should be determined and this seems to be a reasonable assumption. From an accounting standpoint, it is nice to look at a total variance as being the sum of two or more individual variances. This total materials variance is difficult to prove if the materials price variance is established at the point of purchase and the materials usage variance is established as materials are put into production. The units on which the variances are computed are not comparable and a single total variance cannot be computed separately, but must be simply the sum of the two variances, price and usage.

Direct labor variances are likewise the product of both price and usage—often referred to as rate and efficiency. Here, the point of measurement for the two variances is the same—at input. Therefore, the two variances can be added together to obtain the total labor variance which can also be computed separately as a proof factor.

Overhead variances are computed in different ways depending on the information available. The method usually referred to as the two variance method computes a budget variance, which is a combination of spending and efficiency and a volume variance which measures the difference caused by standard hours versus hours budgeted to compute the overhead rate. The two variance method measures variances based on units of output. The three variance method of overhead relies on input units and breaks spending and efficiency variances into separate categories and also computes a volume variance. Also, since the same units are used in computing all overhead variances, a total variance can be computed which is equal to the sum of the other two or three variances.

## THE VARIANCE FORMULAS

The following assumptions are made relative to the costs of a particular product to develop the use of the variance formulas.

| Standard Costs | | |
|---|---|---|
| Materials | | |
| 2,000 units of A @ $1.83 = | $3,660.00 | |
| 400 units of B @ .94 = | 376.00 | |
| | | $4,036.00 |
| Labor | | |
| 200 hours of C @ $4.76 = | 952.00 | |
| 100 hours of D @ 7.16 = | 716.00 | |
| | | 1,668.00 |
| Overhead (budgeted,270 hours) | | |
| 300 hours of V @ $5.10 = | 1,530.00 | |
| 300 hours of F @ 3.80 = | 1,140.00 | |
| | | 2,670.00 |
| Total standard costs | | $8,374.00 |
| Actual Costs | | |
| Materials | | |
| 2,050 units of A @ $1.87 = | $3,833.50 | |
| 390 units of B @ .96 = | 374.40 | |
| | | $4,207.90 |
| Labor | | |
| 207 hours of C @ $4.80 = | 993.60 | |
| 90 hours of D @ 6.91 = | 621.90 | |
| | | 1,615.50 |
| Overhead (budgeted, 270 hours) | | |
| Variable | 1,500.00 | |
| Fixed | 1,140.00 | |
| | | 2,640.00 |
| | | $8,463.40 |

| | |
|---|---|
| Total standard costs | $ 8,374.00 |
| Total actual costs | 8,463.40 |
| Total variances | $( 89.50) |

*Materials variances* in this illustration are computed based on units of input for both price and usage. As previously explained, the price variance can be computed based on units purchased where that amount differs from input. Formulas and solutions for materials variances are as follows based on the preceding assumptions of standard and actual costs.

TMV = total materials variance
MPV = materials price variance
MUV = materials usage variance
SP = standard price per unit
AP = actual price per unit
SU = standard units of usage
AU = actual units of usage
TMV = (SP)(SU) − (AP)(AU) or (See proof below)
TMV = MPV + MUV
MPV = (SP − AP)(AU)
MUV = (SU − AU)(SP)

Proof:

TMV = MPV + MUV
TMV = (SP − AP)(AU) + (SU − AU)(SP)
TMV = (SP)(AU) − (AP)(AU) + (SU)(SP) − (AU)(SP)
TMV = ~~(SP)(AU)~~ − ~~(AU)(SP)~~ + (SP)(SU) − (AP)(AU)
TMV = (SP)(SU) − (AP)(AU)

Material A Variances

| | |
|---|---|
| TMV = (SP)(SU) − (AP)(AU) | |
| TMV = (1.83 × 2,000) − (1.87 × 2,050) | |
| TMV = 3,660.00 − 3,833.50 | |
| TMV = | $( 173.50) |
| MPV = (SP − AP)(AU) | |
| MPV = (1.83 − 1.87)(2,050) | |
| MPV = (−.04)(2,050) | |
| MPV = | $( 82.00) |
| MUV = (SU − AU)(SP) | |
| MUV = (2,000 − 2,050)(1.83) | |
| MUV = (−50)(1.83) | |
| MUV = | $( 91.50) |
| TMV = | $( 173.50) |

Material B Variances

| | |
|---|---|
| TMV = (SP)(SU) − (AP)(AU) | |
| TMV = (.94 × 400) − (.96 × 390) | |
| TMV = 376.00 − 374.40 | |
| TMV = | $ 1.60 |
| MPV = (SP − AP)(AU) | |
| MPV = (.94 − .96)(390) | |
| MPV = (−.02)(390) | |
| MPV = | $( 7.80) |
| MUV = (SU − AU)(SP) | |
| MUV = (400 − 390)(.94) | |
| MUV = (10)(.94) | |
| MUV = | 9.40 |
| TMV = | $ 1.60 |

| | |
|---|---|
| TMV (A) = | $( 173.50) |
| TMV (B) = | 1.60 |
| TMV = | $( 171.90) |

| | |
|---|---|
| Standard Material cost | $ 4,036.00 |
| Actual material cost | 4,207.90 |
| TMV = | $( 171.90) |

> The material price variance, by the formula, (standard price less actual price) (actual units), eliminates any effect of the difference between standard and actual usage.
>
> The materials usage variance by the formula, (standard units less actual units) (standard price), eliminates any effect of the difference between standard and actual price.

*Labor variances* are based on the input of rates and hours and, when measured against the standard rates and hours, produce rate and efficiency variances that are the equivalent of the price and usage variances for materials. Labor variances are computed according to the following formulas and the preceding assumptions of standard and actual costs.

TLV = Total labor variance
LRV = Labor rate variance
LEV = Labor efficiency variance
SR = Standard rate per hour
AR = Actual rate per hour
SH = Standard hours per unit
AH = Actual hours per unit

TLV = (SH)(SR) − (AH)(AR) or (see proof below)
TLV = LRV + LEV
LRV = (SR − AR)(AH)
LEV = (SH − AH)(SR)

Proof:

TLV = LRV + LEV
TLV = (SR − AR)(AH) + (SH − AH)(SR)
TLV = (SR)(AH) − (AR)(AH) + (SH)(SR) − (AH)(SR)
TLV = ~~(SR)(AH)~~ − ~~(AH)(SR)~~ + (SH)(SR) − (AH)(AR)
TLV = (SH)(SR) − (AH)(AR)

<u>Labor C Variances</u>

TLV = (SH)(SR) − (AH)(AR)
TLV = (200)(4.76) − (207)(4.80)
TLV = 952.00 − 993.60
TLV = $ (41.60)

LRV = (SR − AR)(AH)
LRV = (4.76 − 4.80)(207)
LRV = (−.04)(207)
LRV = $ (8.28)

LEV = (SH − AH)(SR)
LEV = (200 − 207)(4.76)
LEV = (−7)(4.76)
LEV = $ (33.32)

TLV = $ (41.60)

Labor D Variances

| | |
|---|---|
| TLV = (SH)(SR) – (AH)(AR) | |
| TLV = (100)(7.16) – (90)(6.91) | |
| TLV = 716.00 – 621.90 | |
| TLV = | $ 94.10 |
| | |
| LRV = (SR – AR)(AH) | |
| LRV = (7.16 – 6.91)(90) | |
| LRV = (.25)(90) | |
| LRV = | $ 22.50 |
| LEV = (SH – AH)(SR) | |
| LEV = (100 – 90)(7.16) | |
| LEV = (10)(7.16) | |
| LEV = | $ 71.60 |
| TLV = | $ 94.10 |
| TLV (C) = | $ (41.60) |
| TLV (D) = | 94.10 |
| TLV = | $ 52.50 |
| Standard labor costs | $1,668.00 |
| Actual labor costs | 1,615.50 |
| TLV = | $ 52.50 |

The labor rate variance by the formula, (standard rate less actual rate)(actual hours), eliminates any effect of the difference between standard and actual hours.

The labor efficiency variance by the formula, (standard hours less actual hours) (standard rate), eliminates any effect of the difference between the standard and actual rate.

*Overhead variances* are somewhat different than either materials or labor variances because the fixed element of overhead is affected by volume, that is the spreading of fixed costs over more or less than budgeted (predetermined) direct labor hours. Overhead variances are computed according to the following formulas and the preceding assumptions.

TOV = Total overhead variance
OSV = Overhead spending variance
OEV = Overhead efficiency variance
OVV = Overhead volume variance
SVR = Standard variable overhead rate per hour
SFR = Standard fixed overhead rate per hour

AH = Actual hours per unit
SH = Standard hours per unit
BH = Budgeted hours
AO = Actual overhead

TOV = SH(SVR + SFR) − AO or (see proof below)
TOV = OSV + OEV + OVV
OSV = (AH)(SVR) + (BH)(SFR) − AO
OEV = (SH − AH)(SVR)
OVV = (SH)(SFR) − (BH)(SFR)

Proof:
TOV = OSV + OEV + OVV
TOV = (AH)(SVR) + ~~(BH)(SFR)~~ − AO + (SH − AH)(SVR) + (SH)(SFR) − ~~(BH)(SFR)~~
TOV = ~~(AH)(SVR)~~ − AO + (SH)(SVR) − ~~(AH)(SVR)~~ + (SH)(SFR)
TOV = (SH)(SVR + SFR) − AO

| | |
|---|---|
| TOV = (SH)(SVR + SFR) − AO | |
| TOV = (300)(5.10 + 3.80) − 2,640.00 | |
| TOV = (300)(8.90) − 2,640.00 | |
| TOV = 2,670.00 − 2,640.00 | |
| TOV = | $ 30.00 |
| OSV = (AH)(SVR) + (BH)(SFR) − AO | |
| OSV = (297)(5.10) + 270 (3.80) − 2,640.00 | |
| OSV = 1,514.70 + 1,026.00 − 2,640.00 | |
| OSV = 2,540.70 − 2,640.00 | |
| OSV = | $( 99.30) |
| OEV = (SH − AH)(SVR) | |
| OEV = (300 − 297)(5.10) | |
| OEV = (3)(5.10) | |
| OEV = | 15.30 |
| OVV = (SH)(SFR) − (BH)(SFR) | |
| OVV = (300)(3.80) − (270)(3.80) | |
| OVV = 1,140.00 − 1,026.00 | |
| OVV = | 114.00 |
| TOV = | $ 30.00 |
| Standard overhead costs | $2,670.00 |
| Actual overhead costs | 2,640.00 |
| TOV = | $ 30.00 |

The overhead spending variance by the formula, (actual hours) (standard variable rate) plus (budgeted hours) (standard fixed rate) less actual overhead, eliminates any effect of standard hours.

The overhead efficiency variance by the formula, (standard hours less actual hours) (standard variable rate), pertains only to the time saving effect at the standard variable rate.

The overhead volume variance by the formula, (standard hours) (standard fixed rate) less (budgeted hours) (standard fixed rate) determines the difference between the fixed overhead based on standard hours and the predetermined fixed overhead—a true volume variance.

Notes on variances:

1. All formulas are arranged to produce negative figures when actual costs exceed standard costs—parentheses indicate negatives—actual over standard.
2. Variances are computed for each type of material and labor rather than in total to pinpoint the sources of the variances.
3. Again, what appears to be favorable may not be when the reason is determined. As an example, both materials A and B were purchased at prices below the standard. The total savings on materials was 4.26% below the standard cost and appears to be substantial and favorable. It is not favorable if excessive materials were purchased to obtain a quantity discount. The real benefit of variance analysis is realized only when the reason for the variance is known.

## CHECKLIST OF CAUSES OF VARIANCES

Variances may be caused by one or a combination of reasons. The following outline is a summary of some common causes for variances.

I. Materials price variance
   A. General price increase or decrease
   B. Change in supplier
   C. Change in material or component
   D. Change in freight rates
   E. Premium for rapid shipment in emergency
   F. Change in order quantity
   G. Effect of order quantity on freight per unit.

II. Materials usage variance
   A. Careless handling
   B. Errors in machining
   C. Theft
   D. Change in quality control
   E. Change in amount of scrap because of change in quality of material

III. Labor rate variance
   A. General wage rate change
   B. Use of higher rate employee where lower rate employee was not available
   C. Overtime and other premiums

IV. Labor efficiency variance
   A. Training time if not treated as overhead

B. Change in machinery utilized
C. Change in processing
D. Rework because of poor quality material
E. Rework because of processing errors
F. Inadequate supervision
G. Timekeeping errors
H. Fatigue in overtime situations
I. Temperature changes
J. Morale
K. Level of production activity

V. Overhead spending variance
A. Change in prices paid for indirect materials
B. Change in usage
C. Change in tax rates or value of assets assessed
D. Change in depreciable lives of equipment
E. Change in insurance rates
F. Change in rates paid indirect labor
G.` Change in payroll tax rates or maximum taxable wages

VI. Overhead efficiency variance
A. Reflects change in input volume on variable costs
B. Usually follows labor efficiency

VII. Overhead volume variance
A. Change in actual volume from planned volume
B. General demand
C. Strikes
D. Shortages
E. Marketing programs
F. Acceptance of new products

## ACCOUNTING FOR THE VARIANCES

All costs of production are put into goods in process, finished goods and cost of sales at standard. The variances are recorded separately for materials, labor and overhead in the accounts and are analyzed in detail through worksheet techniques for further reporting to management. The variances in the preceding example would have been recorded as follows:

| | | | |
|---|---|---|---|
| Goods in process | 141 | 4,036.00 | |
| Materials variances | 780 | 171.90 | |
| Materials | 140 | | 4,207.90 |
| Issue materials | | | |
| Goods in process | 141 | 1,668.00 | |
| Direct labor applied | 702 | | 1,615.50 |
| Direct labor variances | 781 | | 52.50 |
| Transfer to goods in ·rocess | | | |

| | | | | |
|---|---|---|---|---|
| Goods in process | 141 | 2,670.00 | | |
| Overhead applied | 799+899 | | 2,670.00 | |
| Transfer at standard | | | | |
| Variance equals $30.00 overapplied | | | | |
| Finished goods | 142 | 8,374.00 | | |
| Goods in process | 141 | | 8,374.00 | |
| Transfer to finished goods at standard on completion | | | | |
| Materials | 4,036.00 | | | |
| Direct labor | 1,668.00 | | | |
| Overhead | 2,670.00 | | | |
| Total standard cost | 8,374.00 | | | |
| Cost of sales | | 601 | 8,374.00 | |
| Finished goods | | 142 | | 8,374.00 |
| To record cost of sales at standard | | | | |

In this illustration the variances net to only $89.40 and would be closed through cost of sales. If the variances are substantial, they must be allocated according to the amount of goods in process, finished goods and cost of sales to which the variances apply. Substantial variances are also a prelude to reevaluating and perhaps, establishing new standards.

## REPORTING ON VARIANCES

Variance reports should be directed to management and the responsible individual or department. Standards against which actual performance is measured should be realistic in that the standard should be achievable, or perhaps, nearly achievable. Percentage relationships of actual to standard costs are useful in reporting to individuals at all levels. Percentages are comparable from one period to the next in that they are not influenced by the level of activity as dollars are, and percentages reveal the desired information without disclosing the number of dollars. Percentages are also relevant to the degree of efficiency.

Figure 7-2 illustrates a variance report for management based on the preceding examples in this chapter. Sections of this report or abbreviated reports may be presented as often as daily to various departments or department heads as desirable.

## KEEPING STANDARDS CURRENT

Periodically, at a specific time or times during the year, all standard costs should be revised. Also, overhead costs, because of the annual computation of predetermined rates, must be revised at the beginning of each year. All standards should be revised when actual costs vary more than an acceptable amount from the standard costs. Otherwise, confidence is lost in the standards, and management, as well as other personnel, tend to evaluate standards rather than performance when reading the variance reports. Therefore, the lack of revision as necessary tends to erode the effectiveness of the variance reports.

MACHINE MANUFACTURING CORPORATION

Management Variance Report

Month of May 19x8

| | Standard | Actual | Variance | Actual % of Standard |
|---|---|---|---|---|
| MATERIALS PRICE VARIANCE | | | | |
| Material A | $3,751.50 | $3,833.50 | $ ( 82.00) | 102.19% |
| Material B | 366.60 | 374.40 | ( 7.80) | 102.13 |
| Total MPV | 4,118.10 | 4,207.90 | ( 89.80) | 102.18 |
| MATERIALS USAGE VARIANCE | | | | |
| Material A | 3,660.00 | 3,751.50 | ( 91.50) | 102.50 |
| Material B | 376.00 | 366.60 | 9.40 | 97.50 |
| Total MUV | 4,036.00 | 4,118.10 | ( 82.10) | 102.03 |
| TOTAL MATERIALS VARIANCE | $4,036.00 | $4,207.90 | $ (171.90) | 104.26% |
| LABOR RATE VARIANCE | | | | |
| Labor C | $ 985.32 | $ 993.60 | $ ( 8.28) | 100.84% |
| Labor D | 644.40 | 621.90 | 22.50 | 96.51 |
| Total LRV | 1,629.72 | 1,615.50 | 14.22 | 99.13 |
| LABOR EFFICIENCY VARIANCE | | | | |
| Labor C | 952.00 | 985.32 | ( 33.32) | 103.50 |
| Labor D | 716.00 | 644.40 | 71.60 | 90.00 |
| Total LEV | 1,668.00 | 1,629.72 | 38.28 | 97.71 |
| TOTAL LABOR VARIANCE | $1,668.00 | $1,615.50 | $ 52.50 | 96.85% |
| OVERHEAD SPENDING VARIANCE | $2,540.70 | $2,640.00 | $ ( 99.30) | 103.91% |
| OVERHEAD EFFICIENCY VARIANCE | 1,530.00 | 1,514.70 | 15.30 | 99.00 |
| OVERHEAD VOLUME VARIANCE | 1,140.00 | 1,026.00 | 114.00 | 90.00 |
| TOTAL OVERHEAD VARIANCE | $2,670.00 | $2,640.00 | $ 30.00 | 98.88% |
| TOTAL COST VARIANCES | $8,374.00 | $8,363.40 | $ ( 89.40) | 101.07% |

**Figure 7-2**

## SUMMARY

Standard costs can be established for most products. However, actual costing is required for one-of-a-kind, custom manufactured products and probably the best control for these products is a comparison to the original estimated cost.

A parts list should be developed for each product to properly cost each part and component plus assembly time when applicable.

Standard costs can be developed for all repetitive products. The development of the standards should have the input of accounting, purchasing, production and engineering. The standards should be developed by cost accounting and reviewed with the other departments for revisions before being finalized.

Once adopted, the standard costs become a convenient method of costing the inventory flow and speed up the accounting process. Standard costs are also more convenient in pricing a physical inventory.

The following variances are the result of comparing actual costs to standard costs and, when the reasons for the variances are determined, they become an excellent means of evaluating performance and correcting deficiencies.

1. Materials price variance
2. Materials usage variance
3. Total materials variance
4. Labor rate variance
5. Labor efficiency variance
6. Total labor variance
7. Overhead spending variance
8. Overhead efficiency variance
9. Overhead volume variance
10. Total overhead variance

Variances must be reported to management and to the responsible department or department head. The method of reporting and the amount of detail depends on the information needed by the recipient and the amount of information that it is proper to disclose to the recipient.

Variances are normally closed through cost of sales but must be allocated to goods in process, finished goods and cost of sales if substantial in amount.

Care must be taken not to automatically accept costs that are less than standard as favorable or costs in excess of standard as unfavorable. The real meanings of the variances cannot be determined until the causes of the variances are explained.

The standards must be revised periodically, or as dictated by major cost changes, to maintain the degree of reliability that is necessary to command the confidence of management and other personnel.

# 8

# Choosing from Among Inventory Alternatives

## DOES THE MANUFACTURER NEED PERPETUAL INVENTORIES

Attention given to inventory records varies from systems that have instant recall of exact quantities, costs and prices for every component, to no inventory records at all. Some computerized systems trigger reorders based on programs which flag minimum quantities established for each part. Other systems reorder only when the crisis hits, usually an out-of-stock situation. Both extremes are impractical for most manufacturers.

The complete, computerized system is too expensive for many manufacturers and also requires extensive personnel training to gather reliable input and output data. Any system, no matter how automated, is only as reliable as the information it receives to process. Reacting to incomplete or inaccurate data creates some very embarrassing stock situations. One example was a situation where the processing of stock received fell behind stock withdrawn from inventory. Certain items showed negative quantities on the inventory print out, when they had actually been reordered several times based on the reorder triggering system and there was an extreme overstock position. This also caused an unfavorable budget expenditure that was the first indication of the problem.

The lack of any inventory records is purely unacceptable, poor business, which yields inaccurate financial statements and invites trouble with various taxing authorities. An absolute minimum is an accurate, documented, annual physical inventory with reliable inventory estimating procedures during the interim. A physical inventory plus interim spot physical verifications of quantities are also necessary with even the best of perpetual systems.

However, an advantage of keeping reliable perpetual inventory records has to do with the physical inventory count. Physical inventories, when combined with reliable perpetual records, are largely a verification of the reliability of the perpetual records. If the physical count and costing proves the perpetual records are accurate within an acceptable range, the physical inventory may be taken at a date other than the year-end, and the perpetual accepted for the year-end balances. In fact, where definite lines may be drawn between sections of the perpetual inventory, the physical counts can be spread by sections to various month-ends. Counting, costing, extending and totaling the physical inventory is usually the largest single closing procedure for the accountant. By performing this function at other month-ends, the year-end closing time is greatly reduced and the remaining information necessary for writing the reports can be gathered more rapidly to serve the manufacturers needs better and faster.

Most manufacturers benefit from the use of a perpetual inventory system. The real question then becomes the extent of the inventory records. This extent can vary from our previously discussed detail on every component to a system that yields only the total inventory costs. A perpetual system that produces total inventory costs is rather simple and inexpensive, yet increases greatly the reliability of interim financial statements and the measurement of profitability on a monthly or quarterly basis. The simplicity of this system is illustrated by the fact that records are required only to add to inventory the purchases of material and the input of direct labor and manufacturing overhead and the relief from inventory of the cost of sales. This can be accomplished with either a manual or computer system. Such a system must be augmented by regular physical counts of key items as discussed in Chapter 4 on purchasing procedures.

The extent of the detailed information kept on perpetual inventories must be determined by the needs of the individual manufacturers versus the cost of the system. Unfortunately, there is no exact measurement of the future savings and income that will result. Careful, informed judgment is necessary and should not be influenced by either an ingrained mistrust of the computer or an attitude that the computer can solve the inventory problem by itself. The decision can be influenced by the abilities of the personnel and equipment readily available, perhaps already in house, plus a gradual step-by-step refinement of the system.

Consultations between the manufacturer and other knowledgeable personnel, both inside and outside the company, to determine both the extent of the inventory problem and the capabilities and costs of solving the problem are necessary. The decision must be weighed carefully. No move at all or a leap in the wrong direction can be equally dangerous.

## ESTIMATING INVENTORIES BY THE GROSS PROFIT METHOD

It must be emphasized that the gross profit method is purely an estimating method of determining inventory costs, but is a very useful estimate both where perpetual records are not available or as a rule of thumb evaluation of the perpetual records. It is necessary to apply the gross profit technique of estimating to each product sold where there are varying markup percentages on the products. Otherwise the gross profit percent used in the estimate becomes inaccurate as the sales mix of the products changes. Figures 8-1 and 8-2 illustrate the gross profit method for estimating an interim inventory where two products are manufactured and sold follows:

| | | Product | |
|---|---|---|---|
| | Total | Machine A | Machine B |
| Inventory, January 1, 19x8 | $ 70,000 | | |
| Purchases of materials | 180,000 | | |
| Direct labor | 90,000 | | |
| Manufacturing labor | 80,000 | | |
| Goods available | 420,000 | | |
| Sales | 430,000 | $210,000 | $220,000 |
| Gross profit percentages | | .40 | .25 |
| Gross profit | 139,000 | 84,000 | 55,000 |
| Cost of sales | 291,000 | $126,000 | 165,000 |
| Inventory, January 31, 19x8 (goods available less cost of sales) | $129,000 | | |

**Figure 8-1**

Had an overall gross profit percentage of 31% based on the previous year and adjusted for changes in costs and sales prices been used, the results would have been as follows:

| | |
|---|---|
| Goods available (same) | $420,000 |
| Sales (same) | 430,000 |
| Gross profit percentage | .31 |
| Gross profit | 133,300 |
| Cost of sales | 296,700 |
| Inventory, January 31, 19x8 (goods available less cost of sales) | 123,300 |
| Correct estimate—Figure 8-1 | 129,000 |
| Estimate error caused by not computing gross profit on individual products—note | $ 5,700 |

Note: This error distorts both the inventory and the net profit before federal income tax for the month by $5,700.

**Figure 8-2**

## FLOW OF GOODS ASSUMPTIONS

There are three flow assumptions with variations of each that are acceptable when used consistently. They are: (1) FIFO, first-in, first-out, (2) LIFO, last-in, first-out, and (3) averaging methods, namely weighted or moving average. Each method has a different effect on income as determined on a periodic basis, and points for and against each method can be argued. Over a period of years, accountants have almost completely departed from the actual physical flow of goods as an indication of the preferable method. Also, the arguments tend to center around the impact of increasing costs as reflected in the inventories carried in the financial statements.

The first-in, first-out, FIFO method tends to constantly turn over the goods carried in the balance sheet inventory by moving out the oldest inventory items through cost of sales. The end result of FIFO is current, or recent, inventory costs reflected in the balance sheet as a current asset, but older, previous costs are matched against sales at cost of sales in the income statement.

Last-in, first-out, LIFO, conversely, matches the most recent costs against sales in the income statement but reflects older, sometimes antiquated costs in the balance sheet. Practically speaking, LIFO uses higher costs and reduces taxable income. However, here a higher, offsetting income is reported when the old inventory is finally liquidated. Temporary dips into LIFO inventories can be prevented by setting up an allowance when the old, depleted inventory is to be replaced in the next period. This procedure prevents showing abnormal profits unnecessarily or profit manipulation through a temporary sell out of old LIFO inventories.

Averaging inventory methods result in new costs being established based on averaging the beginning inventory with purchases during the current period. The costs obtained through averaging methods fall between the FIFO and LIFO values.

To choose one of the three general concepts over the other two requires somewhat of a compromise of principles or a definite choice as to whether greater precedence is placed on the inventory values as reflected in the income statement or the balance sheet. In many situations the tax impact gets primary consideration—probably incorrectly so from an accounting point of view, as the tax considerations too often result in the selection of LIFO.

There are two objections to LIFO. First, the inventory values carried on the balance sheet become completely outdated for goods that remain in stock and are marketable year after year. FIFO or averaging costs do run behind the selling price, but only to the degree of the amount of time it takes to turn over the inventory. Second, LIFO simply will not work as a perpetual method—or if used perpetually, reflects the inventory values inaccurately until adjusted back to a pure LIFO basis at the end of the year.

Figure 8-3 presents the flow of a single item through the inventory on a perpetual basis and the related problems encountered under differing methods.

FIFO

| Transaction | Number of Units | Cost per Unit | Total Cost | Inventory Value |
|---|---|---|---|---|
| Beginning inventory | 400 | $2.00 | $ 800 | $ 800 |
| Sale 1 | (300) | 2.00 | ( 600) | 200 |
| Purchase 1 | (500) | 2.20 | 1,100 | 1,300 |
| Sale 2 | (300) | 100 @ 2.00 | | |
| | | 200 @ 2.20 | ( 640) | 660 |
| Purchase 2 | 500 | 2.30 | 1,150 | 1,810 |
| Sale 3 | (400) | 300 @ 2.20 | | |
| | | 100 @ 2.30 | ( 890) | 920 |
| Ending inventory | 400 | 400 @ 2.30 | $ 920 | $ 920 |

LIFO

| Transaction | Number of Units | Cost per Unit | Total Cost | Inventory Value |
|---|---|---|---|---|
| Beginning inventory | 400 | $2.00 | $ 800 | $ 800 |
| Sale 1 | (300) | 2.00 | ( 600) | 200 |
| Purchase 1 | 500 | 2.20 | 1,100 | 1,300 |
| Sale 2 | (300) | 2.20 | ( 660) | 640 |
| Purchase 2 | 500 | 2.30 | 1,150 | 1,790 |
| Sale 3 | (400) | 2.30 | ( 920) | 870 |
| | | 100 @ 2.00 | | |
| | | 200 @ 2.20 | | |
| Ending inventory | 400 | 100 @ 2.30 | $ 870 | $ 870 |

AVERAGING

| Transaction | Number of Units | Cost per Unit | Total Cost | Inventory Value |
|---|---|---|---|---|
| Beginning inventory | 400 | $2.00 | $ 800 | $ 800 |
| Sale 1 | (300) | 2.00 | ( 600) | 200 |
| Purchase 1 | 500 | 2.20 | 1,100 | 1,300 |
| Sale 2 | (300) | 1300/600 = | ( 650) | 650 |
| | | 2.167 | | |
| Purchase 2 | 500 | 2.30 | 1,150 | 1,800 |
| Sale 3 | (400) | 1800/800 = | | |
| | | 2.25 | ( 900) | 900 |
| Ending inventory | 400 | 400 @ 2.25 | $ 900 | $ 900 |

**Figure 8-3**

The FIFO method fits naturally into the perpetual inventory system, and the use of the first-in, first-out flow assumption with perpetual records yields an accurate ending inventory that needs adjustments only if errors have occurred. LIFO, however, does not yield a true inventory value—averaging does only if the moving average concept is accepted.

In Figure 8-3 under LIFO, the ending perpetual inventory is 100 units @ $2.00 plus 200 units @ $2.20 plus 100 units @ $2.30 or a total cost of $870. A true LIFO system yields an ending inventory of 400 units, which is the same quantity as the beginning inventory, and under LIFO must be valued at the beginning inventory cost of $2.00 per unit or $800. The ending perpetual inventory is incorrect by $870 less $800 and must be adjusted, as must profit, by the $70 inaccuracy in perpetual costs.

The moving average perpetual inventory value at the end of the period is 400 units at $2.25 or $900, and the moving average cost must be maintained in the perpetual records. Weighed average cost has to be determined as follows at the end of the period if a weighted average cost system is used rather than moving average.

| Transaction | Units | Cost | Total |
|---|---|---|---|
| Beginning inventory | 400 | 2.00 | $ 800 |
| Purchase 1 | 500 | 2.20 | 1,100 |
| Purchase 2 | 500 | 2.30 | 1,150 |
| Totals | 1400 | $2.179* | $3,050 |

**Figure 8-4**

*The weighted average cost is determined by dividing the total units available, 1,400, into the total cost of $3,050. The ending inventory is $2.179 × 400 units or $871.60 necessitating an adjustment down from the $900 in the perpetual records.

In summary only FIFO and moving average perpetual records yield true end of period inventory costs—LIFO and weighted average do not.

## INVENTORY COSTING METHODS

The choice of inventory costing falls between cost and lower of cost or market. However, this choice is not a clear-cut decision that can be made arbitrarily. Whether or not the manufacturer can use lower of cost or market as opposed to cost depends on the flow assumption that has been adopted. There is reasonable support in denying the use of lower of cost or market with LIFO, and this objection should be a consideration when selecting the flow of goods.

LIFO assigns original cost to the first inventory. As inventory quantities increase, new layers are built up at more recent costs. If replacement costs drop below the costs of the first inventory or additional layers, and the LIFO inventory is valued at the lower of cost or market, the basic justification for LIFO—matching current costs and current revenues on the income statement is defeated. Also, the current Internal Revenue Code denies the use of lower of cost or market with LIFO.

Lower of cost or market may receive criticism in any event. Consistency in accounting is an accepted basic concept as is the recording of assets at cost. Lower of cost or market to a degree violates both the consistency and the cost concept. The consistency concept is not seriously violated if lower of cost or market is applied to individual items in the inventory as opposed to groups of items or the entire inventory. The group or entire inventory application of lower of cost or market can result in large segments or total inventory valuation at cost one year and market the next—a definite inconsistency. The violation of the basic cost concept can be justifiably overruled by conservatism in valuating the inventory at its current valuation which is lower than cost. This valuation can be accomplished through an allowance account established to reduce the inventory to market—the allowance may be adjusted annually to reflect the current difference between cost and lower of cost or market with the resulting gain or loss caused by the allowance adjustment being reported as a holding loss or gain. Adequate disclosure requires that the gain or loss be disclosed or reported as a separate item if material in amount. If immaterial the gain or loss may be washed out through cost of goods sold.

## APPLICATION OF LOWER OF COST OR MARKET

The use of lower of cost or market requires the selection of market from among three alternatives for the proper market comparison to cost. If selling prices are considerably above cost or replacement cost and there is at least a normal profit available, the comparison is simply that of cost to market (replacement cost). Where profit margins are narrow or there may be a loss, the selection of the proper market becomes more complicated. Accounting principles define three separate markets as follows:

1. Replacement cost—the cost at which goods can be purchased or reporduced and put into stock at the inventory date.
2. Selling price, less cost to complete and any disposal costs. This is market ceiling cost.
3. Selling price, less cost to complete and sell, disposal costs, and a normal profit margin. This is market floor cost.

Figure 8-5 illustrates the selection of the market that is compared to cost for lower of cost or market. Cost to complete and dispose of will be $5 for each product and normal profit will be an additional $7.

| | | Market | | | | | |
|---|---|---|---|---|---|---|---|
| Product | Selling Price | Replacement | Ceiling (2) less $5 | Floor (2) less $12 | Choice of Market | Cost | Lower of Cost or Market |
| (1) | (2) | (3) | (4) | (5) | (6) | (7) | (8) |
| A | 90 | 79 | 85 | 78 | 79 | 75 | 75 |
| B | 80 | 67 | 75 | 68 | 68 | 70 | 68 |
| C | 70 | 66 | 65 | 58 | 65 | 64 | 64 |
| D | 60 | 57 | 55 | 48 | 55 | 56 | 55 |
| E | 50 | 44 | 45 | 38 | 44 | 47 | 44 |
| F | 40 | 30 | 35 | 28 | 30 | 29 | 29 |
| G | 30 | 17 | 25 | 18 | 18 | 19 | 18 |

Explanations: Replacement market cannot be above ceiling or below floor—a simplification of the selection of market—the proper market is always the market between the two extremes for market.

Reasoning:

(A) Replacement market is below the ceiling but above the floor—selection of proper market is replacement of 79; cost is 75; LCM is 75.

(B) Replacement market is below the ceiling, also below the floor—selection of proper market is floor of 68; cost is 70; LCM is 68.

(C) Replacement market is above floor, also above ceiling—selection of proper market is ceiling of 65; cost is 64; LCM is 64.

(D) Replacement market is above the floor, also above the ceiling; selection of proper market is ceiling of 55; cost is 56; LCM is 55.

(E) Replacement market is below the ceiling and above the floor; selection of proper market is replacement of 44; cost is 47; LCM is 44.

(F) Replacement market is below the ceiling and above the floor; selection of proper market is replacement of 30; cost is 29; LCM is 29.

(G) Replacement market is below the ceiling, also below the floor; selection of proper market is floor of 18; cost is 19; LCM is 18.

**Figure 8-5**

## PHYSICAL INVENTORY CONTROLS

As the accuracy of a perpetual system is verified by physical counts, the control of the physical inventory is verified by perpetual records. That is to say, shortages caused by a lack of physical control are disclosed because the perpetual records say we should have inventory in excess of the physical count. Some items or components are more subject to physical shortages than others. This may be caused by unreported scrapping, uses outside the factory, or simply being misplaced. Those items subject to such shortages should be kept in an enclosed area, and requisitioned and signed for by the user. The employee who controls their issue must be protective and particular by nature to properly control usage and paperwork.

Another element of physical inventory controls is the regularity of the physical verifications. This is not to suggest complete physical counts more often than annually where perpetual records are reasonably accurate, but more frequent spot verification of perpetual records regarding certain items according to their vulnerability to shrinkage. These spot checks on a test basis are not time consuming and may detect shrinkages before they become significant.

Planning for the physical inventory includes selection of specific hours during which to make the count and issuing definite instructions to the personnel who are in any way involved. Activity in the plant including shipping, receiving and production should be halted or at a minimal level during the physical inventory. This is necessary to establish a satisfactory cut-off and to prevent movement of goods during the count. If certain areas can be isolated, no withdrawals made for a required period of time, and adequate control maintained over all goods, the interference with production can be minimized. A common solution is to conduct the count during hours when the plant is closed. This sometimes requires the payment of overtime premiums to inventory people and probably should be governed by current production requirements or weighed against the loss caused by interfering with normal production. The nearer the day and time selected is to a normal cut-off date, as the end of a month or other accounting period, the simpler the reconciliation of the physical count to the end of period records and in turn to the general ledger.

Instructions given to inventory personnel should include specifics on time, place, procedures and each employee's particular assignment. Instructions should be distributed a few days before the inventory taking and should include the means of controlling and accounting for all inventory cards or sheets. A numerical control system with the assignment of responsibility for the issuance of the cards or sheets and their collection and accountability vested in one individual. The instructions should also refer the counters and listers to personnel who can answer their questions regarding the count. They should also be reminded that spot verifications of their counts and listings will be made.

Responsibility for the control of the count should also fall on one individual. He should be responsible for reassignments during the count to properly spread the workload and for seeing that all inventoriable items are included in the count one time.

## CHANGING INVENTORY METHODS

Permission must be obtained from Internal Revenue Service to change inventory methods and the change must be for a reason other than the evasion of taxes.

Accountingwise, the change in method must be disclosed during the year of change, the effect on assets, net income and income per share must be stated along with the reason for the change. The accountant must also state whether or not he concurs with the change.

## SUMMARY

Perpetual inventory records are desirable for most manufacturers. The degree of perpetual records can vary from quantities and costs of every item to a perpetual record on only the total inventory. Each manufacturer must weigh the estimated cost of the perpetual record keeping against the related benefits.

The perpetual records must be reliable. Inaccurate perpetual records can mislead the manufacturer and his personnel and cause the wrong action to be taken or assumed on ordering, usage, etc., which is worse than no action.

A common method of estimating inventories during interim periods is the gross profit method. The gross profit method can be used where there are no perpetual records, to compute inventory losses, or as a rule of thumb against the perpetual records or physical count. The accuracy of the gross profit method of estimating inventories can be distorted by a change in sales mix, price or cost increases or decreases, or any other reason that may cause the estimated gross profit percentage to be incorrect.

The flow of goods assumptions determine the preference for FIFO, LIFO or averaging methods to identify which goods have been sold or issued and which goods are still in inventory. The arguments usually debate FIFO and LIFO, the extremes, with averaging methods usually being a compromise between FIFO and LIFO. In short, FIFO tends to emphasize current values on the balance sheet, and LIFO emphasizes the matching of current revenue and costs on the income statement. FIFO does, however, continually move out the inventory, and, while there is a revenue-cost lag, it is not as pronounced as the antiquated inventory costs that can eventually appear on the balance sheet using LIFO. It should also be remembered that a pure LIFO system and a weighted average system will require end of period adjustments because they cannot be properly reflected in perpetual inventory records. Perpetual records function properly with FIFO or moving average methods.

Inventories should be consistently costed at cost or lower of cost or market. LIFO inventories should not use lower of cost or market as this violates the justification for LIFO of matching current revenue with current costs. When lower of cost or market is used, there is stronger support for applying the LCM concept to individual items rather than the entire inventory or to groups of items. Market, however, is not a single concept. The proper market must be selected from among replacement cost, selling price less cost to complete and sell (the ceiling), and selling price less cost to complete and sell and a normal profit margin (the floor). The proper market is then compared to cost to obtain LCM.

The physical inventory count serves as verification of the accuracy of the perpetual inventory records, and at the same time the perpetual inventory records serve as verification of physical control of the goods. Shortages may be due to errors in the records or physical shrinkages. Therefore, when the physical count is short of the perpetual records, the source of the difference must be determined—the record keeping corrected, physical control tightened, or both.

Planning and written instructions are essential prior to a physical count for a proper cut-off and to enforce a conscientious effort. Inventories represent the biggest category of investments for many manufacturers. Control, both physical and accountingwise, is absolutely necessary.

# 9

# End of Period Entries, Reports and Controls

## MONTHLY ADJUSTING AND REVERSING ENTRIES

To properly reflect income and expense each month during the year, certain monthly account adjustments are necessary. These adjustments are of two types. The first type adjusts the payment of cash or receipt of cash which does not coincide with the earning of the related income or the incurring of the related expenses. This type of adjustment results in accruing or deferring income or expense. An example is interest that is paid quarterly—a portion of the quarterly interest is earned each day, each week, each month, etc.

Another type of adjustment is made to record transactions that occur internally. All of the special journals in which transactions are recorded on a daily basis and totaled at the end of the month involve transactions between the company and an outsider or an employee. Other transactions such as the flow and production of inventory and depreciation of assets occur internally and must be recorded through the general journal as a form of adjusting entries.

It is simpler to reverse certain of these entries each month and compute a new adjustment without regard to previous adjustments at the end of the following month. Generally, all accrual entries, the recording of income and expenses through an adjustment prior to their being paid, should be reversed. Deferral entries, adjustments to prepaid income and expense, should be reversed only if the original transactions were recorded as income or expenses rather than deferred income or expenses.

The following examples illustrate adjustments to various accounts in the order that they appear in the Chart of Accounts in Chapter 2.

Temporary investments require a monthly adjustment to record the interest earned. Assume that the date is April 30, 19x1, and that we purchased a U.S. Treasury Bill that matures in 90 days for $98,500 on April 4, 19x1. If the maturity value is $100,000, the following adjustment should be made on April 30, 19x1:

| | | | | |
|---|---|---|---|---|
| Temporary investments | | 110 | 433.33 | |
| Interest income | | 490 | | 433.33 |
| Days held to April 30 | = | 26 | | |
| Interest earned | = | 26/90 × $100,000 − 98,500 | | |
| | = | 26/90 (1500) | | |
| | = | $433.33 | | |

The computation also serves as the best journal entry explanation. The entry is an accrual entry and should be reversed as of May 1, 19x1.

The allowance for uncollectible accounts should be adjusted at least annually based on an analysis of receivables or perhaps the expense may be determined based on sales. Regardless of the method used, an estimated amount should be charged to expense and credited to the allowance on a monthly basis. If $24,000 is the estimated amount of the uncollectible accounts to be written off, then a monthly entry should be made as follows:

| | | | |
|---|---|---|---|
| Uncollectible accounts expense | 819 | 2,000 | |
| Allowance for uncollectible accounts | 119 | | 2,000 |
| to enter 1/12 of the estimated annual expense—actual amount of allowance to be adjusted at year-end | | | |

Prepaid insurance falls into the deferral category and the original premium payment can be classified as either prepaid insurance or insurance expense. Since different types of premiums are paid for varying lengths of time, a dual standard suits the needs of recording insurance premium payments. Convenience dictates the recording of monthly premiums as expense and annual premiums as prepaid. A schedule for computing prepaid insurance is presented in chapter 10. This procedure should be used at least annually to determine the exact amount of prepaid insurance. As a monthly procedure, the total of the annual premiums to be paid for the year should be estimated as 1/12 of that amount charged to expense each month as follows:

| | | | |
|---|---|---|---|
| Insurance expense | 834 | 3,000 | |
| Prepaid insurance | 134 | | 3,000 |
| Total annual premiums to be charged to prepaid insurance 36,000 × 1/12 | | | |

Since this is a deferral entry that was first recorded as an asset, it requires no reversing entry.

Inventory entries have been discussed in previous chapters. In general, inventories are first recorded as purchased materials, direct labor and manufacturing expenses. The normal recordings in the special journals take care of these entries and the transfer from finished goods to cost of sales. Accounting, according to information furnished by production, must then record by journal entry the transfer of goods between the three inventory categories as follows:

| | | | |
|---|---|---|---|
| Goods in process | 141 | 15,000 | |
| Materials | 140 | | 6,000 |
| Direct labor applied | 702 | | 4,000 |
| Factory expense applied | 799 | | 3,000 |
| Factory overhead applied | 899 | | 2,000 |

To record the cost elements put into process during the month

| | | | |
|---|---|---|---|
| Furnished goods | 142 | 17,000 | |
| Goods in process | 141 | | 17,000 |
| To record goods completed during the month | | | |

Monthly depreciation entries should be made to estimate 1/12 of the annual depreciation by the various categories. These monthly entries should be corrected during the year to give the proper attention to acquisitions and disposals of depreciable assets, both actual and anticipated transactions. The monthly depreciation entry should be recorded as follows:

| | | | |
|---|---|---|---|
| Depreciation—machinery and equipment | 761 | 1,000 | |
| Depreciation—patterns | 763 | 100 | |
| Depreciation—dies and fixtures | 764 | 400 | |
| Depreciation—office furniture and equipment | 860 | 500 | |
| Depreciation—vehicles | 862 | 600 | |
| Depreciation—buildings | 865 | 2,000 | |
| Accumulated depreciation | | | |
| Office furniture and equipment | 160 | | 500 |
| Machinery and equipment | 161 | | 1,000 |
| Vehicles | 162 | | 600 |
| Patterns | 163 | | 100 |
| Dies and fixtures | 164 | | 400 |
| Buildings | 165 | | 2,000 |
| Estimated annual depreciation: | | | |
| Office furniture and equipment | 6,000 × 1/12 = | | 500 |
| Machinery and equipment | 12,000 × 1/12 = | | 1,000 |
| Vehicles | 7,200 × 1/12 = | | 600 |
| Patterns | 1,200 × 1/12 = | | 100 |
| Dies and fixtures | 4,800 × 1/12 = | | 400 |
| Buildings | 24,000 × 1/12 = | | 2,000 |

A schedule for computing actual annual depreciation is presented in Chapter 10. The above accounts can be adjusted to actual during the last month of the year.

Organization costs, according to the Internal Revenue Code, cannot be amortized over less than 60 months. They are almost always amortized over exactly 60 months. This means that 1/60 of the costs should be charged to expense each month. However, as a practical matter, organization costs are often immaterial in amount and the amortization entry is made only annually. The 60 month rule converts the annual amortization to 20 percent of the original cost. If organization costs were a large amount, say $30,000, the monthly entry would be as follows:

| | | | |
|---|---|---|---|
| Amortization of organization costs | 870 | 500 | |
| Organization costs | 170 | | 500 |
| 30,000/60 | | | |

The cost of a patent may be the cost of developing the patent plus legal fees, etc., in registering the patent and defending it; or the patent may have been purchased at a fixed amount. The life of a patent is originally 17 years. A patent should be amortized over its remaining legal life or its useful life, whichever is shorter. A schedule for patent amortization should be developed similar to the depreciation schedule presented in chapter 10. The monthly entry to record patent amortization would be made as follows:

| | | | |
|---|---|---|---|
| Amortization of patents | 871 | 500 | |
| Patents | 171 | | 500 |
| Estimated annual amortization | 6000 × 1/12 = 500 | | |

Goodwill can be recorded as an asset only when purchased—a price paid in excess of the fair market value of the net assets of a company being acquired. A willingness to buy goodwill is usually a result of high earnings, and many formulas have been devised to compute goodwill based on capitalizing earnings at chosen rates, etc. However, regardless of how scientifically goodwill is computed, the end purchase price of a business is always a result of negotiations between the buyer and seller.

Goodwill is to be amortized over a period not to exceed 40 years. As a practical matter, goodwill created by the seller tends to dissipate over a period of time as the customers become acquainted with the buyer. This process usually takes considerably less than 40 years—more like 5 or 10. Assume that a company is purchased as follows:

| | |
|---|---|
| Fair market value of assets acquired | $600,000 |
| Liabilities assumed | 400,000 |
| Net assets | 200,000 |
| Negotiated purchase price | 250,000 |
| Price paid for goodwill | $50,000 |

Expected length of time for goodwill of seller to dissipate—8 years
Annual goodwill amortization = 50,000/8 = 6,250

The monthly amortization entry would be made as follows:

| | | | |
|---|---|---|---|
| Amortization of goodwill | 872 | 521 | |
| Goodwill | 172 | | 521 |
| 6,250/12 = 520.83 | | | |

Life insurance policies, other than term insurance, accumulate a cash surrender value that increases each year after an initial period, say two years. These policies must be owned by the company in order for the cash surrender value to be a company asset, in which case the company is also usually the beneficiary. A schedule of the cash value is usually furnished as a part of the policy and the increases in the cash value are treated as a reduction of the premium which is not deductible for tax purposes. The monthly entry for the increase in cash surrender value is recorded as follows:

| | | | |
|---|---|---|---|
| Cash surrender value of officers' life insurance | 180 | 200 | |
| Officers' life insurance | 880 | | 200 |
| Annual increase 2400/12 = 200 | | | |

Interest receivable on long-term investments should be accrued monthly unless immaterial in amount. Also, if the investments were purchased below or above their maturity value, the difference should be amortized in order that the face value will be the balance in the investment account at the maturity date. Assume that government bonds are purchased for $95,000 on January 1, 19x1, and have a maturity value of $100,000 in five years. The stated interest rate on the bonds is 6% payable annually. Interest at the rate of $6,000 per year would be accrued $500 per month. The $5,000 difference between cost and maturity value, assuming straight-line amortization, would be amortized at $83.33 ($5,000/60 months) per month to interest income. The monthly entry would appear as follows:

| | | | |
|---|---|---|---|
| Long-term investments | 182 | 83.33 | |
| Interest receivable (new account) | 111 | 500.00 | |
| Interest income | 490 | | 583.33 |

This is an accrual type entry which the rule on reversing entries says to reverse each month. However, since it is a repetitive entry each month, it seems more expedient to not reverse this particular entry.

If the long-term investments were in stock rather than interest bearing securities, only dividends which had been declared before the month-end date but not paid would be accrued as a dividends receivable and dividend income. This entry probably should be reversed unless the dividends payment date is more than one month in the future.

Notes payable—short-term are usually for a specific number of days as 60, 90, 120, etc. The interest rate is stated on the note and usually accrues from the date of the note. Assume the note is dated March 2, 19x1, is a 90 day note in the amount of $100,000 and bears interest at the rate of 8 percent. At April 30, 19x1 the accrued interest is computed and entered as follows:

| | | | |
|---|---|---|---|
| Interest expense | 814 | 1,311 | |
| Accrued interest | 214 | | 1,311 |
| $100,000 × 59/360 × .08 = 1,311.11 | | | |

This entry would be reversed and the accrual computed again at May 31, 19x1, if the note were not paid or the interest not paid on May 31, the due date.

Accrued payroll and accrued payroll taxes were discussed and illustrated in chapter 5.

Commissions are accrued and reversed each month according to the amount earned by commission salesmen that has not been paid to them. Each salesman's unpaid commissions are added and a combined entry made as follows:

| | | | | |
|---|---|---|---|---|
| Commissions expense | | 811 | 2,270 | |
| Accrued commissions | | 211 | | 2,270 |
| Salesman A 10,000 × .05 = | 500 | | | |
| Salesman B 14,000 × .05 = | 700 | | | |
| Salesman C 20,000 × .05 = | 1,000 | | | |
| Salesman D 1,000 × .07 = | 70 | | | |
| | 2,270 | | | |

Royalties are paid according to licensing agreements on certain products or components. The amount of the royalty is usually based on gross sales of the product at an agreed percentage or at a fixed amount per unit sold. Royalty payments may be made monthly, quarterly, semi-annually, annually or at other intervals depending on the licensing agreement. There are accrued royalties at the end of any month during which the units of the product are sold under the licensing agreement. The entry for the accrual may be reversed or the accrual account used to accumulate the amount due to the payment date and the payment charged to the accrual account. An accrual entry might be made for the month ended April 30, 19x1 as follows:

| | | | | |
|---|---|---|---|---|
| Royalty expense | | 812 | 700 | |
| Accrued royalties | | 212 | | 700 |
| Product A | | | | |
| Sales $40,000 @ .01 = | 400 | | | |
| Product B | | | | |
| 60 units @ $5 | 300 | | | |
| | 700 | | | |

Contributions to retirement funds may be determined by various formulas or arbitrarily depending on the plan. Some profit sharing plans have the annual contribution determined as a percent of profit, others have the contribution determined annually by the board of directors. Pension plans may have the contribution as a percentage of salaries, or a predetermined fixed amount. Pension plans may also have past service benefits that are amortized plus an interest charge from the inception of the plan. Past service costs are usually amortized over a 10 year period; however, the funding of the past service cost may be more or less than 10 years. If the funding is less than 10 years, a deferred cost is established; if more than 10 years, a liability is created. Assume that the pension plan calls for a normal annual contribution of $18,000 plus past service contributions of $120,000 which are being amortized over 10 years. The monthly accrual which can be left to accumulate, not reversed, for the entire year can be recorded as follows;

| | | | | |
|---|---|---|---|---|
| Retirement benefits | | 813 | 2,500 | |
| Accrued retirement funds | | 213 | | 2,500 |
| Annual-normal 18,000 /12 = | 1,500 | | | |
| Past service | | | | |
| 120,000/10/12 | 1,000 | | | |
| | 2,500 | | | |

Payments may be charged to the accrual account which should be adjusted for any small differences at least annually.

Property tax laws vary from state to state, but in general there is an assessment date on which the value of the taxable property is determined by multiplying the taxable value of the property by the property tax rate. Assume that the assessment date is March 1, 19x1 and that the tax is payable June 15, 19x1 and December 15, 19x1. It is necessary to estimate the assessed value in January and perhaps the rate until it is published by the assessment authority. Assume an assessed value of $200,000 and a rate of 6 percent. The monthly accrual would be recorded as follows:

| | | | |
|---|---|---|---|
| Property tax expense | 821 | 1,000 | |
| Accrued property tax | 221 | | 1,000 |
| 200,000 × .06 × 1/12 = 1,000 | | | |

The June 15 and December 15 payments are to be charged to the accrual account.

State and federal income taxes are both based on net taxable income in most situations. Also, the federal tax and the tax in many states are progressively higher as income increases. The monthly accruals should be based on the amount of income, but the computations should be annualized to prevent the tax from rising sharply as a percent of income as the amount of taxable income increases through the year. First, assume the following tax rates:

| Taxable Income | Federal | State |
|---|---|---|
| First $25,000 | 20% | 2% |
| Second $25,000 | 22% | 3% |
| Over $50,000 | 48% | 5% |

Second, assume that account 222, accrued state income tax, has a balance of $700 at the end of the third month of the current fiscal year and that account 223, accrued federal income tax, has a balance of $6,000. Both balances represent only the accruals for the current fiscal year. Third, assume that taxable income for the first four months is $27,000. The amount to be added to the accruals and the adjusting entry are as follows:

| | | | | |
|---|---|---|---|---|
| Annualized taxable income: | | | | |
| $27,000 × 12/4 = | $81,000 | | | |
| State income tax | | 822 | 223 | |
| Accrued state income tax | | 222 | | 233 |
| $25,000 × .02 = | $ 500 | | | |
| 25,000 × .03 = | 750 | | | |
| 31,000 × .05 = | 1,550 | | | |
| $81,000 | | 2,800 × 4/12 = | $933.33 | |
| Amount previously accrued | | | 700.00 | |
| Adjustment | | | $233.22 | |
| Federal income tax | | 823 | 2,460 | |
| Accrued federal income tax | | 223 | | 2,460 |
| $25,000 × .20 = | 5,000 | | | |
| 25,000 × .22 = | 5,500 | | | |
| 31,000 × .48 = | 14,880 | | | |
| 81,000 | $25,380 × 4/12 = | $8,460 | | |
| Amount previously accrued | | 6,000 | | |
| Adjustment | | $2,460 | | |

The annualized tax may require modifiction for anticipated tax credits, etc. In these cases it is usually simpler to add to the previous accrual than to reverse entries and to enter all payments as charges to the accruals.

The accrual of payroll taxes, withholdings, deposit requirements, etc., were discussed and examples illustrated in Chapter 5. However, there is one other accrual requirement related to payroll that has not been previously discussed. That is the contributions made by the employer to union pension funds and to other union fringe benefits. These costs should be accrued during the month in which the related payroll was paid. The necessary forms to be filed with the payments to the funds should be completed as the basis for the accrual. Since these expenses usually apply to production personnel, an expense account may be set up in the 700 series of factory expenses and the union expenses included as a part of the factory expense applied to production. A monthly accrual might be recorded as follows:

| | | | | |
|---|---|---|---|---|
| Union pension and fringe benefits (new account) | 739 | | 720 | |
| Accrued union pension and fringe benefits (new account) | 239 | | | 720 |
| Pension fund $8,000 × .05 = | | 400 | | |
| Vacation fund 2,000 hours × .10 = | | 200 | | |
| Education fund 600 hours × .20 = | | 120 | | |
| | | 720 | | |

This entry does not need to be reversed if it is more convenient to simply charge payments in the following month to the accrual account.

There are three important dates related to dividends. The declaration date—this is the date the dividend is declared by the board of directors and becomes a liability to the corporation. The date of record, usually a few days later except for closed corporations, is the date that determines, according to ownership of stock on that date, who is to receive the dividend checks. The final date is the dividend payment date. Assume that the board of directors meets on April 1, 19x1, and declares a dividend of $1 per share of 10,000 shares of outstanding common stock. Cash dividends are not paid on treasury stock. The dividend is payable on May 15, 19x1, to stockholders of record as of April 30, 19x1. The accounting entries would be as follows:

| | | | |
|---|---|---|---|
| April 1, 19x1 | | | |
| Dividends on common stock | 350 | 10,000 | |
| Dividends payable | 215 | | 10,000 |
| April 30, 19x1 | | | |
| No entry required | | | |
| May 15, 19x1 | | | |

(This entry would be made through cash disbursements as the checks are issued and charged to dividends payable—account 251. If a special bank account is used for dividends, it might be necessary to record the payment through a general journal entry as a summary of the checks issued.)

Bonds payable require entries for the monthly accrual of interest expense and to amortize the related premium or discount on the bonds. Assume a ten year bond issue, $200,000 face value, issue price $197,600, and interest payable semiannually at an annual rate of 8 percent. The entry to accrue the interest monthly would be as follows:

| | | | |
|---|---|---|---|
| Interest expense | 814 | 1,333 | |
| Accrued interest | 214 | | 1,333 |
| 200,000 × .08 × 1/12 = 1,333 | | | |

The entry to amortize the $2,400 discount on the issue ($200,000 − $197,600) would be recorded as follows:

| | | | |
|---|---|---|---|
| Interest expense | 814 | 20 | |
| Discount on bonds payable | 262 | | 20 |
| 2,400/120 (total months bonds will be outstanding) | | | |

The entry to accrue the interest may be reversed each month and the semiannual interest payments charged to expense, or, if not reversed, the payment may be charged to the accrued interest account.

## THE WORKSHEET APPROACH TO MONTHLY FINANCIAL STATEMENT PREPARATION— EVALUATION AND ELIMINATION

Most textbooks use the worksheet approach as an intermediate step between the general ledger and the financial statements. The headings for the worksheet are presented in Figure 9-1. The usual procedure is to take an unadjusted trial balance, make the necessary adjustments on the worksheet, extend the balance sheet and income statements accounts, enter the adjustments in the general ledger, and prepare the financial statements. There are additional problems involved in keeping the general ledger accounts in agreement with the worksheet and, therefore, in balance.

MACHINE MANUFACTURING CORPORATION

April 30, 19x1

Trial Balance Worksheet

| Account | Account Number | Trial Balance | Adjustments | Balance Sheet | Income Statement |
|---|---|---|---|---|---|
| | | | | | |

**Figure 9-1**

The worksheet is necessary in some instances. For the C.P.A. conducting an audit, the trial balance worksheet serves as a focal point for the audit, as a part of his supporting evidence and, since he cannot record entries in the general ledger, the worksheet gives him a place to record any adjustments necessitated by the findings of the audit.

Where the records are incomplete, usually no general ledger, the worksheet serves a useful purpose. In this situation the trial balance is taken as of the beginning of the period, probably the last set of reliable balances, two extra columns are added to the worksheet, and cash receipts and disbursements are summarized and posted to these columns. This work is followed by the adjustments and extensions to the financial statement columns. Here the worksheet has also served as a sort of general ledger.

When the accountant is preparing financial statements from unfamiliar and difficult-to-follow records, the worksheet can serve to put the entire picture in perspective. However, when the worksheet is used for this purpose, it can usually be eliminated the next time around.

A more expedient procedure is to run a tape of the general ledger after all postings are made from the special journals to prove the equality of debits and credits. Then go through the general ledger account by account to determine and make the necessary adjusting entries. The prior month's adjustments can usually serve as a guide for the next month's adjustments. Post all the adjustments to the general ledger. Run another tape of the trial balance. On this second tape subtotals should be taken after the asset accounts, liability accounts, stockholders' equity accounts, income accounts, and at the end of the tape. These subtotals can be used to verify totals on the financial statements, the most significant of which is the subtotal after the stockholders' equity. This figure is the net income. Each subtotal may be used as a verification as follows:

| | |
|---|---|
| after assets | = total assets |
| after liabilities | = stockholders' equity |
| after stockholders' equity | = net income |
| after income | = expenses |

Once the adjusted general ledger trial balance is proven on the tape or through the computer, the financial statements can be taken directly from the general ledger, thereby eliminating the trial balance worksheet.

## THE DAILY REPORT

The daily report, as presented in Figure 9-2, should be completed at the end of each day's activity. The totals for the cash figures can be taken from the daily deposit and by totaling each day's checks written. The planned shipments per day are determined by dividing the planned shipments for the month by the number of working days in the month. The planned shipments for April, 19x1 were $75,000 divided by 22 working days to get a daily average of $3,409. The word shipments is used instead of sales because sales people tend to call orders received sales. The actual shipments are the totals of each day's invoices. Planned and actual shipments are cumulative totals for each working day during the month.

The daily report may be prepared on columnar paper in pencil. The report should be passed around to management each day and returned to the accountant, or copies may be distributed to each member of management each morning.

An added feature of the daily report is the strengthening of internal control of cash and receivables. Keeping everyone informed makes misappropriations more difficult.

The report also serves as a constant measuring stick for sales—becoming an indirect means of motivation in the area of greatest importance.

MACHINE MANUFACTURING CORPORATION

Daily Report

April, 19x1

| Day of Month | Cash and Temporary Investments: Received | Disbursed | Balance | Shipments: Planned | Actual | Over (Under) |
|---|---|---|---|---|---|---|
| 1 | 3,512 | 1,230 | 52,302 | 3,409 | 2,118 | (1,291) |
| 2 | 6,702 | 1,476 | 57,528 | 6,818 | 5,710 | (2,399) |
| 3 | 4,115 | 1,932 | 59,711 | 10,227 | 9,173 | (1,054) |
| 4 | 1,280 | | 60,991 | 13,636 | 14,187 | 551 |
| 5 | 1,970 | 5,189 | 57,772 | 17,045 | 19,760 | 2,715 |
| 6 | | | | | | |
| 7 | | | | | | |
| 8 | 3,176 | 823 | 60,125 | 20,454 | 21,747 | 1,293 |
| 9 | 947 | — | 61,072 | 23,863 | 24,089 | 226 |
| 10 | 561 | 17,342 | 44,291 | 27,272 | 27,521 | 249 |
| 11 | 2,577 | — | 46,868 | 30,681 | 30,583 | ( 98) |
| 12 | 6,292 | 4,787 | 48,373 | 34,090 | 32,076 | (2,014) |
| 13 | | | | | | |
| 14 | | | | | | |
| 15 | 5,487 | 2,186 | 51,674 | 37,499 | 36,413 | (1,086) |
| 16 | 326 | 181 | 51,819 | 40,908 | 38,029 | (2,879) |
| 17 | 1,234 | 2,857 | 50,196 | 44,317 | 41,761 | (2,556) |
| 18 | 2,096 | 178 | 52,114 | 47,726 | 44,807 | (2,919) |
| 19 | 766 | 5,311 | 47,569 | 51,135 | 48,211 | (2,924) |
| 20 | | | | | | |
| 21 | | | | | | |
| 22 | 7,009 | 121 | 54,457 | 54,544 | 52,303 | (2,241) |
| 23 | 972 | 800 | 54,629 | 57,953 | 58,774 | 821 |
| 24 | 1,711 | — | 56,340 | 61,362 | 63,098 | 1,736 |
| 25 | 1,387 | 9,079 | 48,648 | 64,771 | 66,146 | 1,375 |
| 26 | 407 | 5,283 | 43,772 | 68,180 | 70,275 | 2,095 |
| 27 | | | | | | |
| 28 | | | | | | |
| 29 | 4,175 | — | 47,947 | 71,589 | 74,729 | 3,140 |
| 30 | 3,734 | 1,404 | 50,277 | 75,000 | 77,931 | 1,931 |

**Figure 9-2**

## DECISION MAKING BASED ON ANALYSIS OF SALES, COSTS OF SALES AND GROSS PROFIT

Figure 9-3 presents an analysis of sales, cost of sales and gross profit by product for the Machine Manufacturing Corporation. This type of analysis should be prepared on a monthly basis throughout the year to keep the manufacturer constantly informed as to which products are being sold and how each contributes to gross profit both in dollars and as a percent of the selling price. We are often inclined to overemphasize the percentage—both the dollars contributed and the percentage of gross profit should influence our decision making. At this point let's look at each product and the various possibilities based on the information in Figure 9-3.

*Machine 1* The gross profit percentage of 21.11% is below average and we should ask ourselves the following questions: Are we in a competitive position that will allow us to raise the price of machine 1? Have there been production problems or procurement problems that have affected the costs of the machine that will not be repetitive—if so, how will their correction affect profits? One should be very careful in evaluating answers to this problem to be assured that the same or other problems will not pop up again. If we cannot improve the profit margin substantially on machine 1, could we attempt to divert marketing efforts to more profitable items successfully? Certainly, machine 1 is an important product to us. It is second in total sales and also second in total gross profit contributed. The primary emphasis needs to be placed on improving the gross profit percentage without a significant sacrifice in sales volume.

*Machine 2* This machine falls into the same general category as machine 1.

It would be interesting to see a sales trend and gross profit trend for both machines. We should also look at the length of time since a model change has been made of these two machines. Any improvements would help justify price increases.

MACHINE MANUFACTURING CORPORATION

Analysis of Sales, Cost of Sales and Gross Profit

Year Ended March 31, 19x1

| Product | Net Sales | Cost of Sales | Gross Profit Contributed | Gross Profit Percentage |
|---|---|---|---|---|
| Machine 1 | $180,000 | $142,000 | $ 38,000 | 21.11% |
| Machine 2 | 160,000 | 131,000 | 29,000 | 18.31 |
| Machine 3 | 87,000 | 60,000 | 27,000 | 31.03 |
| Custom machines | 208,000 | 141,000 | 67,000 | 32.21 |
| Repair parts | 62,000 | 34,000 | 28,000 | 45.16 |
| Service | 18,000 | 10,000 | 8,000 | 44.44 |
| Totals | $715,000 | $518,000 | $197,000 | 27.55% |

**Figure 9-3**

*Machine 3* More volume appears to be the desired improvement for machine 3. The gross profit percentage is significantly better than machines 1 and 2. However, we should not be complacent because of the higher percentage. Can we reduce costs or increase the selling price of machine 3? Perhaps increased efforts should be made in advertising and promotion of machine 3 because of its higher profit percentage.

*Custom Machines* This is our most important product. The gross profit percentage is good, we are performing a unique service for our customers which they will remember, we are constantly exploring new areas of usage that can develop new standard products, and with the volume of custom machines we are carrying enough fixed overhead to decrease the costs of the entire line of manufactured products.

*Repair Parts* The profit margin on repairs should be reasonably high, as it is, because of the captive market. A higher profit margin is also justified because each sale is small when compared to complete machines, and the same volume requires more paper work and administrative time.

*Service* Although small in volume, service should always be offered to customers. Personal service is an excellent opportunity to promote the company and its products. Personal service should always be of the highest quality and strive to solve customers' problems thoroughly rather than partially.

The same sales and gross profits can be analyzed in many ways. Here we have illustrated an analysis by products. They can also be analyzed by states, sales territories, cities, divisions, etc. The author once performed a complete analysis of sales for a manufacturer by geographic area. The project went like this:

Sales for a year were first coded by type of customer using the Standard Industrial Code to determine who were the customers for the products. Since the customers were other manufacturers, a recent census of manufacturers was used to determine where the markets were. Next the actual sales were analyzed by market areas. The results showed weak sales in certain areas according to the potentials. One area showed the potential to be 27 times actual sales. Increased efforts were made to establish dealerships in the areas that showed the greatest promise. The results were excellent and have continued to improve over the years.

## PLANNING THROUGH UNITS OF PRODUCT SOLD TALLY

Part of the information that accounting must accumulate for accurate costing and inventory relief includes the number of units of each product sold each month. An accumulation of this data by units of products in addition to the normal dollar figures becomes a guide for purchasing quantities, minimum stocking requirements and the size of production runs. An example of a tally by quarter is presented in Figure 9-4.

As a guide for purchasing and production runs, assume that part 101 is used on machines 1 and 2, on approximately one half of the custom machines and, of course, as a repair part. Units of 101 used per year are as follows:

| | |
|---|---|
| Machine 1 | 190 |
| Machine 2 | 170 |
| Custom machines | 70 |
| Repair parts | 200 |
| Total | 630 |

Depending on lead time, anticipated changes, economical purchase quantities and production runs, the recorded annual usage serves as an excellent guide to stocking requirements, buying and processing.

Another benefit that can be derived from the units of product sold tally is that of absolute growth or decline in sales of various products. It is possible, through the comparison of annual tallies over a period of years, to establish sales trends for each product and to pinpoint highs and lows during the year. The unit tally is more useful for these purposes than dollars of sales because units eliminate the effect of price changes over a period of time.

MACHINE MANUFACTURING CORPORATION

Units of Product Sold Tally

Year Ended March 31, 19x1

| | Quarter | | | | |
|---|---|---|---|---|---|
| | First | Second | Third | Fourth | Year |
| Machine 1 | 70 | 40 | 30 | 50 | 190 |
| Machine 2 | 50 | 20 | 60 | 40 | 170 |
| Machine 3 | 40 | 30 | 50 | 20 | 140 |
| Custom machines | 20 | 40 | 60 | 20 | 140 |
| Repair parts | | | | | |
| 101 | 30 | 40 | 60 | 70 | 200 |
| 102 | 80 | 90 | 80 | 60 | 310 |
| 103 | 60 | 50 | 60 | 40 | 210 |
| 104 | 20 | 30 | 40 | 20 | 110 |
| 105 | 40 | 20 | 30 | 40 | 130 |

**Figure 9-4**

In this analysis there is one possibility of being misled—that is by one or a few large sales of a single product that may not be repetitive. This possible distortion must be kept in mind when planning future purchases and production runs.

## MONTHLY ACCOUNTING CONTROL SYSTEM

There has to be supporting data to substantiate the balance in every general ledger account. The balance sheet accounts are supported by counts, reconciliations, subsidiary records and lists, and computations. The income statement accounts are largely supported by an accumulation of data on an annual basis. Computations support other accounts, such as depreciation and accrued income or expense accounts, that are directly related to other balance sheet accounts. All of this information must be available and should be verified at least annually. Specific accounts should be cross checked with supporting data on a monthly basis. Many accounts are supported by our previously described monthly adjustments. Other monthly control features are as follows:

*Petty cash*—count, reconcile expenses and count to balance and adjust.

*Cash in bank*—reconcile bank statement to general ledger balance, adjust those items that are general ledger corrections.

*Accounts receivable—trade*—tape or prepare aging of subsidiary, locate differences between general ledger and subsidiary records, correct subsidiary, correct and adjust general ledger.

*Accounts receivable —affiliates*—verify that balances are in agreement with intercompany accounts on the affiliates' records, adjust where necessary.

*Travel advances*—list or tape, tie-in to general ledger balance, adjust for general ledger corrections.

*Accounts payable—trade*—tape subsidiary, remittance advices or open invoices depending on record keeping system, correct as necessary, adjust for general ledger corrections.

*Notes payable—short term*—list and tie-in to general ledger balance.

*Common stock and preferred stock*—a list of stockholders at par, or original selling price for no-par stock, should be tied-in to the general ledger balance each month if there is significant activity in the stock accounts.

## SUMMARY

Certain accounts have to be adjusted every month. Some entries for these adjustments can be similar each month, such as uncollectible accounts expense, the write-off of prepaid insurance and depreciation, unless there are significant changes. Other accruals and deferrals must be computed each month. Reversing entries should be made where convenient.

Generally, where the accountant is familiar with the general ledger, there is no need to use a worksheet for monthly financial statements, as they can be pulled directly off the general ledger after the monthly adjustments have been posted.

A daily report on the cash position and actual shipments versus planned shipments should be given to each member of management every working day. This not only keeps management informed, but also serves as a motivation for more sales and as an internal control feature for cash.

Sales, cost of sales and gross profit should be continually analyzed by product, territory, division and every other practical way to emphasize the sources of profits or losses. This enables the manufacturer to locate areas that need attention and to push the sources of greatest profits.

Sales should also be accumulated and reported by units of products. This is of great aid to purchasing in substantiating usage. It also establishes trends that are real—not influenced by price increases, etc.

Every accountant must follow certain control procedures every month on key general ledger accounts. Passing by a single month in exercising proper controls can cause costly errors, embarrassment and greater amounts of time in searching several months to locate mistakes. One cannot afford errors that destroy the confidence in monthly reports.

# 10

# Making Lease, Purchase, and Financing Decisions on Plant and Equipment—Related Insurance Accounting

## THE ROLE OF THE ACCOUNTANT IN ASSISTING THE MANUFACTURER AND HIS CUSTOMERS

The accountant has a genuine opportunity to serve the manufacturer and his customers in making the correct decisions on plant and equipment. The accountant's participation in plant and equipment decisions is particularly important because of his knowledge in computing return on investment, imputed interest, financing methods and, perhaps, because he can weigh the advantages and disadvantages more rationally than those members of management who are directly involved in using the assets considered for acquisition. These same abilities can be used to convince customers that investments in the manufacturer's product will yield favorable returns or profits.

The accountant is also, in most cases, the more conservative part of management and is inclined to look a situation over carefully before spending the dollars. Other members of management such as production, engineering, and sales may be more aware of specific assets that can be utilized by the manufacturer. The accountant must justify in dollars their worth verses present or alternative assets and methods. A president of a manufacturing firm once commented that the author tended to make all decisions based on dollars and cents; then as an afterthought he replied to his own remark that he guessed that's how they should be made. This is nearly correct—occasionally an intangible benefit must also be considered.

## ACCOUNTING FOR PLANT AND EQUIPMENT PURCHASES AND DISPOSALS

Many methods of recording purchases and disposals of depreciable assets have been widely discussed and proposed. Among these are recording acquisitions at list price and recognizing gain or loss on a trade-in, recording the acquisition at the fair market value of the trade-in plus the boot paid, recording the new asset at its cash price and recognizing gain or loss on the trade, and recording the acquisition at the book value of the trade-in plus the boot paid.

Recording an acquired asset at list price and recognizing gain or loss on a trade has had little practical use for as long as the author can remember. This is mainly because the acquisition price is usually negotiated; any sizeable asset can be bought for less than the list price, and the trade-in allowance is simply a means of adjusting the price of the new asset.

Recording the new asset at the fair market value of the trade-in plus boot presents the problem of arriving at a reliable valuation of the traded asset and also seems to be a departure from our accepted cost concept.

Recording the new asset at its cash price and recognizing gain or loss on the trade corrects over or under depreciation of the traded asset when it is replaced. This method may be logical, but has to be influenced by whether the asset acquired and traded are like assets or unlike assets and has been used only on a limited basis.

Recording the acquired asset at the book value of the old asset traded in plus the boot paid has been widely used and is acceptable for tax purposes. This method tends to correct over or under depreciation on the old asset over the life of the new asset. Because of its wide usage this method will be used in examples presented in this book.

It should be noted that all costs related to the acquisition of an asset are included as a part of the cost of the asset. These costs include freight, sales tax, import duties, insurance while in transit, other taxes, installation, start up costs, fix up costs and used assets, and any other costs incurred in acquiring the asset or getting it ready for use. Cash discounts for prompt payment reduce the cost of the asset, although the manufacturer may elect to treat the finance charge as a part of the cost for investment tax credit purpose.

The following is a comparative example of recording an asset at its cash price versus recording an asset at the book value of the asset traded in plus the boot paid.

| | |
|---|---|
| Cash Price | $10,000 |
| Asset traded in—cost | $12,000 |
| Accumulated depreciation | 8,000 |
| Book value | $ 4,000 |
| Boot paid | $ 5,000 |

| | | |
|---|---|---|
| Entry at cash price: | | |
| New asset | 10,000 | |
| Accumulated depreciation—old asset | 8,000 | |
| Old asset | | 12,000 |
| Cash | | 5,000 |
| Gain on trade | | 1,000 |
| Entry at book value plus boot paid: | | |
| New asset | 9,000 | |
| Accumulated depreciation—old asset | 8,000 | |
| Old asset | | 12,000 |
| Cash | | 5,000 |

Assuming a five year life and straight-line depreciation, the comparative effect is as follows:

| Year | Cash Price | Book Plus Boot |
|---|---|---|
| 1 Gain | $(1,000) | $ |
| 1 Depreciation | 2,000 | 1,800 |
| 2 Depreciation | 2,000 | 1,800 |
| 3 Depreciation | 2,000 | 1,800 |
| 4 Depreciation | 2,000 | 1,800 |
| 5 Depreciation | 2,000 | 1,800 |
| Total expense—net | $9,000 | $9,000 |

When an asset is sold, gain or loss, which is the difference between the selling price and the book value of the asset, must be recorded.

Assume a selling price of $15,000 for an asset that cost $28,000 and has accumulated depreciation to date of sale of $10,000.

| | | | |
|---|---|---|---|
| Cash | | 15,000 | |
| Accumulated depreciation | | 10,000 | |
| Loss on sale of asset | | 3,000 | |
| Asset | | | 28,000 |
| Proof: | | | |
| Cost | $28,000 | | |
| Accumulated depreciation | 10,000 | | |
| Book value | 18,000 | | |
| Selling price | 15,000 | | |
| Loss on sale | $ 3,000 | | |

When assets are acquired at a lump sum, a reasonable basis must be determined for allocating the cost to each asset purchased. If an entire business is purchased, any excess over the fair market value of the net assets may be goodwill.

## ACCOUNTING FOR PLANT AND EQUIPMENT MANUFACUTRED OR CONSTRUCTED

When the firm manufactures equipment for its own use, the cost is recorded much the same as that of manufactured products for resale, that is, the inclusion of material, direct labor and overhead. Components that have standard costs may be included at standard if the standard approximates the actual cost. Nonstandard parts, assembly, start up, etc., must be included at actual cost with the normal amount of overhead applied at the current rate.

Assets constructed, such as a building, should include materials, direct labor, and overhead directly related to the construction project. It is unlikely that a manufacturer will build any sizable project using his own labor unless construction projects are continuous. Therefore, the cost is more likely to include materials, subcontracts and direct overhead, or a contract with a general contractor plus direct overhead. There is some disagreement regarding capitalizing such costs as interest on construction loans, property tax on the site during construction, and certain administrative costs during the construction period. There seems to be some tendency toward capitalizing more of these costs—the author feels that costs to be capitalized should be necessary costs in all similar construction projects and should add value to the structure. This could include those previously mentioned, but careful consideration should be given to each situation until clearer guidelines are established.

## ALTERNATIVE DEPRECIATION METHODS

One of the first decisions to be made relating to depreciation is the fraction of a year to be used in computing depreciation in the year of acquisition and in the year of disposal of an asset. Four alternatives are suggested, (1) compute depreciation from the nearest month end in the year of acquisition and to the nearest month end in the year of disposal; (2) take a full year in the year of acquisition and none in the year of disposal; (3) take none in the year of acquisition and a full year in the year of disposal; (4) take a half year in year of acquisition and a half year in the year of disposal. Text books seem to favor the nearest month end approach; a full year in year of acquisition gives the fastest tax write-off; and accountants like to use the half year method because it is reasonably equitable and doesn't require referral back to the first year to determine how many months have been depreciated. It is simpler. The author prefers a dual concept; the half year in year of acquisition and half year in year of sale for most assets, but to the nearest month end for major assets such as a new plant or entire assembly line. We will use the half year method in our examples.

There are four basic methods of depreciation being used with various modifications of these methods to include interest factors, groups and composites, etc. The four basic methods are straight-line, sum of the years' digits, declining-balance, and units of production which can be based on either input, such as direct labor hours, or output, such as units of the product produced. The straight-line, sum of the years' digits and declining-balance methods all result in depreciation based on the passing of time and depreciation becomes a fixed cost. The units of production methods cause depreciation to become a factor directly related to production and therefore a variable cost.

Assuming that an asset has a cost of $16,000 and a salvage value of $1,000, a five year life and that the half year in year of acquisition and year of disposal or last year is equitable, depreciation is computed as follows:

Straight-line method

| Year | Depreciation | Computation |
|---|---|---|
| 1 | $ 1,500 | 16,000 − 1,000 = 15,000 × .2 × ½ |
| 2 | 3,000 | 15,000 × .2 |
| 3 | 3,000 | 15,000 × .2 |
| 4 | 3,000 | 15,000 × .2 |
| 5 | 3,000 | 15,000 × .2 |
| 6 | 1,500 | 15,000 × .2 × ½ |
| Total | $15,000 | |

Sum of the year's digits method*

| Year | Depreciation | Computation |
|---|---|---|
| 1 | $ 2,500 | 16,000 − 1,000 = 15,000 × 5/15 × ½ |
| 2 | 4,500 | 15,000 × 5/15 × ½ plus<br>15,000 × 4/15 × ½ |
| 3 | 3,500 | 15,000 × 4/15 ×½ plus<br>15,000 × 3/15 × ½ |
| 4 | 2,500 | 15,000 × 3/15 × ½ plus<br>15,000 × 2/15 × ½ |
| 5 | 1,500 | 15,000 × 2/15 × ½ plus<br>15,000 × 1/15 × ½ |
| 6 | 500 | 15,000 × 1/15 × ½ |
| Total | $15,000 | |

Double declining-balance method

| Year | Depreciation | Computation |
|---|---|---|
| 1 | $ 3,200 | 16,000 − .2 × 2 × ½ |
| 2 | 5,120 | 16,000 − 3,200 × .2 × 2 |
| 3 | 3,072 | 16,000 − 8,320 × .2 × 2 |
| 4 | 1,843 | 16,000 − 11,392 × .2 × 2 |
| 5 | 1,106 | 16,000 − 13,235 × .2 × 2 |
| 6 | 659 | 16,000 − 1,000 − 14,341 |
| Total | $15,000 | |

$$*SYD = N\left(\frac{N+1}{2}\right)$$

SYD = 6 (6/2)

SYD = 15

Units of production method (assume 7,500 units)

| Year | Depreciation | Usage | Computation |
|---|---|---|---|
| 1 | $ 1,400 | 700 | 700 × $2 rate per unit |
| 2 | 3,400 | 1,700 | 1,700 × $2 rate per unit |
| 3 | 2,800 | 1,400 | 1,400 × $2 rate per unit |
| 4 | 3,200 | 1,600 | 1,600 × $2 rate per unit |
| 5 | 2,200 | 1,100 | 1,100 × $2 rate per unit |
| 6 | 2,000 | 1,000 | 1,000 × $2 rate per unit |
| Totals | $15,000 | 7,500 | |

## FEDERAL INCOME TAX BENEFITS AND CONSEQUENCES

The use of double declining-balance depreciation or sum of the year's digits depreciation results in larger deductions from revenue in arriving at taxable income in the early life of an asset and smaller deductions in the later life of an asset. The advantage is the deferral of federal income tax and the use of tax dollars for working capital, etc., until it is later paid back. However, these accelerated methods result in a depreciation recapture and greater taxes if the asset is sold. Both methods are acceptable for tax purposes for new tangible personal property having a life of three years or more. Used tangible personal property with a life of three years or more can be depreciated using declining-balance at 150 percent of the straight-line rate.

There is also available an additional first year depreciation for tangible, personal property having a life of six years or more. It is limited to 20 percent of $10,000 cost or $2,000 for a corporation, an affiliated group of corporations and a partnership. The basis of the asset for computing regular depreciation is reduced by the amount of the additional first year depreciation. A proprietor is allowed up to $4,000, or 20 percent of $20,000, additional first year depreciation if he files a joint return.

Buildings purchased or constructed after July 24, 1969, can be depreciated at 150 percent of the straight-line rate. Special rules apply to residential rental property.

Investment tax credit is available on tangible personal property having a useful life of at least three years. The credit applies during the year the assets are placed in service as follows:

| Depreciable Useful Life | |
|---|---|
| 3 or 4 years | Cost × 1/3 × 10% |
| 5 or 6 years | Cost × 2/3 × 10% |
| 7 years or more | Cost × 10% |

This credit is a direct reduction and must be paid back if the asset is retired or disposed of before it has been held the number of years on which the credit was based, except for casualty losses. However, if a seven year asset is held five years, etc., only the excess credit claimed or a third need be paid back. The credit is limited to the amount of the tax up to $25,000 and one half of the tax in excess of $25,000. Unused credits may be carried back three years and forward seven years. Starting in 1977 an election can be made to carry the credit forward only. Used equipment purchases are limited to $100,000 annually in applying the credit.

## USING DIFFERENT DEPRECIATION METHODS FOR ACCOUNTING AND TAX PURPOSES

On major asset purchases the choice of depreciation methods becomes more important for both accounting and tax purposes. However, the two purposes have different objectives. Accounting attempts to reflect depreciation as realistically as possible while the tax objective should be the conservation of dollars. Because of these differences, it may be necessary to use an accelerated method for tax purposes and straight-line depreciation for the financial statements. This results in a different amount of taxable income on the annual tax returns than on the financial statements, but the same amount of taxable income on both over the entire life of the depreciable asset. The federal income tax expense for financial statement purposes is computed on taxable income per the financial statements, but the current liability is the amount payable on the tax return. The difference is a deferral, as illustrated in Figure 10-1.

## PHYSICAL AND ACCOUNTING CONTROL OF EQUIPMENT

Every manufacturer must keep subsidiary records on all depreciable assets and the related depreciation. Each piece of equipment should be assigned a serial number for absolute identification, and periodic inventories of equipment should be taken by referring to the subsidiary records.

The subsidiary equipment records may take the form of a ledger with a page for each asset and the accumulated depreciation, it may be stored and a printout run through the computer or the subsidiary may simply be a worksheet as presented in Figure 10-2.

| | |
|---|---|
| Asset cost | $160,000 |
| Salvage value | 10,000 |
| Depreciable base | $150,000 |

Estimated useful life—5 years
Financial statement method—straight-line
Tax return method—sum of the years' digits
Tax rate—48%

| | Net Income Before Depreciation | | Depreciation | | Taxable Income | | Tax | | |
|---|---|---|---|---|---|---|---|---|---|
| Year | Financial Statements | Tax Returns | Financial Statements | Tax Return | Financial Statements | Tax Return | Financial Statements | Tax Return | Deferred Tax |
| 1 | $120,000 | $120,000 | $ 30,000 | $ 50,000 | $ 90,000 | $ 70,000 | $ 43,200 | $ 33,600 | $ 9,600 |
| 2 | 140,000 | 140,000 | 30,000 | 40,000 | 110,000 | 100,000 | 52,800 | 48,000 | 4,800 |
| 3 | 160,000 | 160,000 | 30,000 | 30,000 | 130,000 | 130,000 | 62,400 | 62,400 | — |
| 4 | 180,000 | 180,000 | 30,000 | 20,000 | 150,000 | 160,000 | 72,000 | 76,800 | (4,800) |
| 5 | 200,000 | 200,000 | 30,000 | 10,000 | 170,000 | 190,000 | 81,600 | 91,200 | (9,600) |
| Totals | $800,000 | $800,000 | $150,000 | $150,000 | $650,000 | $650,000 | $312,000 | $312,000 | $ -0- |

**Figure 10-1**

The deferred tax account is carried as a deferred credit on the balance sheet until it becomes a current liability, which would be during the last year of the depreciable life of the related asset.

MACHINE MANUFACTURING CORPORATION

Schedule of Equipment and Accumulated Depreciation

| Asset | Serial Number | Date Acquired | Cost | Depreciation Rate | Depreciation Method | Accumulated Depreciation 3-31-19x3 | Depreciation Expense 3-31-19x4 | Accumulated Depreciation 3-31-19x4 |
|---|---|---|---|---|---|---|---|---|
| Jay 17″ lathe | 101 | 6-30-19x1 | 10,000 | 10% | SL | 1,500 | 1,000 | 2,500 |
| Jay 15″ lathe | 102 | 9-30-19x1 | 7,000 | 10% | SL | 1,050 | 700 | 1,750 |
| ABC mill | 103 | 10-31-19x1 | 4,000 | 10% | SL | 600 | 400 | 1,000 |
| G & P grinder | 104 | 1-31-19x2 | 3,000 | 10% | SL | 450 | 300 | 750 |
| G & P buffer | 105 | 2-28-19x2 | 2,000 | 10% | SL | 300 | 200 | 500 |
| Comet saw | 106 | 6-30-19x2 | 3,000 | 10% | SL | 150 | 300 | 450 |
| Lift crane | 107 | 7-31-19x2 | 1,000 | 10% | SL | 50 | 100 | 150 |
| Paint booth | 108 | 8-31-19x2 | 2,000 | 10% | SL | 100 | 200 | 300 |
| Blitz welder | 109 | 9-30-19x2 | 5,000 | 10% | SL | 250 | 500 | 750 |
| Arrow drill | 110 | 9-30-19x2 | 2,000 | 10% | SL | 100 | 200 | 300 |
| | | | 39,000 | | | 4,550 | 3,900 | 8,450 |

**Figure 10-2**

## LEASE OR BUY DECISION MAKING

The primary guide in lease or buy decisions should be the comparative cost of the two alternatives. Generally, it costs less to buy those assets that are to be used on a regular and continuous basis, but this should not be accepted without examining the alternative costs. It should also be kept in mind that the cost of owning an asset only starts with the purchase. After the asset is acquired there are continuing costs for interest, either actual or imputed, property tax, depreciation, insurance, maintenance and space costs.

The tax advantage of either alternative is usually of little consequence. The deductible rent expense for leased equipment is offset by the costs of ownership for purchased equipment. It should also be noted that the investment tax credit may also be available in both situations, as it may be passed on to the lessee with lessor permission.

Availability can be an important factor in lease or buy decisions for those items needed on an occasional basis. Even though it may be cheaper to rent when considering the cost of the equipment, other factors such as customer service, production hold ups, and product quality may favor purchasing the equipment. Another alternative to leasing or buying, where use is only occasional or skill is insufficient, is to have certain functions performed by other manufacturers or machine shops. More than one source should be sought for outside work as a hedge against future service problems.

Probably the most common reason for leasing equipment that is to be used on a continuing basis is that leasing requires little or no initial cash outlay. This in itself may be sufficient reason for leasing where working capital is a critical problem. However, the contracted rental payments will be an additional working capital drain for the life of the lease.

The accountant should definitely share in lease or buy decisions. Some leasing companies tend to emphasize only their side of the picture when discussing leased equipment. A client once explained to the author how he could now deduct the cost of his equipment since he had decided to lease it. He was not aware that all the costs of ownership including depreciation were also tax deductible.

Occasionally, a contract that is called a lease is actually a purchase. Any so-called lease which gives permanent possession of the leased asset to the lessee before the expiration of the useful life of the asset for less than its value at the expiration of the lease, is actually a purchase. Such transactions must be accounted for as a purchase rather than a lease.

## ACCOUNTING FOR FINANCE CHARGES ON INSTALLMENT PURCHASES

An installment purchase should state the cash price of the asset plus the finance charge. If not, the current value should be determined and the difference between the current value and the total contract treated as a finance charge. These finance charges should be charged to interest expense over the life of the installment contract based on the unpaid principal balance. This can be done by determining the interest rate through an annuity table and computing the interest each time a payment is made based on the previous unpaid balance. Similar results can be obtained by using a sum of the digits approach with the number of installments used to compute the sum of the digits.

The initial contract may be set up in two ways—either gross or net. The contract should always be set up gross, including the finance charges, if the finance charge cannot be cancelled by a payoff prior to the final installment. If the finance charge can be cancelled, the contract may be set up net. An example follows:

| | | |
|---|---|---|
| Cash price of asset | $ 9,972 | |
| Finance charge | 1,332 | |
| Total payments | $11,304 | |
| Terms—36 monthly payments of $314 each | | |
| Entry to record the acquisition—gross method: | | |
| Deferred interest | 1,332 | |
| Asset | 9,972 | |
| Installment contract payable | | 11.304 |
| Entry to record the acquisition—net method: | | |
| Asset | 9,972 | |
| Installment contract payable | | 9,972 |

Interest payable in each $314 installment using the sum of the digits method is computed as follows:

$$\text{Sum of digits} = N\left(\frac{N+1}{2}\right)$$
$$= 36\left(\frac{37}{2}\right)$$
$$= 666$$

Finance Charge Amortization Schedule

| Payment | Fraction | Multiplier | Interest |
|---|---|---|---|
| 1 | 36/666 | 1,332 | 72 |
| 2 | 35/666 | 1,332 | 70 |
| ⋮ | ⋮ | ⋮ | ⋮ |
| 36 | 1/666 | 1,332 | 2 |
| Totals | 666/666 | | 1,332 |

The entry to record the first payment using the gross method is made as follows:

| | | |
|---|---|---|
| Installment contract payable | 314 | |
| Interest expense | 72 | |
| Cash | | 314 |
| Deferred interest | | 72 |

The entry to record the first payment using the net method is made as follows:

| | | |
|---|---|---|
| Installment contract payable | 242 | |
| Interest expense | 72 | |
| Cash | | 314 |

Each succeeding entry is the same except for the decrease in the amount of interest expense according to the finance charge amortization schedule and a comparable increase in the amount of the payment applied to the principal.

## COMPUTATION OF RETURN ON INVESTMENT THROUGH ADDITIONAL SALES AND COST REDUCTIONS

Investments in plant and equipment must be based on need, not want, and need should be defined in terms of increasing profits. Profits should be forecast in terms of both increased income and reduced costs as compared to alternative production methods. Production people, at times, are inclined to suggest the acquisition of new equipment or facilities based on expediency alone—without an understanding of the comparative costs or possible alternative uses of available funds. The accountant must be prepared to put the pencil to investments in fixed assets with the long-run picture in mind. The accountant should also know the availability of funds and understand the possibility of overextension.

As an example assume that an expenditure of $100,000 can be made to set up and equip a new production line which is basically a replacement of the current line. Sales are expected to increase by the use of the new line because of improved product availability and minor changes in the product that can be made economically by using the new procedures. The sales increase has been set at $50,000 per year with 28 percent of this amount or $14,000 in additional profits. Regular sales are projected at an average of $500,000 per year for the next five years and the cost savings on these sales will be reduced by saving 2,000 hours of labor per year which would cost $10 per hour including fringe benefits and direct overhead. The new line is expected to have a useful life of five years at which time the cost of dismanteling will equal the salvage value.

The additional costs of owning the new production line are computed as follows:

Additional cost:

| | |
|---|---|
| Depreciation | $100,000 |
| Interest—average investment of $50,000 × 9% × 5 years | 22,500 |
| Property tax—average depreciated cost of $50,000 × 2% × 5 years | 5,000 |
| Increase in space occupied—600 square feet at $3 per year for 5 years | 9,000 |
| Insurance—$800 per year | 4,000 |
| Total cost | 140,500 |
| Less $2,000 per year decrease in maintenance | 10,000 |
| Net additional cost | $130,500 |

Additional income:

| | |
|---|---|
| Profit on additional sales—$14,000 per year for 5 years | $ 70,000 |
| Increased profits on regular sales through labor savings of $20,000 per year for 5 years | 100,000 |
| Total | 170,000 |
| Less total additional costs of line above | 130,500 |
| Return on investment | $ 39,500 |

Annual return on investment equals—

$$\frac{\text{Average annual return}}{\text{Average investment}} \quad \frac{\frac{39{,}500}{5}}{\frac{100{,}000}{2}} = \frac{7{,}900}{50{,}000} = 15.8\%$$

Once the annual percentage of return on investment is determined, alternative uses of the funds should be evaluated including a judgement of the amount of risk involved and how the investment fits the manufacturer's long run objectives.

## COMPUTATION OF CASH PAYBACK PERIOD

The cash payback period for an asset may be determined by dividing the cost of the asset by the annual savings and increased income plus depreciation or, in other words, dividing the cost by the annual cash flow. Using the same example as previously used in computing return on investment, the cash payback period would be as follows:

$$\text{Cash payback period} = \frac{\text{Original cost}}{\text{Annual income plus depreciation}}$$

$$= \frac{100{,}000}{7{,}900 + 20{,}000}$$

$$= 3.58 \text{ years}$$

The cash flow used in this example would have to be reduced by any taxes to be paid on the $7,900 profit.

## DISCOUNTED CASH FLOW ANALYSIS

Income and cost savings that are to be realized over a period of years do not have the same value as current funds and must be discounted in arriving at a current value. The same technique has been used by the author in determining that inventory items should be purchased when lower costs were available through the utilization of automatic machining that was available only for larger quantities. Current values are determined by using a present value table as presented below.

Present value of $1.00

| | Compound Discount Rate | | | |
|---|---|---|---|---|
| Year | 6% | 10% | 15% | 20% |
| 1 | .943 | .909 | .870 | .833 |
| 2 | .890 | .826 | .756 | .694 |
| 3 | .840 | .751 | .658 | .579 |
| 4 | .792 | .683 | .572 | .482 |
| 5 | .747 | .621 | .497 | .402 |
| 6 | .705 | .564 | .432 | .335 |
| 7 | .665 | .513 | .376 | .279 |
| 8 | .627 | .467 | .327 | .233 |
| 9 | .592 | .424 | .284 | .194 |
| 10 | .558 | .386 | .247 | .162 |

**Figure 10-3**

In evaluating our previous example, the discounted cash flow analysis, assuming an interest rate of 10 percent and income available at the end of the year, would be computed as follows:

| Year | Cash Flow | Discounted Rate at 10% | Discounted Cash Flow |
|---|---|---|---|
| 1 | $27,900 | .909 | $ 25,361 |
| 2 | 27,900 | .826 | 23,045 |
| 3 | 27,900 | .751 | 20,953 |
| 4 | 27,900 | .683 | 19,055 |
| 5 | 27,900 | .621 | 17,326 |
| Total | | | $105,740 |
| Initial outlay | | | 100,000 |
| Discounted net cash flow | | | $ 5,740 |

## CONSIDERATIONS ON PLANT SIZE

Again, the initial cost of manufacturing facilities is only the beginning of the costs. Such costs as property taxes, insurance, interest either imputed or on the mortgage note, utilities, maintenance and depreciation continue as long as the building is owned. Buildings are surprisingly expensive, and when these costs are projected it becomes apparent that a building can be paid for twice in a few years.

Buildings have tended to appreciate in value over the past years—but so will funds wisely invested elsewhere. Also, the cost of providing additional space currently must be compared to expected future costs of providing the same space when needed.

A trend analysis of operations should be prepared by the accountant in an effort to project future space requirements as new facilities are considered. This trend analysis combined with current building costs, the previously mentioned carrying costs, projected future costs, available funds and their alternative uses should serve as the basis for a carefully thought out plan on new plants.

The author believes that it is less critical to find that additional space is needed in the future than to carry excess space for an extended period of time. The best protection for future space requirements is to acquire excess land on which to expand the manufacturing plant rather than carrying excess building capacity. The cost of carrying excess land is considerably less than the cost of carrying excess building capacity. The old cliche, "Don't build it too small," should be ignored, as should certain other advice from so-called experts, as carefully planned expansion is undertaken.

## NECESSARY INSURANCE FOR THE MANUFACTURER

Closely related to the manufacturer's ownership of plant and equipment is the need for adequate insurance coverage. Fire and extended coverage must be carried on the plant and equipment that is owned by the manufacturer and on certain leased plant and equipment according to the terms of the lease. Generally, this building and contents coverage also covers the inventory. The current fair market value (replacement value) of building and contents should be reviewed periodically to ascertain that adequate coverage is provided. Book value or original cost is often insufficient during periods of rising prices.

Most fire and extended coverage insurance can be written with a co-insurance clause. This clause lets the firm share a part of the risk and reduces the premium. Co-insurance should be purchased only where a total loss at one location is highly unlikely or the manufacturer is willing to assume part of the risk. The co-insurance clause may require that a potential loss be at least 80 percent insured. This means that a $100,000 building is insured for only $80,000 with the manufacturer assuming the other $20,000 risk. If the co-insurance requirement is not met, the claim on any loss is reduced proportionately. In this example if the $100,000 building is insured for only $70,000 under the 80 percent co-insurance clause, the insurance company is liable for only ⅞ of any loss up to a maximum claim of $70,000.

Most fire and extended coverage polices are written for three years. This assures the manufacturer of the same rates for a three year period. However, the premium can be paid annually, or in many cases the entire insurance program can be combined into monthly payments to conserve cash for other requirements.

Along with the fire and extended coverage insurance, the manufacturing firm should consider business interruption insurance to replace income during the period of recovery after the manufacturing facilities have been damaged or destroyed.

General liability insurance must be carried to provide protection on visitors to the manufacturer's place of business. This insurance should provide enough coverage to protect the firm against possible damage claims for injuries, etc., for which a liability could occur.

Of particular importance to the manufacturer is the insurance of valuable papers, molds, dies, patterns, fixtures, etc. Part of these items may be covered under the building and contents policy, but valuable papers and assets not located on the premises may not be covered. The valuable papers are of particular significance since they include the drawings used to manufacture the products. Perhaps, in addition to insurance, these drawings or key drawings should be duplicated and stored elsewhere.

Workmen's compensation and employee liability insurance are required by law. The rates for these coverages normally depend on the various job categories of employees. These categories should be reviewed with the insurance auditor to determine that each employee is classified correctly.

Vehicles should be insured with high coverages for property damage and liability. Insurance should also be carried to protect the firm when employees use their own vehicles for company business.

MACHINE MANUFACTURING CORPORATION

Prepaid Insurance Schedule

March 31, 19x2

| Agency | Insurance Company | Policy Number | Coverage | Face of Policy | Term of Policy | Date Paid | Amount Paid | Term of Premium | Fraction Prepaid | Amount Prepaid |
|---|---|---|---|---|---|---|---|---|---|---|
| Pruner | Etna | F1027 | Fire and E.C. | $ 400,000 | 4-1-x1 to 3-31-x4 | 3-25-x2 | $ 5,000 | 4-1-x2 to 3-31-x3 | 12/12 | $ 5,000 |
| Dunlap | Etna | BI770 | Business Interruption | 300,000 | 4-1-x1 to 3-31-x4 | 3-25-x2 | 3,000 | 4-1-x2 to 3-31-x3 | 12/12 | 3,000 |
| Jones | American | G8070 | General Liability | 500,000 | 4-1-x1 to 3-31-x4 | 3-25-x2 | 7,000 | 4-1-x2 to 3-31-x3 | 12/12 | 7,000 |
| Crown | Crown | WC106 | Workmen's Compensation | Statute | 9-1-x1 to 8-31-x2 | 8-25-x1 | 6,000 | 9-1-x1 to 8-31-x2 | 5/12 | 2,500 |
| Jones | American | EL106 | Employee Liability | Statute | 9-1-x1 to 8-31-x2 | 8-25-x1 | 4,800 | 9-1-x1 to 8-31-x2 | 5/12 | 2,000 |
| Jones | American | VP107 | Valuable Papers | 180,000 | 8-1-x1 to 7-31-x4 | 7-25-x1 | 3,000 | 8-1-x1 to 7-31-x2 | 4/12 | 1,000 |
| Jones | American | V2043 | Vehicles | 800,000 | 8-1-x1 to 7-31-x2 | 7-25-x1 | 9,000 | 8-1-x1 to 7-31-x2 | 4/12 | 3,000 |
| Jones | American | B6433 | Burglary | 80,000 | 4-1-x1 to 3-31-x4 | 3-25-x2 | 2,000 | 4-1-x2 to 3-31-x3 | 12/12 | 2,000 |
| Jones | American | P4770 | Product Liability | 500,000 | 7-1-x1 to 6-30-x4 | 6-25-x2 | 9,000 | 7-1-x2 to 6-30-x3 | 3/12 | 2,250 |
| Jones | American | U1766 | Umbrella | 5,000,000 | 7-1-x1 to 6-30-x4 | 6-25-x2 | 5,000 | 7-1-x2 to 6-30-x3 | 3/12 | 1,250 |
| Jones | American | EB477 | Employee Bonds | 100,000 | 7-1-x1 to 6-30-x4 | 6-25-x2 | 1,000 | 7-1-x2 to 6-30-x3 | 3/12 | 250 |
| Cross | Cross | H3662 | Health and Accident | — | 1-1-x2 to 12-31-x2 | 3-25-x2 | 4,000 | 4-1-x2 to 4-30-x2 | 1/12 | 4,000 |
| | | | | | | | $58,800 | | | $33,250 |

**Figure 10-4**

In many cases burglary insurance should be carried on company products, as these items may not be insured against theft under the fire and extended coverage policy.

Products must be insured under a product liability policy to protect the firm against injuries resulting through the use of the manufactured product.

A growing form of insurance is the umbrella policy. In general, this is a large liability policy that picks up where other coverages leave off. The manufacturer should require detailed information from the insurance company as to what risks are covered by the umbrella policy.

Employee dishonesty may be insured against—this type of policy should cover large defalcations that could prove damaging to the firm. In fact, this reasoning should be the basis for all insurance.

Other types of insurance may be carried as protection for the firm or as employee benefits including life insurance, health and accident insurance, and salary or wage replacement indemnity.

Periodically, an insurance schedule should be prepared to both summarize the coverage and to compute the amount of insurance that is prepaid. Figure 10-4 is a prepaid insurance schedule.

## SUMMARY

The accountant must be in a position to evaluate the acquisition of plant and equipment for the manufacturing firm and in many cases for the manufacturer's customers. To do this adequately the accountant needs to understand both the accounting and tax consequences of acquisitions and disposals of assets and the related depreciation methods.

Other decisions need to be made based on properly evaluating leasing versus buying including the alternative that may require accounting for finance charges on installment purchases.

Tools for consideration in determining the advisability of investing in additional plant and equipment are the computation of return on investment, cash payback period and a discounted cash flow analysis.

The accountant must also maintain equipment records to substantiate general ledger balances in the asset and accumulated depreciation accounts. These records may also serve as a basis for physical inventories of assets as necessary.

The responsibility to see that the manufacturer carries proper insurance is also shared by the accountant because of his knowledge of the firm's risks. Prepaid insurance schedules should be prepared as a part of the accounting process and as a summary of the various coverages. The actual prepayment of insurance premiums should be kept to a minimum, with monthly premiums arranged to conserve cash outlays whenever feasible.

# 11

## Profit Planning and Forecasting Techniques

### PURPOSES AND BENEFITS OF PROFIT PLANNING AND FORECASTING

Planning and forecasting are a definite part of the management process as it applies to the entire manufacturing operation. The management process has been described as plan, organize, motivate and control. One can see elements of each step in profit planning and forecasting, but particularly planning and controlling as actual results are compared to the plan.

The profit plan gives the firm direction and established boundaries within which to operate. The total plan consists of:

1. The operating plan which is the preparation of future income statements.
2. The capital expenditures plan which plans for the acquisition of needed capital assests.
3. The cash flow forecast which determines that cash is available to carry out the first two steps of the plan.
4. The planned balance sheet which shows the effect of the operating plan, capital expenditures plan and the cash projection of the financial condition at the end of the planning period.

When the manufacturer uses the entire plan as a guide, he is shooting for targeted objectives that are reasonably within range, has established that the resources will be available to finance the plan and has set up financial guidelines that will require adjustments if the firm finds it necessary to either shrink or expand the operating plan.

Preparing the profit plan requires the use of accounting techniques, and an accountant must certainly be the technician in drawing up the plan. The accountant should remain flexible enough in his approach to planning to prevent the plan from becoming a straightjacket for operations. He should be willing, in fact suggest, that the plan be revised as needed to meet the overall objectives of the manufacturer as dictated by more current information. Too many times the author has seen operations restricted because something was not in the budget, when it was apparent that profit could have been improved immediately if a revision had been made.

Profit planning should be a continuous process of determining the uncontrollable, external forces that affect operations and reacting by manipulating the controllable, internal forces to maximize long run profits, assuming that this is the primary objective of the manufacturer.

## EIGHT PRINCIPLES OF PROFIT PLANNING

1. *Assign responsibility for developing and revising the plan.* One individual must assume primary responsibility; it may be his only responsibility or one of many responsibilities; he may perform the task alone or have a staff of assistants depending on the size of the particular manufacturer.

The profit planner should work closely with accounting to obtain much of the needed information. He should be capable of forming a liaison between profit planning and all departments in order to properly coordinate the entire plan.

The planner must also be backed up by a planning committee to advise and make decisions on company objectives, to assist in selecting alternatives and to resolve departmental and other conflicts. The committee can also serve as a convenient culprit for the profit planner in explaining his unpopular decisions.

2. *Determine the number of years to be planned and the reasonable breakdown into subperiods.* Every manufacturer needs to plan several years in advance to assure the availability of resources, including personnel, finance and production capacity, necessary to augment the operating plan. Plans that extend beyond the immediate future do not need to be broken down into periods of less than one year. The immediate future, perhaps the next 12 months, should be divided into months or quarters. This monthly or quarterly forecast should be revised and extended at the end of each month and quarter based on what has happened in the previous months and quarters, and, because as time progresses, more reliable information on future operations becomes available. In other words planning and forecasting is a continuous process that is constantly moving forward as time passes and more reliable information is available.

For our example we will prepare a plan for one year with the first three months planned individually and the remainder of the year by quarters.

3. *Predicting the effect of external forces and planning to use internal actions to obtain the desired results.* Numerous external forces can affect the operations of the manufacturer.

These external forces are generally the doings of other groups over which the manufacturer has no direct control. They include government projects, legislation, and executive or judicial decisions. Many actions of the government affect the sale of the products of specific manufacturers either favorably or adversely. Certain legislation may also affect the type of product that may be produced and sold, while other legislation may simply affect general economic conditions. Costs can be affected by government action on such items as interest rates, taxes, tax favors for special industries, or just an attempt to influence the marketability of one product versus another.

Other uncontrollable external forces can include the actions of competitors, consumer behavior, population growth rates, population shifts, shortages caused by weather, etc., to an almost endless list of unforeseeable happenings.

Internal forces can be controlled in an effort to push the plan in the direction that will meet the firm's objectives. These internal forces include advertising, developing or acquiring new products, excellent quality products, excellent customer service, policies that properly develop and motivate personnel, and an endless list of items under varying circumstances to enhance the firm's long run profit position or to offset undesirable external forces.

4. *Define those factors that will determine the level of operations.* Usually the limiting factor is sales volume. However, if there are other limiting factors, they may be determined and eliminated through a detailed profit plan. These other limiting factors are usually the availability of resources to meet the sales potential. These resources include finance, production capacity and skilled or knowledgeable personnel. These resource shortages can be eliminated with proper action in the long run if continuously profitable sales can be obtained.

There is another overriding limitation on the size of operations and amount of expansion of some manufacturers. This limitation is based on the established policy by management to be very conservative about growth or not to grow beyond a certain size. This limitation, although not a consideration in many firms, is perfectly valid. In manufacturing it is usually necessary to add products to the line or to produce new products that are significantly different than those on which the original success was built, if the firm is to grow rapidly. This step, or other new steps, may also require the manufacturer to attempt to penetrate new markets with which he is not familiar. These departures from previously successful products and markets can push the firm into areas where knowledge is inadequate—often the attempt fails and drags down a previously successful manufacturer. Perhaps the risk is simply too great and management prefers not to grow beyond a size or enter into areas that can be personally controlled with confidence. Profits with minimal risk, not size, may be a policy that becomes the limitation.

5. *Coordinate the needs of the entire firm.* In every firm there are spending limitations and in some new, struggling or rapidly growing firms the availability of financial resources may be the key limitation. This puts a greater burden on the profit planner of allocating available financing. In this situation there simply isn't enough money to meet the requirements of each department within the firm. Priorities must be determined with the sanction of the planning committee to allocate available finances to those areas which will give the most benefit to the overall manufacturing operation. Without this coordination, mistakes, including spend it when you get it, will be numerous.

6. *Analyze prior years' operations in formulating the profit plan.* The value of this principle is evident when you consider the comparison of forecasting accurately for a firm that has been operating for a period of years versus a new firm. Obviously, what has occurred in the past is one of the best guides to what will occur in the future. What happened yesterday may be the best guide to what will happen today.

In analyzing prior years' operations it is often possible to establish a trend. This trend, tempered with the knowledge of things you intend to do differently and the expected changes in external forces, may be the best guide to forecasting future operations.

By looking into revenue and expenditures for the various months within the years of past operations, it is also possible to determine high and low levels of operations within each year. This information is not only useful in forecasting sales for each month within the year, but also lets the manufacturer plan the best time within the year for such functions as inventory building, vacations, special maintenance and other housekeeping projects.

7. *Get assistance from all departments in formulating the plan.* There are two basic reasons for this profit planning principle. One is to use the knowledge that each department head has about the needs and expectations he has for his department. Everyone should know more about his individual function than anyone else. Therefore, the best information available comes from each department. The second reason for enlisting aid from all departments in formulating the plan is to make them feel a part of the planning process. Without this it is more difficult to ask them to live with the plan. In other words every department will be more willing to conform to the plan if they have a hand in designing the plan.

Information should be fed to the planner from each department. He should coordinate this information as in principle number 5 with the aid of the planning committee. Changes in departmental forecasts and requirements should be discussed and explained to the department planner before being finalized. This is only being fair to the department, and there might be additional feedback on information that has been overlooked by the planner and the committee.

8. *Compare the planned performance to actual performance.* This step has three benefits. It determines what has happened to cause actual performance to vary from the plan. It finds errors in the plan and assists in improving the planning process in the future. Portions of the comparison can be given to the various departments as a self-evaluation technique. This total comparison is a part of the management control function.

## DEVELOPMENT OF THE PROFIT PLAN

As previously mentioned the four parts of the profit plan are the operating plan, the capital expenditures plan, the cash flow forecast and the projected balance sheet. Each of these parts is dependent on the success of the other and may require revisions if the entire picture does not fit together properly.

In our plan we will prepare a one year operating plan broken down into months for the first quarter and into quarters for the last three quarters of the year. The capital expenditures plan and the cash flow forecast will be made for the same time periods. The balance sheet, which should be acceptable if the rest of the plan is successful, will be projected at the end of the year only.

In actual practice the plan should be extended and revised as necessary as each month progresses. Also, the time periods will be broken down into months so that we are always planned three months in advance, and a new quarterly projection made in order to always be a year ahead by quarters at the end of each quarter. Annual projections may be made for several years and revised and extended at least annually.

## THE OPERATING PLAN

The operating plan starts with the sales forecast which should come from the sales department. The planner should provide assistance to the sales manager relating to those forces which will affect sales outside the firm and outside the sales department. As the sales forecast comes to the planning department it is to be referred to the planning committee for their scrutiny and suggestions. More emphasis is put on this part of the operating plan than any other. Marketing, in most manufacturing companies, leads the way for the rest of the operations.

Costs of production based on sales and any changes in inventories follow the sales forecast. Probably cost accounting, engineering and the production department can provide the best input on production costs after being provided with the quantities of each product to be produced.

Departmental costs, such as general and administrative, are also dependent to some extent on sales. Much of this information can be provided by department heads—other parts may come directly from the members of the planning committee.

The various parts of the operating plan are presented as follows:

Planned Revenue—Figure 11-1
Planned Cost of Goods Manufactured and Sold—Figure 11-2
Planned General and Administrative Expenses—Figure 11-3
Planned Income Statement—Figure 11-4

The sequence of these parts of the operating plan provide the information to proceed logically.

MACHINE MANUFACTURING CORPORATION

Planned Revenue

Year Ending March 31, 19x8

| | April | May | June | Second Quarter | Third Quarter | Fourth Quarter | Total Year |
|---|---|---|---|---|---|---|---|
| Revenue | 70,000 | 80,000 | 80,000 | 250,000 | 240,000 | 260,000 | 980,000 |

**Figure 11-1**

MACHINE MANUFACTURING CORPORATION

Planned Cost of Goods Manufactured and Sold

Year Ending March 31, 19x8

| | April | May | June | Second Quarter | Third Quarter | Fourth Quarter | Total Year |
|---|---|---|---|---|---|---|---|
| Finished goods inventory, beginning of month | 88,000 | 98,000 | 98,000 | 98,000 | 98,000 | 98,000 | 88,000 |
| Goods in process, beginning of month | 82,000 | 82,000 | 82,000 | 82,000 | 82,000 | 82,000 | 82,000 |
| Materials | | | | | | | |
| Inventory, beginning of month | 46,000 | 46,000 | 46,000 | 46,000 | 46,000 | 46,000 | 46,000 |
| Net purchases | 35,890 | 34,160 | 34,160 | 106,750 | 102,480 | 111,020 | 424,460 |
| Materials available | 81,890 | 80,160 | 80,160 | 152,750 | 148,480 | 157,020 | 470,460 |
| Less inventory, end of month | 46,000 | 46,000 | 46,000 | 46,000 | 46,000 | 46,000 | 46,000 |
| Materials issued | 35,890 | 34,160 | 34,160 | 106,750 | 102,480 | 111,020 | 424,460 |
| Direct labor | 12,780 | 10,720 | 10,720 | 33,500 | 32,160 | 34,840 | 134,720 |
| Manufacturing overhead | | | | | | | |
| Indirect labor | 2,100 | 2,400 | 2,400 | 7,500 | 7,200 | 7,800 | 29,400 |
| Repairs | 280 | 320 | 320 | 1,000 | 960 | 1,040 | 3,920 |
| Depreciation | 1,500 | 1,500 | 1,500 | 4,500 | 6,000 | 6,000 | 21,000 |
| Factory supplies | 500 | 560 | 560 | 1,750 | 1,680 | 1,820 | 6,870 |
| Utilities | 280 | 320 | 320 | 1,000 | 960 | 1,040 | 3,920 |
| Insurance | 420 | 480 | 480 | 1,500 | 1,440 | 1,560 | 5,880 |
| Building maintenance | 70 | 80 | 80 | 250 | 240 | 260 | 980 |
| Payroll taxes | 800 | 800 | 800 | 2,500 | 2,400 | 2,600 | 9,900 |
| Property taxes | 140 | 160 | 160 | 500 | 480 | 520 | 1,960 |
| Retirement benefits | 280 | 320 | 320 | 1,000 | 960 | 1,040 | 3,920 |
| Cost variances | 70 | 80 | 80 | 250 | 240 | 260 | 980 |
| Miscellaneous | 140 | 160 | 160 | 500 | 480 | 520 | 1,960 |
| Total manufacturing overhead | 6,580 | 7,180 | 7,180 | 22,250 | 23,040 | 24,460 | 90,690 |
| Total goods in process | 137,250 | 134,060 | 134,060 | 244,500 | 239,680 | 252,320 | 731,870 |
| Less goods in process, end of month | 82,000 | 82,000 | 82,000 | 82,000 | 82,000 | 82,000 | 82,000 |
| Cost of goods manufactured | 55,250 | 52,060 | 52,060 | 162,500 | 157,680 | 170,320 | 649,870 |
| Total goods available | 143,250 | 150,060 | 150,060 | 260,500 | 255,680 | 268,320 | 737,870 |
| Less finished goods inventory end of month | 98,000 | 98,000 | 98,000 | 98,000 | 98,000 | 98,000 | 98,000 |
| Cost of goods manufactured and sold | 45,250 | 52,060 | 52,060 | 162,500 | 157,680 | 170,320 | 639,870 |

**Figure 11-2**

MACHINE MANUFACTURING CORPORATION

Planned General and Administrative Expenses

Year Ending March 31, 19x8

| | April | May | June | Second Quarter | Third Quarter | Fourth Quarter | Total Year |
|---|---|---|---|---|---|---|---|
| Officers' salaries | 6,000 | 6,000 | 6,000 | 18,000 | 18,000 | 18,000 | 72,000 |
| Clerical salaries | 1,667 | 1,667 | 1,666 | 5,000 | 5,000 | 5,000 | 20,000 |
| Engineering salaries | 2,000 | 2,000 | 2,000 | 6,000 | 6,000 | 6,000 | 24,000 |
| Sales salaries | 3,000 | 3,000 | 3,000 | 9,000 | 9,000 | 9,000 | 36,000 |
| Repairs | 100 | 100 | 100 | 300 | 300 | 300 | 1,200 |
| Depreciation | 166 | 166 | 168 | 500 | 500 | 500 | 2,000 |
| Utilities | 100 | 100 | 100 | 200 | 500 | 500 | 1,500 |
| Telephone and telegraph | 300 | 300 | 200 | 700 | 700 | 800 | 3,000 |
| Insurance | 300 | 300 | 300 | 900 | 900 | 900 | 3,600 |
| Building maintenance | 100 | 100 | 100 | 300 | 300 | 300 | 1,200 |
| Payroll taxes | 800 | 800 | 800 | 1,900 | 300 | 2,600 | 7,200 |
| Property tax | 100 | 100 | 100 | 300 | 300 | 300 | 1,200 |
| State income tax | 200 | 300 | 300 | 800 | 800 | 800 | 3,200 |
| Travel and entertainment | 400 | 400 | 300 | 1,000 | 1,000 | 1,100 | 4,200 |
| Advertising | 400 | 400 | -0- | 400 | 600 | 600 | 2,400 |
| Office supplies | 100 | 100 | 100 | 400 | 400 | 400 | 1,500 |
| Dues and subscriptions | 100 | 100 | 100 | 300 | 300 | 300 | 1,200 |
| Professional services | 200 | 200 | 2,000 | 200 | 200 | 200 | 3,000 |
| Uncollectible accounts | 67 | 67 | 66 | 200 | 200 | 200 | 800 |
| Interest expense | 180 | 170 | 160 | 490 | 410 | 390 | 1,800 |
| Retirement benefits | 300 | 300 | 300 | 900 | 900 | 900 | 3,600 |
| Miscellaneous | 100 | 100 | 100 | 300 | 300 | 300 | 1,200 |
| Totals | 16,680 | 16,770 | 17,960 | 48,090 | 46,910 | 49,390 | 195,800 |

**Figure 11-3**

MACHINE MANUFACTURING CORPORATION

Planned Income Statement

Year Ending March 31, 19x8

| | April | May | June | Second Quarter | Third Quarter | Fourth Quarter | Total Year |
|---|---|---|---|---|---|---|---|
| Net Sales | 70,000 | 80,000 | 80,000 | 250,000 | 240,000 | 260,000 | 980,000 |
| Cost of Goods Manufactured and sold | 45,250 | 52,060 | 52,060 | 162,500 | 157,680 | 170,320 | 639,870 |
| Gross Profit | 24,750 | 27,940 | 27,940 | 87,500 | 82,320 | 89,680 | 340,130 |
| General and Administrative Expenses | 16,680 | 16,770 | 17,960 | 48,090 | 46,910 | 49,390 | 195,800 |
| Income Before Federal Income tax | 8,070 | 11,170 | 9,980 | 39,410 | 35,410 | 40,290 | 144,330 |
| Federal Income Tax | 2,580 | 4,070 | 3,500 | 15,015 | 13,115 | 15,450 | 53,730 |
| Net Income | 5,490 | 7,100 | 6,480 | 24,395 | 22,295 | 24,840 | 90,600 |

**Figure 11-4**

## THE CAPITAL EXPENDITURES PLAN

The firm expects to install a new line during the last half of the fiscal year at a cost of $60,000 with $30,000 being paid in each of the last two quarters. The capital expenditures plan precedes the cash flow forecast and the planned balance sheet, as information from the expenditures is required for these subsequent parts of the plan. Depreciation on the new capital assets has been taken on the income statement. The capital expenditures plan is presented in Figure 11-5.

MACHINE MANUFACTURING CORPORATION

Capital Expenditures Plan

Year Ending March 31, 19x8

| | April | May | June | Second Quarter | Third Quarter | Fourth Quarter | Total Year |
|---|---|---|---|---|---|---|---|
| Expenditures —new line | — | — | — | — | 30,000 | 30,000 | 60,000 |

**Figure 11-5**

## CASH FLOW FORECAST

The cash flow forecast, presented in Figure 11-6, requires the conversion from an accrual to a cash basis. To do this the planner must understand the collection and payment lags. Accounting and credit should be able to furnish the needed information. In our cash flow forecast we have made the following assumptions:

Accounts receivable collections—

¼—month of sale
½—month after sale
¼—2 months after sale

Cost of goods manufactured payments—

Materials, ½ month of purchase, ½ month following purchase
Direct labor, all in month of cost
Overhead, ½ in month of cost, ½ following month, less depreciation

General and administrative expense—

Payments—½ in month of expense, ½ following month, less depreciation
Federal income tax—paid as due with estimates fully paid
Capital expenditures—as incurred
Mortgage note payable—equal monthly on principal, interest included in expenses
Dividends—after end of each quarter

MACHINE MANUFACTURING CORPORATION

Cash Flow Forecast

Year Ending March 31, 19x8.

| | April | May | June | Second Quarter | Third Quarter | Fourth Quarter | Total Year |
|---|---|---|---|---|---|---|---|
| Beginning balance | 52,400 | 46,686 | 62,037 | 56,085 | 59,000 | 46,595 | 52,400 |
| Cash receipts | 77,000 | 83,500 | 77,500 | 247,000 | 243,000 | 253,000 | 981,000 |
| Total cash available | 129,400 | 130,186 | 139,537 | 303,085 | 302,000 | 299,595 | 1,033,400 |
| Cash disbursements | | | | | | | |
| Cost of goods manufactured | 53,880 | 51,075 | 50,560 | 157,180 | 152,250 | 162,640 | 627,585 |
| General and administrative expenses | 16,334 | 16,574 | 17,392 | 48,240 | 46,540 | 48,610 | 193,690 |
| Federal income tax | | | 15,000 | 25,165 | 13,115 | 15,450 | 68,730 |
| Capital expenditures | | | | | 30,000 | 30,000 | 60,000 |
| Mortgage note payable | 500 | 500 | 500 | 1,500 | 1,500 | 1,500 | 6,000 |
| Dividends | 12,000 | | | 12,000 | 12,000 | 12,000 | 48,000 |
| Total cash disbursements | 82,714 | 68,149 | 83,452 | 244,085 | 255,405 | 270,200 | 1,004,005 |
| Ending balance | 46,686 | 62,037 | 56,085 | 59,000 | 46,595 | 29,395 | 29,395 |

**Figure 11-6**

## PLANNED BALANCE SHEET

The planned balance sheet is presented in Figure 11-7 as a comparison to the balance sheet at the end of the previous year. This presentation will actually have to be completed after the planned balance sheet is completed, as the planning precedes the year-end. Balances in the planned balance sheet reflect the transactions in the previous parts of the plan, as accounts receivable equals beginning balance plus sales less collections, etc.

## MACHINE MANUFACTURING CORPORATION

### Balance Sheet at March 31, 19x7 and Planned Balance Sheet at March 31, 19x8

#### Assets

| | March 31, 19x7 | March 31, 19x8 |
|---|---|---|
| Current Assets | | |
| Cash in bank and on hand | 42,000 | 29,395 |
| Temporary investments | 10,400 | — |
| Accounts receivable trade | 91,000 | 87,000 |
| Less allowance for uncollectible accounts | 3,000 | 3,000 |
| | 88,000 | 84,000 |
| Inventories | 216,000 | 226,000 |
| Prepaid expenses and advances | 2,600 | 2,600 |
| Total current assets | 359,000 | 341,995 |
| Plant and Equipment | 341,800 | 401,800 |
| Less accumulated depreciation | 76,000 | 99,000 |
| | 265,800 | 302,800 |
| Other Assets—Cash surrender value of officers' life insurance | 3,200 | 4,500 |
| | 628,000 | 649,295 |

#### Liabilities and Stockholder's Equity

| | March 31, 19x7 | March 31, 19x8 |
|---|---|---|
| Current Liabilities | | |
| Accounts payable—trade | 40,000 | 41,395 |
| Current portion of mortgage note payable | 6,000 | 8,000 |
| Accrued and withheld payroll taxes | 3,000 | 3,000 |
| Accrued salaries and wages | 4,000 | 4,000 |
| Accrued federal income tax | 15,000 | — |
| Other accrued taxes and expenses | 8,000 | 6,300 |
| Total current liabilities | 76,000 | 62,695 |
| Long-term liability | | |
| Mortgage note payable | 200,000 | 194,000 |
| Less current portion above | 6,000 | 8,000 |
| | 194,000 | 186,000 |
| | 270,000 | 248,695 |
| Stockholders' Equity | | |
| Common stock | 60,000 | 60,000 |
| Retained earnings | 298,000 | 340,600 |
| | 358,000 | 400,600 |
| | 628,000 | 649,295 |

**Figure 11-7**

## SUMMARY

Profit planning and forecasting provides guidance for the manufacturer and prevents financial errors and overextensions. The plan should be constantly updated and revised as necessary to improve the profit potential.

There are eight principles of profit planning summarized as follows:

1. Assign responsibility.
2. Determine planning and forecasting years and subperiods.
3. Predict external forces and plan internal actions.
4. Define the factors that will determine the operating level.
5. Coordinate the needs of the entire firm.
6. Analyze prior years.
7. Get assistance from all departments.
8. Evaluate actual performance and the plan.

The plan is developed in four parts—the operating plan, the capital expenditures plan, the cash flow forecast and the planned balance sheet. Each part is interdependent and may require revisions based on another part of the plan.

The final evaluation based on the plan and actual performance is a part of the control feature in managing a manufacturing company. In the total plan we are actually planning and controlling—valuable services to management to which accounting is a key contributor.

# 12

# Sharpening Audit Responsibilities of Auditor and Client

## REASONS FOR AN ANNUAL AUDIT

An audit is a means of verifying that the financial statements presented by the manufacturer are materially accurate, that the accounting principles used in preparing the financial statements are consistent with the principles used for the preceding year, and that all facts are disclosed that could have an impact on the financial position of the company. Audits are more than this in most situations, and the audit will be further discussed throughout the chapter.

The auditor expresses an opinion as to the fairness of the financial statements and supplementary schedules. His audit is conducted in accordance with accepted auditing standards for field work. His qualifications and competence are dictated in accordance with other prescribed standards, and the minimum contents of the audit report are set forth by a third set of standards. The contents of his report were discussed in Chapter 1.

Audits are often requested by lending institutions, stockholders, particularly nonmanagement stockholders, and other third parties. Audits are also an aid to management in evaluating the performance of accounting and to accounting as a form of self-evaluation.

In many situations the auditor actually suggests and presents to the client adjustments to the accounting records prior to preparing the annual financial statements. The auditor may also go through a similar process in preparing unaudited financial statements at interim dates, such as at the end of fiscal quarters. Where the auditor performs these additional services, he is acting to some extent not only as an auditor but as a public controller. Here he must be careful as to the additional services he performs not to prejudice his independence in expressing an opinion on the fairness of the client's financial statements.

The audit adds precedence to the manufacturer's financial statements, is an aid to his accounting department, prevents delays in obtaining credit, and adds to management and stockholder confidence relating to the financial position of the firm.

## BENEFITS TO THE MANUFACTURER AND HIS ACCOUNTANT

Any outsider who has had manufacturing accounting experience can see areas for improvements in the existing procedures or system. A management letter suggesting various alternative methods and procedures, corrections, tax precautions, tax saving ideas, and general management considerations should be a product of every audit. The auditor gains a wide range of knowledge through his education, which is continuous, and through his wide range of accounting engagements. It is a part of his responsibility to share with the client what he has learned about the firm through conversations and various observations.

Much of the auditing work is truly a housekeeping function—that is, just getting things cleaned up and in order. This tidyness is in itself of significant benefit, for it not only puts things in order but actually absorbs part of the workload. But probably the greatest benefit can come from the extra ten percent effort in looking for and suggesting better ways of doing things to the client. This extra ten percent, if not volunteered by the auditor, should be requested by the manufacturer.

## SHARING AUDIT RESPONSIBILITIES

The audit is not the sole responsibility of the auditor; it is a joint responsibility of auditor and client. The auditor should request and the client should volunteer his assistance in every practical aspect of the audit. This sharing of audit responsibilities is of benefit to the auditor, the client, and to the personnel who actually assist the auditor.

An auditor is a trained professional who has invested a minimum of seven years, in most cases, to obtain his credentials. His services are in great demand and can be utilized more economically by relieving him of every clerical function that is practical to delegate to client personnel. Some procedures must continue to be controlled or performed by the auditor as not to compromise his auditing standards, but many others, with his guidance, can be wholly or partially performed by client personnel. The auditor must keep the best interests of the client in mind and request the needed assistance. The client in his own best interests must offer the needed assistance.

The principal benefits to the manufacturer are a reduction of the audit fee and a learning process for his personnel. The auditor, when relieved of clerical functions, makes his time more valuable.

## CLIENT PARTICIPATION IN PREPARATION OF WORKPAPERS, SCHEDULES AND OTHER INFORMATION

The auditor must approach the request for client assistance correctly. First, he must make the request to an individual who has the authority to get the job done and who understands its importance in relation to other functions—usually the controller or other officer. Second, the auditor must be specific—he should furnish the paper to be sure that it fits in neatly with the rest of his audit workpapers; he should head up each workpaper and explain exactly what he wants to the client. The author has observed a couple of useless efforts by clients who did not understand what the auditor wanted—what the client is to do must be set forth plainly by the auditor.

The following is a list with explanations of numerous areas where the client can share responsibilities for the audit.

*Petty cash* The petty cash custodian can reconcile and have petty cash reimbursed on the last day of the year. This gets the expenses recorded in the proper period and eliminates any need for a petty cash reconciliation or adjustment by the auditor. The client can prepare a schedule totaling petty cash reimbursements and expenses for the year, give the auditor a copy of the year-end reconciliation, and be prepared to pull petty cash vouchers and invoices as requested by the auditor.

*Cash in bank* Here the client can furnish the auditor with a copy of the year-end reconciliation, a list of outstanding checks, prepare the bank confirmations, request a cut-off statement to be mailed directly from the bank to the auditor and, with the auditors instructions, prepare a proof of cash for the entire year on each bank account. The client can also assist in locating the items needed to reconcile receipts and disbursements per books to deposits and withdrawals per bank.

*Temporary investments* This account should be analyzed with interest income. The client can prepare a schedule for the auditor starting with a list of investments in the beginning balance, purchases, sales and maturities during the year, and interest accrued at the beginning of the year, earned during the year and accrued at the end of the year. In addition the client can prepare a confirmation for the auditor.

*Accounts receivable—trade* The auditor should be furnished an aging schedule for accounts receivable at the year-end. From this aging he can select the accounts to be confirmed, and the client can prepare the confirmation forms. The client, under the auditor's supervision, can also assist in putting the forms and return envelopes in envelopes prior to mailing. In some cases the client can prepare a summary of the source of activity in the accounts receivable account during the year.

*Allowance for uncollectible accounts* This account has to be analyzed in connection with accounts receivable and uncollectible accounts expense. The auditor can be furnished a list of write-offs and recoveries during the year with explanations and documentation as requested. He should also be given a copy of the analysis in establishing the balance of the allowance account at the audit date.

*Accounts receivable—employees* The auditor should be given a list—he may have the list signed as verification by the employees or send them confirmations as necessary.

*Accounts receivable—affiliates* A copy of the intercompany account from the affiliate's general ledger can be furnished to the auditor.

*Travel advances* The auditor can be given a list to verify with the employees—this account should be analyzed with travel and entertainment expense with the auditor given a schedule according to the amounts he chooses to vouch.

*Prepaid insurance* This account should be analyzed with insurance expense. A prepaid insurance schedule as presented in Chapter 10 should be given to the auditor along with a schedule of other insurance expense.

*Inventories* Inventory lists and summaries should be available to the auditor. He should also be furnished an analysis of costing procedures, cut-off procedures and the instructions for counting the physical inventory. Inventories are an important area for client assistance. They are large in dollar amount and the paper work is voluminous. The client can save hours of audit time by preparing neat, accurate inventory lists and summaries with easy to follow trails from the physical to the final summary. Extreme care should be exercised in costing, extending and totaling the inventories. Errors on inventories can easily be for material amounts and should be avoided.

*Goods on consignment-out* A list by customer and costs should be furnished to the auditor along with the requested confirmation forms.

*Plant and equipment and accumulated depreciation* The auditor should be furnished a schedule as presented in Chapter 10 and a list of additions and disposals along with the documentation of the costs and selling prices.

*Patents* A list should be prepared for the auditor with costs and documentation for additions. Explanations should be furnished to substantiate the useful life assigned to each patent.

*Goodwill* If newly acquired, the auditor should be furnished contracts and other documentation of the purchase—he probably should have been consulted on the acquisition originally. Also, the amortization period assigned to the goodwill must be substantiated.

*Cash surrender value of officers' life insurance* Confirmations can be prepared by the client for the auditor, and the client can prepare a schedule showing the CSV at the beginning of the year plus the increase in the CSV on each policy during the year and the ending cash values of each policy. This asset should be analyzed with a schedule of life insurance expense showing premium payments and the net amount of the nondeductible insurance expense.

*Special funds* A list of contributions and withdrawals should be prepared with an analysis of the investments in the fund and the income earned.

*Long-term investments* The auditor should be furnished a complete schedule showing the beginning balances of each investment, the purchases and sales during the year, the gains and losses on sales, and income earned. This account should be analyzed with the related income accounts.

*Accounts payable—trade* The auditor should be given a list of accounts payable from which to select the accounts he wishes to confirm. The client can prepare the confirmation forms and assist the auditor in getting them ready for mailing. The client can also prepare a summary of the source of entries in the general ledger account.

*Notes payable—short-term* A schedule of the activity in the notes payable account, starting with the balance at the beginning of the year and ending with the notes open at the end of the year, can be prepared for the auditor. This account should be analyzed with the related interest expense and accrual. The confirmation requests on notes payable can be prepared by the client for the auditor.

*Accrued liabilities* Accruals and many of the related expenses can be analyzed for the auditor. Computations of accruals should be copied and given to the auditor. Schedules of related expense accounts should be prepared and available to the auditor along with the supporting documents.

*Mortgage note payable* A schedule of payments broken down between principal and interest should be prepared for the auditor. The interest on the mortgage note should be tied in to the interest expense account along with other interest expense to substantiate the total interest expense for the year. The client can prepare a confirmation for the auditor.

*Bonds payable and discount or premium on bonds payable* A copy of the bond indenture should be given to the auditor and a schedule prepared to show the balances in bonds payable, premium or discount and interest payable at the beginning of the year, an analysis of activity in the accounts during the year and a list of outstanding bonds at the end of the year. The interest on the bonds for the year becomes another source of interest expense, and the correct computation to amortize premium or discount must be provided for the auditor.

*Capital stock accounts* A list of stock issued, the issue price of each certificate and a list of the stockholders by certificate number must be provided for the auditor. The proper allocation between capital stock and additional paid-in capital on each certificate must be a part of the analysis.

*Treasury stock* A list of treasury stock acquired, the cost and certificate numbers should be prepared for the auditor.

*Retained Earnings* A schedule of all activity in the account should be prepared for the auditor. In most cases there are no entries to retained earnings since the previous audit.

*Dividends* Copies of the minutes in which the dividends were declared will support the entries in the account. The client must be prepared to support the amount of dividends paid to each stockholder.

*Revenue* Schedules of revenue accounts can be prepared for the auditor as he selects for tests. Particular attention should be paid to year-end cut-offs by the client with explanations of cut-off procedures available for the auditor.

*Returned sales* Internal control of credit memos must be adequate and explained to the auditor. Documentation of credits must be available as requested by the auditor.

*Cost of sales* The cost of sales must be documented by cost records and a trail available to tie individual entries on cost of sales to the related sales.

*Salaries and wages* A tie-in of the general ledger accounts to payroll tax returns should be prepared for the auditor. Director's minutes, union contracts and personnel files must be available to substantiate the amounts paid to various groups of employees.

*Taxes* All tax returns must be available for payroll taxes, income taxes, sales taxes, property taxes, etc. Expenses should be scheduled as requested by the auditor.

*Expenses* Schedules and supporting invoices should be prepared and pulled as requested by the auditor.

*Other documents* Copies of minutes of stockholders' meetings, board of directors' meetings and certain committee meetings should be given to the auditor as requested. Contracts, leases and other documents which have an impact on the financial position of the company should be copied for the auditor. Other letters such as the letter to the attorneys and the management representation letter should be prepared for the auditor.

*Accounting records* Above all else, the accounting records should be completed and orderly with adequate detail or explanation provided for every recorded transaction. All documents such as checks, purchase orders, invoices, etc., should be filed where they are instantly available.

All of these procedures save time, reduce the cost of the audit and put responsibility for the audit on both the client and the auditor as it should be.

## PREVENTION OF MISUNDERSTANDINGS BETWEEN THE AUDITOR AND THE CLIENT

An engagement letter should be prepared by the auditor to indicate the types of services he expects to perform for the client. In this letter the auditor should be specific about the type of opinion he expects to give on the clients' financial statements and whether or not an audit is actually being conducted.

Certified public accountants have many clients for which they do not audit the records. In many of these C.P.A.-manufacturer relationships, the C.P.A. acts more as a public controller than as an auditor. This can be a very rewarding type of service for the manufacturer. It costs less to engage a qualified accountant for a few hours each month, quarter, etc., than to hire a qualified accountant on a full time basis. Again, in this type of engagement, there needs to be a written agreement between the C.P.A. and the manufacturer as to the types of services and opinions to be rendered by the accountant.

Certain information must be included in annual and interim financial reports. Often it is preferable from a usefulness standpoint to include other schedules, analyses and narratives. However, before these additions are made to the reports, they should be explained to the client. These extras are usually only a small part of the total report, and should be suggested to the client where they will add to the thoroughness of the reporting process.

Fees are always of interest to both the accountant and the manufacturer. The author agrees that the client is entitled to an estimate of the cost of the C.P.A.'s services, but does not believe in set fees either on a monthly or annual basis. With set fees someone always gets cheated. The C.P.A. is either overpaid or underpaid and, unfortunately, services that the client should have are sometimes neglected because the accountant receives no additional compensation for additional services. In short, fees should be based on time with allowances for wasted time, training and other wheel spinning.

Both the C.P.A. and the manufacturer should constantly look for new ways to improve the financial reports. This search for improvements can be in two areas—information and appearance. Excellent quality financial reports are good publicity for both the manufacturer and the accountant.

Probably the most important aspect of the client-accountant relationship is that of always being open and leveling with each other. The tasks they engage in are of mutual interest. What is best for the client is usually also best for the accountant; however, the accountant must maintain absolute independence and always abide by generally accepted accounting principles, auditing standards and professional ethics.

## ASSISTING THE MANUFACTURER TO IMPROVE PROCEDURES

Suggestions to improve procedures need not occur only as a by-product of the audit. Often a procedures review should be made as a separate engagement when both the C.P.A. and the manufacturer can concentrate their efforts toward objectives other than financial reports.

The knowledge of other specialists, perhaps others from the same accounting firm, can be utilized to augment that of the accountant who has primary responsibility for the manufacturing client—note the word augment not replace. The accountant who has previously worked with the manufacturer has acquired an understanding of the existing system, the physical layout and the flow of goods and paperwork. He is also aware of management policies, either written or unwritten. This familiarity with the firm is time-consuming to duplicate. Therefore, the accountant who has the responsibility for the majority of the services to the manufacturer should conduct or assist with any systems review.

Parts of what can be done in a systems review have been described in previous chapters, namely the marketing audit, the purchasing audit, multiple ideas on the general and cost accounting systems and numerous internal reports. However, the possibilities for assisting the manufacturer in systems improvements are nearly endless.

The objectives of a systems or procedures review may be many and varied, but in general we are usually looking for ways to save time, develop more useful information for management, improve accounting and management controls and simply put the housekeeping in order.

## SUMMARY

The auditor presents an opinion on the fairness of the manufacturer's financial statements and in many situations presents adjustments to the accounting records as a part of his services. His opinion adds precedence to the financial reports and adds to the confidence that management, stockholders and third parties have in the reports.

The auditor, as a part of his audit, should submit a letter to management suggesting improvements in the existing system and procedures. This may be the greatest benefit of the audit, requires little extra effort and strengthens relationships between the auditor and the manufacturer.

The responsibility for the audit must be shared by both the manufacturing firm and the auditor. This sharing of responsibilities can reduce the audit fee and increase the value of the auditor's time. The auditor must request assistance from an individual who has decision making authority. The chapter suggests many areas in which the client can assist. The auditor must carefully instruct client personnel and lay out the work papers that are to be prepared for him.

There should be an engagement letter setting forth the types of services the C.P.A. expects to provide for the manufacturer and the type of opinion he expects to give on the financial statements. Whether or not an audit is conducted must be set out clearly—this engagement letter represents a form of agreement between the auditor and client to prevent misunderstandings.

Special service engagements can be provided by the accountant with the assistance of other technicians. These special engagements are of particular value as they allow the C.P.A. and manufacturer to concentrate on specific problem areas, rather than the usual financial reporting.

# 13

# Selecting the Best Form of Business Organization for the Manufacturer

## THE PROPRIETORSHIP

*General* The proprietorship can have only one owner who usually is also the manager of the business. Proprietorships are generally small businesses, and while 46 percent of the manufacturers in the United States are proprietorships, they account for only one percent of manufacturing receipts and two percent manufacturing net profit.

*Favorable Attributes* The proprietorship is the easiest, least expensive type of business to organize, as it has fewer legal requirements than either the partnership or corporation. It is also simpler to terminate a proprietorship.

The proprietorship is a very flexible form of business. The owner can make decisions and act without the consent of partners, stockholders or the board of directors. He can give precise answers to customers and associates on the spot. The proprietor has complete freedom in making decisions; he can react immediately to any situation; and he can add or delete certain business at his own choosing. This freedom in decision making enables the proprietor to adjust to changing conditions more rapidly without accountability to other parties.

The proprietor can plan, act and react in complete secrecy, although in most circumstances the knowledge of other trusted associates should be utilized.

Owners of proprietorships are highly motivated concerning the success of the business, as their personal success is tied directly to the profitability of the firm.

In many states proprietorships escape certain taxes that apply to corporations. The proprietor also escapes the double taxation that applies to corporate dividends. He can also take funds out of the business and make additional investments in the business as practical without restrictions. Business income or losses can be used on the owner's individual tax return to offset other income or losses. The manufacturer, who operates as a proprietorship, can also convert his business from manufacturing to an investment oriented business without risking the passive income restrictions that apply to a corporation. The proprietor also escapes part of the payroll taxes and insurance requirements on his own income that would have to be paid on a corporate salary. Long-term business capital losses may be used to offset personal capital gains or ordinary income for a proprietor—they must be offset by corporate capital gains in a corporation.

*Unfavorable Attributes* Many loyal, trained and valued employees wish to be owners and share in the profits of the business; salaries may not be adequate motivation, and the owner may find it desirable to be a partnership or corporation in order to grant ownership and share profits with employees he wishes to keep in running or perpetuating the business.

The owner of a proprietorship has unlimited liability for business obligations. This means that his personal assets, as well as business assets, are always on the line. However, even if the manufacturer is incorporated, the owner will be asked to guarantee most major obligations, thus making it difficult to escape the liability. This leaves only open business credit and catastrophes as the obligations against which incorporating limits the owner's liability. He should not be in business if he anticipates needing protection against open credit; catastrophes should be insured against; he may still be liable if personally negligent. Nevertheless, there is still some degree of risk in a proprietorship for these losses that an owner may avoid in a corporation, and his peace of mind may be a personal consideration.

A proprietorship is more limited in methods and ranges of raising capital than either a partnership or corporation. In a proprietorship the owner alone can invest additional funds, and borrowing is limited to his credit procurement only. Also, a proprietorship, because it is more difficult to perpetuate, may find long-term borrowing more difficult to obtain.

The income of a proprietorship, when included on the tax return of the proprietor, may cause his total income to be taxed at an excessively high rate. Also, the business has to use the same tax year as the owner, which is almost always the calendar year. This probably creates more of a problem for the accountant than the manufacturer, but may influence the availability of accounting service and may force the manufacturing business to end its year at an inconvenient part of its annual cycle.

One of the greatest disadvantages of a proprietorship is the transfer of ownership. This transfer of ownership is necessary when the proprietor wishes to leave the business, dispose of part of the business, retire or if he dies. The transfer can be accomplished more easily through the sale of stock in a corporation rather than the sale and purchase of all assets and liabilities. Stock is also easier to divide into smaller units of ownership. Because of these difficulties, the manufacturer who operates as a proprietorship should plan through a will or agreement for an orderly takeover by a member of his family, his employees or an interested outside party. Perhaps an insured buy-and-sell agreement should be prepared by the owner, his accountant and his attorney.

Many small manufacturing businesses simply outgrow the proprietorship form of business. The steps to incorporate are discussed later in this chapter. The manufacturer should consult with his attorney and accountant to carefully weigh the advantages and disadvantages of incorporating before changing his form of business. He should consider the Subchapter S corporation which is also discussed later in this chapter.

## THE PARTNERSHIP

*General* The partnership has more than one owner, but otherwise is somewhat similar to the proprietorship. Only seven percent of the manufacturers in the United States operate as partnerships. They account for only one percent of total manufacturing receipts and one percent of manufacturing net profit. The partnership is a workable form of business organization, generally where there is a limited number of compatable owners.

*The Partnership Agreement* Great care must be taken in selecting partners—disputes can be prevented by drafting a carefully prepared partnership agreement which should include, but not be limited to, the following:

1. Type of business to be engaged in
2. Principal objectives of the business
3. Name of the firm
4. Location of the business, both manufacturing and offices
5. Names of the partners
6. Investments of each partner, detailing the assets and liabilities and their value to be contributed by each partner
7. How each partner is to be compensated for his services, interest to be paid on each partner's capital and how remaining profits and losses are to be distributed
8. Duties and authority of each partner
9. Restrictions on each partner
10. Draw for each partner
11. Pricing of sales to a partner and his family
12. Provisions for admissions and withdrawals of partners
13. How the portion of income is to be determined for a deceased partner

14. The source of funds for buying out a partner backed up with a buy-and-sell agreement
15. Method of accounting
16. Fiscal or calendar year of the partnership
17. Duration of the partnership
18. How the partnership may be dissolved and liquidated and how assets are to be valued and divided on liquidation
19. How disabled partners are to be compensated and for how long
20. How differences among the partners are to be settled
21. All other areas of possible dispute

The partnership agreement should be observed in decision making and amended as improvements are deemed necessary.

*Favorable Attributes* Management responsibilities in a partnership can be divided among partners according to their special abilities, thereby, spreading responsibilities and utilizing the knowledge of each more fully.

Partners should be motivated by sharing directly in the profits of the partnership. Other employees may be motivated by the possibility of becoming a partner and sharing in company responsibilities and profits.

A partnership files only an information tax return and each partner picks up his proportionate share of partnership income or loss on his individual return. This enables the partnership to spread its income or losses among the partners and may reduce the tax rate on total income. Partners also pay less payroll taxes and insurance than would be required on corporate salaries. Partners escape some state taxes that apply to corporations and the double taxation on dividends. Passive income is not the tax problem for a partnership that it may be for a corporation. Generally, partnership income passes through the partnership to the partners without a change in form. This gives partners the advantage of offsetting capital losses against ordinary income—not possible in a corporation. Partners may offset their share of partnership net income or loss against losses or income from other sources.

Partners must be fairly compensated for their services to the partnership. An inactive partner may not be compensated in excess of his proportionate share of ownership. If a partner has no management responsibilities, he may be treated as a limited partner which restricts the amount of his partnership liability.

A partnership may have greater borrowing capacity by combining the borrowing power of all the partners.

Partnerships can perpetuate the life of the business through a buy-and-sell agreement among the partners. The means of funding the agreement should be considered to strengthen it and avoid undue hardship on the remaining partners.

*Unfavorable Attributes* Because a third party does not understand a partner's authority, he is usually justified in accepting acts of a partner in behalf of the partnership. Any partner can commit the business by his acts.

Partners, except limited partners, have unlimited liability for partnership obligations. This means that the total personal assets of a partner are on the line for partnership debt. Many risks may be insured against, some, but not all, can be diminished by incorporating.

Partners must pay taxes on their individual shares of partnership net income even if the income is left in the business. Drawings by a partner do not measure the amount taxable to a partner.

A partnership must obtain permission to use a fiscal year where the partners are individuals. This privilege is automatically available to a corporation.

## THE CORPORATION

*General* Most large manufacturers are incorporated. Corporations represent 47 percent of the manufacturing firms which do 98 percent of the manufacturing business and account for 97 percent of manufacturing net profit.

*Corporate Charter* The charter, which is also called articles of incorporation, certificate of incorporation, etc., in various states, grants permission to the incorporators to operate under the laws of a state. Ownership in a corporation is evidenced by shares of stock issued to the owners in exchange for value received. The charter authorizes the number of shares and types of stock that can be issued. Every corporation must have voting stock issued which is usually common stock. The life of a corporate charter is usually perpetual. The charter must state the purpose of the corporation which can be defined broadly to allow great latitude, or narrowly to restrict the range of operations. Other items of importance usually in the corporate charter are the location of the business, names of the incorporators, and the minimum amount of beginning capital. Various other items are sometimes included in the corporate charter.

*Stockholder Rights* Common stockholders usually have voting rights at one vote for each share of stock owned. Common stockholders share in the net earnings of the corporation which may be distributed as dividends or retained as needed by the corporation.

Preferred stockholders have a prior claim to common stockholders in the event of corporate liquidation. Preferred stockholders also have a prior right to dividends, but generally do not share in retained earnings or have voting rights. The methods of determining preferred stock dividends can vary from issue to issue and must be determined carefully to fit the needs of each situation.

Stockholders are generally liable only for their initial investment or the par value of the stock if it was purchased at a discount. However, major stockholders are often asked to guarantee corporate debt, may be liable for mismanagement or personal negligence. Other stockholder rights include:

1. The right to transfer ownership through the sale and endorsement of stock certificates except as restricted by agreements between the stockholders or between a stockholder and the corporation
2. The right to vote for directors, transfer of corporate property, major purchases of real estate, etc., corporate combinations, sale of real estate, policy changes and liquidation
3. The right to restrain corporate management authority to the extent granted by law, charter or by-laws
4. The right to protect minority stockholders (minor holdings) against the majority
5. The right to a proportionate share of corporate dividends
6. The right to receive or purchase a proportionate share of any new stock issue of the same class; this right may be waived
7. The right to a proportionate share of any liquidation proceeds

*The Board of Directors* The board is elected by the voting common stockholders to attend to the overall management of the corporation. The board of director duties include but are not limited to the following:

1. Attend board meetings
2. Keep written minutes of meetings and resolutions
3. Adopt by-laws, usually at the first meeting, setting forth the rules under which the corporation is to operate
4. Elect officers to manage the corporation. Officers are usually elected at the annual meeting or at special meetings as necessary. Officers should include at least the following:
   President—chief executive officer
   Vice President—special duties in special areas; available to replace the president
   Secretary—signs, or attests to the corporate seal or other signatures on corporate documents
   Treasurer—chief financial and accounting officer
5. Declare officers' annual compensation
6. Understand corporate policy and organization
7. Declare dividends
8. Not to use corporate information for personal advantage
9. Protect the rights of all stockholders
10. Act in the best interest of the corporation
11. Note dissent when not in agreement with the majority
12. Act on all major corporate decisions
13. Get stockholder approval as required by the rights of the stockholders

Directors may be liable for negligence, failure to produce the required reports or misuse of authority as stated in the charter or by-laws.

In small corporations, the stockholders, directors and officers may be the same people.

*Favorable Attributes* Corporations are separate legal entities and as such are taxed separately from the stockholders. This allows stockholders who are employed by their corporation to receive salaries from the corporation for their services, thereby splitting income between themselves and the corporation. The current corporate tax rates are as follows on ordinary income:

| | |
|---|---|
| First $25,000 | taxed at 20% |
| Next $25,000 | taxed at 22% |
| Over $50,000 | taxed at 48% |

The effect of splitting income between management-stockholders and the corporation may have the effect of taxing total income at lower rates.

A corporation, as previously mentioned, can limit the liability of a stockholder for business obligations to some extent. A proprietorship or partnership should consider all advantages and disadvantages of incorporating, not just limited liability, before incorporating the manufacturing business.

Corporate ownership is easily transferrable, as the stock can be traded from one stockholder to another. This ease in changing ownership makes it less complicated to assure the continuity of the business. Buy-and-sell agreements can be written to protect the corporation, the stockholders and their heirs. Such an agreement can restrict the sale of stock prior to its being offered to the corporation or other stockholders at an agreed price. The price should be determined annually by the board of directors unless the stock is publicly traded. In the event of death of a stockholder, the corporation or other stockholders can be obligated to purchase the stock of the deceased owner. This part of the agreement may need to be funded by life insurance. In any buy-and-sell agreement there should be a restrictive endorsement placed on the certificates to prohibit their sale to an outsider. The services of both the C.P.A. and attorney should be used along with the input of the stockholders in writing a buy-and-sell agreement.

A corporation can obtain additional capital through the sale of stock to current or new stockholders. Also, the corporation usually has greater borrowing power because of its continuity of existence. The corporation may retain earnings for expansion. The stockholders do not pay taxes on retained earnings unless the corporation has elected to be taxed as a Subchapter S corporation.

Certain fringe benefits are available to stockholder-employees that are not available as deductible business expenses in the proprietorship or partnership. These are medical reimbursement plans, group life insurance, group health insurance, indemnity policies and greater pension benefits. Care must be taken that the costs of being nondiscriminatory in such plans don't exceed the benefits received.

*Unfavorable Attributes* Corporations are less flexible than other forms of businesses because of restrictions in the charter, by-laws, and the statutes. More time and involvement are necessary in getting board of director and stockholder approval or resolutions—formalities not required of a proprietor and often not required in a partnership.

Dividends in excess of $100 per stockholder, paid from retained earnings on which the corporation has paid taxes, are taxed again to the stockholders—double taxation. The corporation is required to pay all payroll taxes and insurance on stockholder-employees that are paid on other employees.

When a corporation does business outside the state of incorporation, it should determine if it is necessary to obtain permission prior to beginning operations. Failure to do so can cause difficulties in collecting billings or other penalties.

There are numerous advantages and disadvantages to operating as a corporation, especially for the small manufacturer. Some small manufacturers should incorporate, some should not, some of both will.

## INCORPORATING THE MANUFACTURING BUSINESS

A corporation may be formed as an entirely new business or a corporation may be formed to take over a business previously operated as a proprietorship or partnership. The actual incorporating procedures are the same, but the acquisition of assets by a corporation formed as a new business may differ from the transfer of assets and liabilities from an existing business to a corporation.

A proprietorship or partnership may incorporate tax free by transferring the assets and liabilities to a corporation at their tax basis for stock and securities, if the owners get 80 percent or more control of the corporation. Liabilities may be assumed by the corporation to reduce the basis of the stock issued; but if tax avoidance is the objective or if the liabilities exceed the basis of the assets received, there may be a taxable gain.

There can, and many times should be, a change in accounting methods when a new corporation is formed. This is particularly true where the predecessor company operated on a cash basis. Particular care must be exercised in this situation that the corporation does not collect income or pay expenses of the former business. The result can be double taxation or a loss of the expense deduction. The accountant should be consulted on accounting procedures to be followed by both the former manufacturing business and the new corporation.

Numerous decisions must be made when incorporating, and every aspect of the incorporating procedures should be scrutinized by the attorney, the C.P.A. and the incorporators.

The corporate name deserves careful consideration, as it can be the most important promotional tool of the manufacturer. The name should describe the type of manufacturing. Often the name of one or more of the principals incorporating can be used to benefit from previous and even new associations. Perhaps, if a going manufacturing business is being incorporated, the name of the former business should be used by the new corporation. However, a name change should always be considered when incorporating because it is an opportune time to make a change and may gain extra publicity.

The location of the principal office and the resident agent need to be determined early but may be changed as necessary.

The purpose of the business must be defined with emphasis on the scope allowed by the charter. The purpose may be defined narrowly if the object is to limit the scope or broadly if a wide degree of freedom is to be allowed. The exact wording should be selected with the aid of the attorney.

The capital composition of the corporation should be given careful consideration. Usually, more stock should be authorized than needed and consideration should be given to voting and nonvoting stock to get control where desired—at present and in the future. However, the authorized stock can be changed by amending the charter, but there may be a psychological advantage to having stock other than voting common in the initial authorization. The possibility of debt financing may be advisable. Both stock and bonds may be subscribed prior to issue if a degree of uncertainty exists.

Officers and directors should be chosen and listed with names and addresses—original compensation must be determined for officers.

The assets and liabilities transferred to the corporation should be properly valued to gain the best tax advantage and to treat the incorporators equitably. Whether payment is to be made with stock, cash or debt must be determined.

Proper notification should be given to all creditors, customers, etc., whose accounts will be transferred to or handled by the new corporation. Likewise, all leases, contracts, titles, etc., must be properly assigned or transferred.

Application must be made with Internal Revenue Service for an employer identification number. Forms should be obtained for the deposit of payroll taxes and income taxes. Proper transfer of unemployment tax ratings, workmen's compensation insurance ratings, etc., should be arranged. Other licenses, etc., should be applied for or transferred as necessary.

The stockholders should meet to elect the board of directors immediately after incorporating; the board should then meet to adopt the by-laws, elect officers, declare the officers' salaries, and make any necessary resolutions. They should select a fiscal year with the aid of their C.P.A.

When a going concern is incorporated, the C.P.A. should carefully explain that there is no longer the freedom to withdraw capital as there was in the proprietorship or partnership.

The decision to incorporate is a major one—careful consideration should be given to every aspect with the aid of the attorney and the accountant, including the selection of a tax status—either a regular or Subchapter S corporation as discussed next.

## THE SUBCHAPTER S CORPORATION

The Subchapter S Corporation is very similar to a regular corporation from a legal point of view. It is a separate legal entity and must follow all the requirements for any corporation. The difference is in how the Subchapter S corporation is taxed. Taxable income for federal and usually for state tax purposes is taxed directly to the stockholders in proportion to the percentage of stock each of them owns. However, not all corporations can qualify as a Subchapter S—the necessary qualifications are as follows:

1. The corporation can initially have not more than 10 stockholders. Husband and wife who are joint stockholders are considered one stockholder. Other joint stockholders are considered more than one. The number of stockholders may be increased to 15 during the first five years if by inheritance. The number of stockholders may be increased to 15 for any reason after five years.
2. Stockholders must be individuals, estates or certain qualifying trusts; they cannot be partnerships, corporations or nonqualifying trusts.
3. There may be only one class of stock issued. Unissued or treasury stock may be of a different class.
4. There can be no nonresident alien stockholders.
5. The corporation cannot be a member of an affiliated group eligible to file a consolidated return.
6. The corporation must be a domestic corporation.
7. All stockholders must consent to be taxed as Subchapter S corporation.
8. Not more than 20 percent of receipts may be passive in nature—namely from royalties, rents where significant services are not performed, dividends, interest, annuities, or gains and losses on sale of stock or other securities. There is an exception to the 20 percent rule if the passive income is not in excess of $3,000 in the first and succeeding tax years.
9. Not more than 80 percent of receipts may come from outside the United States.

These qualifications must exist on the first day of the taxable year for which the election is made or by the date of the election if later than the first day of the taxable year.

The election must be filed on Internal Revenue Service Form 2553 with the consent of all stockholders including both husband and wife for jointly held stock. The election must be filed within one month before or after the beginning of the taxable year. For a new corporation the first month begins when the corporation has stockholders, acquires assets or begins doing business.

To revoke the election all stockholders must consent to revocation within the first month of the taxable year for which the revocation is to apply. The first year cannot be revoked. After the election has been revoked, the corporation cannot elect to be taxed again as a Sub S corporation for five years without the consent of Internal Revenue Service.

The election may be involuntarily revoked by:

1. Increasing the number of stockholders to more than allowed for a qualifying corporation.
2. Transferring or issuing stock to a nonqualifying trust, partnership or corporation.
3. Transferring or issuing stock to a nonresident alien.
4. Issuing a second class of stock.
5. Violating the 20 percent rule for passive income.

6. Violating the 80 percent rule for foreign income.
7. Becoming a member of an affiliated group of corporations eligible to file a consolidated return.
8. Affirmative refusal to be taxed as a Subchapter S corporation filed by a new stockholder within 60 days after he acquires the stock.

An involuntary revocation can cause an assessment for taxes for each year beginning with the year in which the revocation occurred. This would create a serious problem for the manufacturer if the cash had been reinvested or distributed which would be the usual case. The accountant should carefully review each year to prevent an involuntary revocation. Also a buy-and-sell agreement among the stockholders can be used to prevent any stockholder from performing any act that would cause a revocation without first offering his stock to the corporation or the other stockholders.

Care must be taken to prevent locking earnings in the corporation on which stockholders have already been taxed. Undistributed, previously taxed earnings become retained earnings of the corporation if not distributed prior to revocation of the election. Subsequently, they become dividends if distributed.

To determine if a corporation should make the Subchapter S election, the C.P.A. should analyze the past, present and future tax status (taxable income and amount of tax) for each stockholder and the corporation by contrasting the tax effect on all parties of the Subchapter S corporation and the regular corporation.

Other tax consequences must also be considered in determining if the Subchapter S election should be filed. These include loss carryforwards in an existing corporation that can be lost once the election is made; the possibility of using income averaging on the stockholders' returns when Subchapter S income is included or when a corporate loss is excluded; the differing treatment of capital gains and losses on corporate returns, individual returns or in the Subchapter S corporation; the effect on pension benefits between the Subchapter S and regular corporation; differing effects on state taxes; and other considerations and plans of individual stockholders.

Once the election is made for a new corporation, a resolution to conform to Section 1244 of the Internal Revenue Code needs to be made that allows a loss on the corporate stock to be treated as an ordinary rather than capital loss. If an existing corporation elects to be taxed as a Subchapter S, a shareholders' statement of consent must be filed immediately assuming any liability for future investment tax credit recapture to prevent recapture at the time the Subchapter S election is made. See Figure 13-1.

Dividends must be handled carefully in the Subchapter S corporation to properly defer taxes. If there is undistributed taxable income at the end of the corporate year, only the amount distributed within 75 days after the end of the year can be treated as dividends from that year. After the 75 days, dividends become a distribution from the current year, if earnings are available, and are taxable when received. Many times individual taxes can be deferred by paying dividends within the 75 day period or not paying dividends until after January 1 for the calendar year individual return. A fiscal year corporation can be used to the advantage of the stockholders if the timing of dividends is handled correctly.

Date

District Director
Internal Revenue Service
Address
City, State Zip Code

Re: Shareholders' Statement of Consent

Dear Sir:

In the event any Section 38 property of Machine Manufacturing Corporation is disposed of by, or ceases to be Section 38 property with respect to, the corporation during a taxable year of the corporation for which the election under Section 1372 is effective, the undersigned agrees (a) to notify the District Director of such disposition or cessation, and (b) to be jointly and severally liable to pay to the District Director an amount equal to the increase in tax provided by Section 47.

| | |
|---|---|
| ______________________ | ______________________ |
| Corporation | Individual |
| By: ______________________ | ______________________ |
| | Address |
| ______________________ | ______________________ |
| Address | Social Security Number |
| ______________________ | ______________________ |
| Employer I.D. Number | District Office |
| ______________________ | |
| District Office | |

**Figure 13-1**

## SUMMARY

There are three basic forms of business organizations available for the manufacturer. The following table summarizes the percentage of firms and receipts for each type of manufacturing firm:

| Type of Organization | Percent of Manufacturing Firms | Percent of Manufacturing Receipts | Percent of Manufacturing Profits |
|---|---|---|---|
| Proprietorship | 46% | 1% | 2% |
| Partnership | 7 | 1 | 1 |
| Corporation | 47 | 98 | 97 |
| | 100% | 100% | 100% |

As the table indicates, larger firms tend to be corporations.

Proprietorships have greater freedom of action, are simpler to organize, and have greater flexibility because of fewer legal restraints.

Both the proprietorship and partnership, except for limited partners, have unlimited liability for business debt. The stockholders of a corporation do have limited liability except for personal actions and when asked to guarantee corporate debt, which is common for major stockholders in close corporations.

Proprietors cannot reward employees with ownership without changing the form of organization. Partnerships can add new partners and corporations can transfer stock ownership or issue additional stock to employees.

Capital procurement is more limited in the proprietorship because the partnerships can use the resources of all partners and corporations can issue additional stock. Corporations also have an advantage in long-term borrowing because of their perpetual existence.

Both proprietorship and partnership income is taxed directly to the owners. Corporations pay their own tax, except for Subchapter S corporations whose earnings are taxed proportionately to the stockholders.

The transfer of ownership in a proprietorship is difficult, especially where the owner is inseparable from the manufacturing operation. A partnership may transfer ownership to other partners, and stock in a corporation is easily transferable, except in a close corporation that is run much as a proprietorship.

A proprietorship is run by the owner; a partnership is governed by the partnership agreement and run by the partners; a corporation must abide by its charter and by-laws. In a corporation the stockholders elect a board of directors who see to the overall functions of the business; the board elects officers who operate the business day-to-day.

Careful consideration must be given to legal and tax consequences of incorporating a business. An attorney should assist in forming the corporation with attention given to the name, purpose, types of stock authorized and issued and other means of financing through borrowed capital. The incorporators, the attorney and the accountant need to function as a team to make the correct initial decisions and to follow the correct legal and tax procedures when incorporating.

A major decision for most small corporations is the selection of a regular or Subchapter S tax status. The C.P.A. should make a careful study for both the corporation and its owners to determine the better of the two alternatives.

A thorough understanding of the different consequences of each form of business organization must be available to the new manufacturer in selecting the form best fitted to his needs. Likewise, an existing firm must carefully research the effect of changing from one form of organization to another.

# 14

# Acquisitions, Liquidations, and Capital Procurement

## WHAT TO LOOK FOR IN AN ACQUISITION

Profit, automatically any investor would look for profit in an acquisition, but there is more to look for and different things to look for in determining what the profit might be. There are also a number of questions the manufacturer should ask himself before acquiring another business.

Prior years' financial statements should be reviewed by an accountant who understands the accounting concepts of the industry. The primary purpose of this review, or perhaps audit if the statements being reviewed are not audited or are suspect, is to determine that the financial statements offered by the seller are reliable. More specifically, do they reflect assets, liabilities, income and expenses with reasonable accuracy.

Next, are the managers of the business adequately compensated? There should be adequate compensation plus enough profit to have an attractive return on investment. If not, profits should be discounted by amounts necessary to provide attractive salaries.

What else should be done differently and how will the changes affect future investments and profits? Now we are looking not only at the initial investment, but also at any additional investments required. Now we are also adjusting profits by the changes that will occur. These steps give us a new investment figure against which to compare future profits—the true return on investment that can be anticipated.

Can we squeeze any of the purchase money out of the company being acquired? This is possible. The purchase may be financed by an initial partial payment and future payments, either to the former owners or an outside lender, made by the acquired firm. Squeezing may mean reducing a previously carelessly controlled, fat inventory—or getting receivables shaped up—or speeding up the production procedures for faster turnover of goods in process. Maybe the former owners were absentee, salaried management, or the chief executive did not perform a function; previous salaries could be available for debt retirement.

Do you have knowledgeable and loyal people to run the acquired firm? Knowledgeable may mean someone from the acquired firm—loyal may mean a present company employee. If both knowledge and loyalty aren't present, the acquisition is precarious.

How will the acquisition benefit your present manufacturing business? Are you buying a customer or supplier? Are the customers of the two companies complementary—that is, will one or both companies get new customers because of the other?

Can you reduce overhead costs by eliminating duplicate management, employees or facilities? Can some or all operations of the two firms be merged to reduce overhead costs for one or both? Know what you expect to change when the acquisition is being considered and made. How often have we heard new management say they don't anticipate any changes? That's ridiculous and unfair to the personnel of the acquired company who deserve the right to face the future with an honest degree of certainty. New management that doesn't foresee changes is admitting ignorance or dishonesty. This is the one time personnel expect changes—let them know what the plans are and enlist their aid and ideas in making the changes.

Are there personnel in the acquired business whose knowledge is needed in the present firm, and is buying the business the best way to get them?

How does the acquired firm fit the financial needs of the present business? If the present business is short on working capital, can the new company help improve the situation or will it be an additional drain? If the present business is facing an accumulated earnings problem, can its profits be increased and its working capital be used effectively in a growing acquisition?

Does the acquisition meet the best objectives of the owners of the present company? Could they obtain greater satisfaction, security and peace of mind by accumulating personal wealth aside from more business expansion?

What are the alternative uses of the available financing? Would it be wise and safer to make further investments in the present business where your understanding is probably greater?

Finally, if you are buying a corporation, you must decide whether to buy the stock or net assets. If the purchase is made at more than book value, it may be possible to increase the basis of depreciable assets and have larger depreciation deductions subsequent to the acquisition. You may also be justified in assigning value to a lease purchased (leasehold) which can be amortized in future years. By purchasing net assets you may also be entitled to investment tax credit on tangible personal property having a life of three years or more. The seller may object to the sale of assets and liabilities rather than stock because of investment tax credit recapture on assets that have been owned less than the qualifying length of time.

Conversely to buying above the book value, if an acquisition is made below book value, the current depreciable assets base may be higher than that available by buying net assets. Therefore, the purchase of stock may be preferable, but the available investment tax credit, if assets are purchased—plus other assignable values—must also be considered.

## DEGREE OF CERTAINTY REQUIRED

All questions regarding a proposed acquisition must be answered with differing degrees of certainty depending upon their individual importance. Their final relative importance must be aimed at the probabilities of the overall success of the acquisition—how sure of success must the final analysis of the variables be?

I have heard it stated by a learned finance professor that there must be no doubt. This is nearly true but depends on the amount being risked and what the possible rewards may be. As an example, a company with $5,000,000 to invest in acquisitions can risk losing $50,000, perhaps $500,000, but certainly not the entire $5,000,000. They can take a chance for $50,000, but when the $5,000,000 is at stake, there should be no doubt.

Every successful management tries new things, takes some reasonable risks and makes some mistakes. But the mistakes must be affordable mistakes—the same applies to acquisitions.

## STEP-BY-STEP LIQUIDATION PROCEDURES FOR A CORPORATION

The objective of liquidating a manufacturing company is to avoid double taxation on property sold at a gain. To avoid double taxation the correct procedures must be followed and the right conditions must prevail.

The first necessary condition is that the manufacturer has been in business more than three years. Otherwise, the corporation may be termed a collapsible corporation and the special liquidation treatment will not be available to it.

It is also necessary in planning a liquidation to understand the meaning of the word property—the sale of which may result in a gain to be passed on directly to the stockholders. Property is generally defined as capital assets—long-term investments, depreciable assets and land used in the business. The courts seem to have also upheld the position that inventory may also be treated as property where it is substantially all sold as a part of a bulk sale.

There are two sections under which a corporation may be liquidated. Section 333, a one-month liquidation, usually is not practical for a manufacturing corporation. Therefore, our discussion will concentrate on Section 337, the one-year liquidation.

An attorney and a C.P.A. who are familiar with state corporate statutes, corporate and individual taxes, and liquidation should assist in planning the liquidation and distributing the proceeds. Although procedures may differ slightly from state to state, the following list can be used in sequence as a general outline.

1. Obtain an unconditional sales agreement for all property.
2. Immediately hold a stockholders' meeting to approve the sale of the property and adopt a resolution approving the liquidation under Section 337 of the Internal Revenue Code. The resolution should be drafted by the attorney with specific input by the C.P.A. to assure that it meets Internal Revenue Service requirements.
3. File Form 966 with Internal Revenue Service along with a copy of the resolution to liquidate within 30 days of the adoption of the resolution. The copy must be certified as a true copy by the corporate secretary.
4. Sell all assets and pay all debts—cease operations.
5. Prepare final state and federal tax returns. Show capital gains on property sold—do not pay corporate tax on capital gains, but attach a note stating that they are being passed on to the stockholders under a Section 337 liquidation. Hold returns—do not file yet.
6. Submit the proper state forms to the Employment Security Division for final audit clearances.
7. File required documents with other state tax divisions for final audit clearance.
8. Most states require a newspaper notice for creditors before final dissolution.
9. Await clearances from state tax divisions.
10. File final tax returns on receipt of clearances.
11. Distribute cash left in corporation to stockholders. A small amount may be placed in escrow for final settlements if necessary.
12. File final dissolution papers with state of incorporation.
13. File Forms 1096 and 1099L on liquidating dividends to the stockholders.

If preferable, assets instead of cash may be distributed to the stockholders at fair market value.

## SOURCES OF CAPITAL

Capital is available from three different sources: (1) capital invested by stockholders, partners or the proprietor, (2) capital retained out of business earnings, and (3) borrowed capital.

Invested capital must be a part of any new venture and can be a source of additional capital for an existing firm. However, additional capital put into an existing firm is usually desirable only under certain circumstances. Those circumstances always must be judged by what is most beneficial to the present owners and can be enumerated as follows:

1. Additional investment by present owners to raise capital needed to pursue new profit opportunities.
2. Additional investment by present owners necessary to increase their equity to an amount that will allow the business to borrow the remaining capital needed to pursue new profit opportunities, with a return that is greater than the cost of the borrowed capital.
3. Additional investment by present owners to bail present operations out of a tight situation with prospects of acceptable earnings in the future.
4. Additional investments from other than present ownership where the new investments will somehow enhance the position (present or future) of present owners.
5. Additional outside investments to bail the business out of a tight situation; this type of investment will most likely be costly to the position of present ownership and may be a last resort effort.

Capital retained out of business earnings can be only the amount left after the payment of taxes on those earnings. Otherwise, perhaps not technically but theoretically, the part of the retained earnings that represents a tax paid by the owners becomes an additional investment by them. Earnings retained by a regular corporation do not face this problem, as the corporation pays its own taxes. However, in a Subchapter S corporation, a partnership, or a proprietorship the taxes are paid by the owners, and if distributions are not made at least equal to the taxes that must be paid, the owners are paying taxes for the business.

Borrowed capital is the primary area to be concentrated on in this chapter. We will not consider short-term borrowing as capital, although many of the procedures discussed in relation to long-term borrowing can be utilized in obtaining short-term money.

Sources of long-term debt financing are numerous. The most common sources are:

1. Bank term loans
2. Loans to purchase equipment—installment contracts
3. Real estate mortgages
4. Bonds payable
5. Small Business Administration loans
6. Finance and lending companies
7. Personal loans

## PRESENTATIONS TO LENDERS

Whenever the amount of long-term borrowing is significant or if the borrower is a new enterprise, projections must be prepared to illustrate to the lender that funds will be available to repay the loan. These projections should be for at least three years. The procedures for making the projections are similar to those for the operating plan discussed in Chapter 11. However, standard projections usually consist of only annual totals. Here the format is slightly different and the projection should include notes disclosing the basis for the assumptions made in putting the projections together. Also, the lender should be presented with a pro-forma balance sheet—what the balance sheet will look like after the loan is obtained.

In the following projection, we are assuming a new business wishes to borrow $80,000 to add to the $20,000 being invested by the incorporators. The $100,000 total is to be used as follows:

| | |
|---|---|
| Cash (working capital) | $25,000 |
| Inventory | 40,000 |
| Equipment | 35,000 |
| Total | $100,000 |

With this information the preparation of the pro-forma balance sheet is a simple procedure, and it would be presented as follows:

NEW MANUFACTURING, INC.

Pro-Forma Balance Sheet

January 1, 19x6

| ASSETS | | |
|---|---|---|
| Current Assets | | |
| Cash | $ 25,000 | |
| Inventory | 40,000 | |
| Total current assets | | $ 65,000 |
| Equipment | | 35,000 |
| | | $100,000 |
| **LIABILITIES AND STOCKHOLDERS' EQUITY** | | |
| Current Liabilities | | |
| Current portion of term loan | | $ 10,000 |
| Long-Term Liabilities | | |
| Term loan payable—9% payable $10,000 per year | $ 80,000 | |
| Less current portion above | 10,000 | |
| | | 70,000 |
| | | 80,000 |
| Stockholders' Equity | | |
| Common stock, no par value, 1,000 shares authorized, 100 shares issued and outstanding | | 20,000 |
| | | $100,000 |

**Figure 14-1**

NEW MANUFACTURING, INC.

PROJECTED INCOME STATEMENTS

| | Year Ending December 31, | | |
|---|---|---|---|
| | 19x6 | 19x7 | 19x8 |
| Sales | $300,000 | $345,000 | $395,000 |
| Cost of Goods Sold | 180,000 | 207,000 | 237,000 |
| Gross Profit | 120,000 | 138,000 | 158,000 |
| General and Administrative Expenses | | | |
| Officer's salary | 24,000 | 25,000 | 26,000 |
| Clerical salaries | 16,000 | 17,500 | 19,000 |
| Utilities | 1,000 | 1,200 | 1,400 |
| Telephone | 1,700 | 1,800 | 1,900 |
| Insurance | 1,800 | 1,900 | 2,000 |
| Payroll taxes | 4,000 | 4,300 | 4,500 |
| Property tax | — | 1,800 | 2,100 |
| State income tax | 400 | 400 | 500 |
| Travel and entertainment | 300 | 300 | 300 |
| Advertising | 600 | 600 | 600 |
| Office supplies | 1,200 | 600 | 600 |
| Dues and subscriptions | 400 | 400 | 400 |
| Professional services | 2,200 | 1,600 | 1,600 |
| Uncollectible accounts | 1,000 | 1,200 | 1,300 |
| Interest expense | 7,200 | 6,300 | 5,400 |
| Rent | 1,000 | 1,000 | 1,000 |
| Miscellaneous | 10,000 | 10,000 | 10,000 |
| Federal income tax | 5,600 | 14,600 | 23,000 |
| | 78,400 | 90,500 | 101,600 |
| Available for Debt Retirement | 41,600 | 47,500 | 56,400 |
| Depreciation | 3,500 | 3,500 | 3,500 |
| Net Income | $ 38,100 | $ 44,000 | $ 52,900 |

**Figure 14-2**

NEW MANUFACTURING, INC.

BASIS FOR PROJECTED INCOME STATEMENTS

YEARS ENDING DECEMBER 31, 19x6, 19x7 AND 19x8

Sales

Sales for 19x6 are based on estimated orders per four major customers who have agreed to quotes prior to actual production as follows:

| | |
|---|---|
| A Company | $ 70,000 |
| B Company | 60,000 |
| C Company | 55,000 |
| D Company | 35,000 |
| Quotes in hand | 220,000 |
| Other—seven quotes totaling $180,000—expect to get at least one-third | 60,000 |
| Minimum small job work, etc. | 20,000 |
| Projected sales, 19x6 | $300,000 |
| Annual increase—at least 15% | 45,000 |
| Projected sales, 19x7 | $345,000 |
| Annual increase—at least 15% = $51,750—round to | 50,000 |
| Projected sales 19x8 | $395,000 |

Cost of Goods Sold

An analysis of material, labor, and overhead costs has been made for quoting purposes. Cost per quotes, with projected annual increases in both costs and sales, average 57% of sales prices. Another 3% has been allowed for unforeseen contingencies in arriving at costs that are 60% of sales.

Officer's Salary

James New will serve as president and general manager starting at $24,000 with a projected increase of $1,000 per year for 19x7 and 19x8. If income exceeds projections, Mr. New will be considered for an annual bonus which is not a part of the projected expenses. Other officers are serving only in advisory capacities without salary for the first three years.

Clerical Salaries

Clerical salaries include a bookkeeper-typist and a sales-purchasing job. Each is to start at $8,000 per year with increases projected at $750 each per year.

**Figure 14-2 (continued)**

NEW MANUFACTURING, INC.

BASIS FOR PROJECTED INCOME STATEMENTS

YEARS ENDING DECEMBER 31, 19x6, 19x7, and 19x8

**Utilities** Utility companies have assisted in determining annual usages as follows:

| | 19x6 | 19x7 | 19x8 |
|---|---|---|---|
| Electricity | $1,100 | $1,200 | $1,400 |
| Water | 100 | 100 | 100 |
| Gas | 2,000 | 2,200 | 2,400 |
| Totals | 3,200 | 3,500 | 3,900 |
| Allocated to cost of goods sold | 2,200 | 2,300 | 2,500 |
| Net to G & A | $1,000 | $1,200 | $1,400 |

**Telephone**

| | 19x6 | 19x7 | 19x8 |
|---|---|---|---|
| Base rate | $1,400 | $1,500 | $1,600 |
| Estimated long distance | 300 | 300 | 300 |
| Totals | $1,700 | $1,800 | $1,900 |

**Insurance** A multiperil package has been projected based on the most acceptable quote as follows:

| | 19x6 | 19x7 | 19x8 |
|---|---|---|---|
| Per quote | $3,000 | $3,200 | $3,400 |
| Allocated to cost of goods sold | 1,200 | 1,300 | 1,400 |
| Net to G&A | $1,800 | $1,900 | $2,000 |

**Payroll Taxes** Payroll taxes are estimated at 10% of salaries with those pertaining to production costs included in cost of goods sold.

**Property Tax** There will be no property tax the first year because of the December 31 assessment date. The second and third years are estimated as follows:

| | | |
|---|---|---|
| 19x7 | Equipment at cost | $35,000 |
| | Inventory at cost | 55,000 |
| | Assessed value | 90,000 |
| | Approximate rate | .02 |
| | Payable—19x7 | $ 1,800 |

**Figure 14-2 (continued)**

NEW MANUFACTURING, INC.

BASIS FOR PROJECTED INCOME STATEMENTS

YEARS ENDING DECEMBER 31, 19x6, 19x7 AND 19x8

| | | |
|---|---|---|
| 19x8 | Equipment at cost | $35,000 |
| | Inventory at cost | 60,000 |
| | Assessed value | 95,000 |
| | Approximate rate | .022 |
| | Payable—19x8—rounded | $ 2,100 |

**State Income Tax** State income tax is at a rate of 3% gross profit less a 90% exclusion as follows:

| | 19x6 | 19x7 | 19x8 |
|---|---|---|---|
| Gross profit | $120,000 | $138,000 | $158,000 |
| 90% exclusion | 108,000 | 124,200 | 142,200 |
| Taxable | 12,000 | 13,800 | 15,800 |
| Rate | .03 | .03 | .03 |
| Tax—rounded | $ 400 | $ 400 | $ 500 |

**Travel and Entertainment** Customers for the first three years are expected to be local and they understand that James New is in a start-up position. Travel and entertainment are to be minimal at $300 per year.

**Advertising** Advertising will be only yellow pages at $600 per year.

**Office Supplies** Office supplies are expected to cost $1,200 the first year, but only $600 additional supplies will be needed in subsequent years.

**Dues and Subscriptions** Only two trade journals and a local organization to which two customers belong are included for a total of $400 per year.

**Professional Services** Legal and accounting services have been projected as slightly higher the first year because of getting started. Estimates are as follows:

| | 19x6 | 19x7 | 19x8 |
|---|---|---|---|
| Legal | $ 700 | $ 400 | $ 400 |
| Accounting | 1,500 | 1,200 | 1,200 |
| Totals | $2,200 | $1,600 | $1,600 |

**Figure 14-2 (continued)**

NEW MANUFACTURING, INC.

BASIS FOR PROJECTED INCOME STATEMENTS

YEARS ENDING DECEMBER 31, 19x6, 19x7 AND 19x8

Uncollectible Accounts — All major customers will pay their accounts. Uncollectible projected at 5% of small job work.

19x6—$20,000 × .05 = $1,000
19x7— 23,000 × .05 = 1,200
19x8— 26,450 × .05 = 1,300

Interest Expense

19x6—$80,000 × .09 = $7,200
19x7— 70,000 × .09 = 6,300
19x8— 60,000 × .09 = 5,400

Rent — Rent is $6,000 per year per lease; $5,000 has been included in cost of goods sold.

Miscellaneous — Set at $10,000 per year for contingencies.

Federal Income Tax

| | 19x6 | 19x7 | 19x8 |
|---|---|---|---|
| Net income before federal income tax | $43,700 | $58,600 | $75,900 |
| Tax 25,000 × .2 | 5,000 | 5,000 | 5,000 |
| 18,700 × .22 | 4,100 | | |
| 25,000 × .22 | | 5,500 | 5,500 |
| 8,600 × .48 | | 4,100 | |
| 25,900 × .48 | | | 12,500 |
| Total | 9,100 | 14,600 | 23,000 |
| Less investment tax credit | 3,500 | | |
| Net tax | $ 5,600 | $14,600 | $23,000 |

**Figure 14-2 (continued)**

## SUMMARY

There are numerous things to look for and many questions to ask in any proposed acquisition including the following:

1. Profit?
2. Management compensation?
3. What will be changed to produce more profit?
4. Can working capital be squeezed?
5. Is required knowledge and loyalty available?
6. How will the new company complement the present firm?
7. Are you buying any additional customers or supplies?
8. Can overhead be reduced because of duplicate capabilities?
9. Can personnel be motivated by changes?
10. Is talent being obtained that will help the present business?
11. Does the acquired firm help solve financial problems of the present firm?
12. Does the acquisition meet the objectives of the owners?
13. What is available to finance the acquisition?
14. Should you acquire net assets or stock?

There should be no question as to the success of any acquisition where the amount risked is large. Smaller amounts can be risked with less certainty.

Manufacturing corporations can be liquidated and avoid double taxation on property sold at a gain. This type of liquidation usually must follow the requirements of Section 337 of the Internal Revenue Code. An attorney and accountant familiar with liquidations must assist to assure that proper procedures are followed.

Capital is available from three general sources—investments by the owners, retained earnings and borrowing. When capital is to be borrowed, a presentation including a pro-forma balance sheet, and income statement projections must be put together to show the lender that repayment of the debt is a likely expectation.

# INDEX

## A